"This engagingly written book takes us above and beyond traditional judgment and decision-making studies and the heuristics and biases of behavioral economics to explore how people develop explanatory models and concepts in the domain of economics. It contains many fascinating insights into the challenges laypeople have in understanding seemingly simple but deeply complex phenomena and economic entities (e.g. money), as well as offering a bold new direction for research into a topic where greater lay understanding has enormous social policy consequences."

Frank Keil, Yale University, USA

"For decades economists have tidily cultivated their own scientific gardens and forgotten that complex socio-economic issues may be effectively tackled with better knowledge of human beings on top of sophisticated equations. A plea for a multi-disciplinary approach, this book is a much-needed attempt to foster dialogue and bridge the cognitive segmentation of social sciences."

Elsa Fornero, University of Turin, Italy

"In recent years, many economists have used psychology to understand the economy better. In their enlightening new book, Leiser and Shemesh use psychology to explain why most people understand economics so poorly. Economics insights often butt against deep-rooted ways of thinking about the world. And even when the lessons of economics are intuitive, economists' rhetoric is not. *How We Misunderstand Economics and Why It Matters* is a great book for anyone who wants to understand the economy – or explain it to others."

Bryan Caplan, George Mason University, USA

HOW WE MISUNDERSTAND ECONOMICS AND WHY IT MATTERS

This is the first book to explain why people usually misunderstand economic phenomena. From the cognitive short-cuts we use to make sense of complex information, to the metaphors we rely on and their effect on our thinking, this important book lays bare not only the psychological traits that distort our ability to understand such a vital topic, but also what this means for policy makers, and civil society more widely.

Accessibly written, the book explores the range of cognitive strategies laypeople employ when thinking about money, finance, and the wider economy. From the intentionality fallacy, whereby all economic phenomena are assumed to have been caused deliberately rather than to have come about by the interplay of different factors, to the role of ideologies in framing how economic thinking is expressed, the book discusses how we interpret important issues such as unemployment, inflation, and how we conceive of money itself.

Exposing the underlying biases and assumptions that fatally undermine financial literacy, and concluding with recommendations for how policies and ideas should be framed to enable a clearer understanding, this will be essential reading not only for students and researchers across psychology and economics, but also anyone interested in progressive public policy.

David Leiser is Full Professor of Economic and Social Psychology at Ben-Gurion University of the Negev, Israel. He is Past President of the International Association for Research in Economic Psychology, and President of the Economic Psychology Division of the International Association of Applied Psychology. He studies lay conceptions, especially in the economic domain.

Yhonatan Shemesh holds a BA and MA in cognitive science from Ben-Gurion University of the Negev, Israel. His research focuses on the ways the human evolutionary cognitive endowment affects how people think and act in the modern world.

HOW WE MISUNDERSTAND ECONOMICS AND WHY IT MATTERS

The Psychology of Bias, Distortion and Conspiracy

David Leiser and Yhonatan Shemesh

LONDON AND NEW YORK

First published 2018
by Routledge
2 Park Square, Milton Park, Abingdon, Oxon OX14 4RN

and by Routledge
711 Third Avenue, New York, NY 10017

Routledge is an imprint of the Taylor & Francis Group, an informa business

© 2018 David Leiser and Yhonatan Shemesh

The right of David Leiser and Yhonatan Shemesh to be identified as authors of this work has been asserted by them in accordance with sections 77 and 78 of the Copyright, Designs and Patents Act 1988.

All rights reserved. No part of this book may be reprinted or reproduced or utilised in any form or by any electronic, mechanical, or other means, now known or hereafter invented, including photocopying and recording, or in any information storage or retrieval system, without permission in writing from the publishers.

Trademark notice: Product or corporate names may be trademarks or registered trademarks, and are used only for identification and explanation without intent to infringe.

British Library Cataloguing-in-Publication Data
A catalogue record for this book is available from the British Library

Library of Congress Cataloging-in-Publication Data
A catalog record has been requested for this book

ISBN: 978-1-138-93892-2 (hbk)
ISBN: 978-1-138-93893-9 (pbk)
ISBN: 978-1-315-67534-3 (ebk)

Typeset in Bembo
by Out of House Publishing

For Geneviève

CONTENTS

Preface   *xiii*

1   Introduction: folk-economic beliefs   1
How to understand what you cannot? 5

2   Why is economics so hard?   10
Economists focus on the aggregate; non-economists think
    of individuals 11
Direct and indirect effects 15
Equilibrium as an explanation 17
Morality 20

3   Cognitive hurdles   23
Cognitive structure: a flashlight in the basement 26
    WM – short range *26*
    LTM – narrow scope *27*
Thinking, fast and slow 30
The intentionality bias 30
Consequences 31
    Opportunity cost neglect *33*
    Aggregate effects *34*
    Ignoring the equilibrium *34*
    Uni-dimensionality and the halo effect *35*
    The denial of tradeoffs *37*

x Contents

4 Unemployment and inflation   40
  Unemployment 41
    Three causes for individual unemployment 43
  Inflation 47
    The central psychological core of "inflation" 49

5 The "good begets good" heuristic: the relations between
  macroeconomic variables   52
  The "good begets good" heuristic 53
  Macroeconomic consequences of the GBG heuristic 57

6 What is the economy like? How metaphors shape our
  understanding of economics   60
  Metaphors as structure mapping 63
    When are metaphors most influential? 65
  Metaphors in problem solving and decision making 65
  Economic metaphors in the media 67
    The economy is an organism 68
    The economy is a machine 68
    The most common economic metaphors 70
  Intuitive theories: the source of metaphorical sources 70
    Intuitive theories at work: folk-psychology 72
  Concluding remarks 75

7 Ideology: lay understanding of capitalism   77
  Contrasting views of capitalism 79
  Moral-psychological roots of lay views of capitalism 83
    Self-interest 83
    Fairness 86
    Ideology and personality 90
  Concluding remarks 93

8 Money and wealth   96
  Supply and demand – money as tool 96
  Money supply 98
  Fiat money 101
  Emotional value of money – money as drug 102
  Emotions are extended to fiat money 103
  Fungibility 104
  Real money vs. money on paper 106

Contents **xi**

9 Financial and economic literacy 109

Financial literacy and education 109

How much financial literacy does the public possess? 110
Consequences of deficient financial knowledge 111
The promise of financial literacy training 112
Financial training is mostly disappointing 112
Correlation is not causation 114

Economic literacy to fight simplistic policies 115

Reforms and economic knowledge: Elsa Fornero 116
Literacy and public policy 118
In praise of informed skepticism: Peter Davies 119

Final words 121

10 Public policy consequences 122

The mismatch 122

Consequences 126

Recommendations 129

Personal finances 131
Governance 134

References *137*

Index *160*

PREFACE

This book is the first to explore how the general public understands economics, or rather, how it systematically misunderstands it. Economics has developed such advanced and unintuitive ways of thinking that ordinary people without proper training simply cannot grasp it. Yet they are expected, by others and by themselves, to do so. We marshal a wide range of principles and insights, coming from cognitive, social, and political psychology, to identify the tools laypeople can bring to bear to achieve a semblance of comprehension.

This preface will remain brief, but there are two comments that we wish to make. In discussing the specificities of lay understanding of economics, we use neo-classic economic theory as a reference, and hope this will not annoy proponents of alternative currents. Convenience and familiarity guided our choice, and as humble psychologists we are in no position to endorse a particular school. More importantly, we submit that, had this book been written by a Libertarian or a Marxist, most of our points would have been unaffected, or only slightly amended. Additional kin-dred points can no doubt be formulated and explored, and if this book serves to encourage such investigations, we would be delighted.

The second comment is that our perspective owes much to the work of Jean Piaget. Laypeople don't understand much of what economists are talking about, while economists don't get what there is to understand, and are frustrated at the public's failure to see the obvious. In the body of the text, we avoided making ref-erence to the Piagetian framework, because it is foreign to most of our expected readers, but here, we would observe that the mismatch and mutual incomprehen-sion between laypeople and economists is analogous to that between one Piagetian stage to the next. Another helpful framework is to consider that gap as that between two Kuhnian paradigms. The two are closely related: Thomas Kuhn made a point of acknowledging how Piaget's work had influenced his own, and when I went to meet him in the course of a sabbatical at MIT, he presented me with a book, and

xiv Preface

stated that the paper on Piaget it includes (Kuhn, 1977) was "the best thing I ever wrote."

Piaget and Kuhn were united in their view that describing deficient knowledge only as a failure to attain the normative form is insufficient. A proper account must strive to analyze how the incomplete knowledge is structured in its own terms. We too attempt to describe *how* people think, as opposed to measuring the extent to which laypeople fail, or documenting points of disagreement between the general public and trained professionals. It is gratifying to acknowledge this filiation to the work of my erstwhile "*patron*."

It is with great pleasure that we acknowledge the help and encouragements of many: Carmela Aprea, Meir Bing, Ivo Bischoff, Bryan Caplan, Eyal Carmel, Nofar Duani, Elsa Fornero, Zeev Kril, David Laibson, Shabnam Musavi, Tobias Rötheli, Michael Sarel, Robert Shiller, Avia Spivak, Nicolas Weill, and Eyal Winter. Amongst "those without whose" (Booth, 1974), I am especially grateful to Bill Congdon, whose many insightful comments were particularly helpful and set my mind thinking about policy implications. I also wish to thank Rector HaCohen and Ben-Gurion University for granting me an extended sabbatical, and to Sacha Bourgeois-Gironde and the Department of Economics at Paris II (Panthéon-Assas) for inviting me to work on this book in a pleasant and stimulating environment.

David Leiser

1
INTRODUCTION
Folk-economic beliefs

> If I were to pick the field of economics I am most anxious to see adopt behaviorally realistic approaches, it would, alas, be the field where behavioral approaches have had the least impact so far: macro-economics.
>
> *(Richard Thaler, 2015, p. 349)*

Economists, especially those who formulate public policy, often express dismay at the failure of the general public to understand economics. This is not a matter of ignorance as in the way non-specialists cannot say much about the workings of, say, the spleen. No one expects us to possess extensive knowledge about this fine organ. We are not exposed to any information about it nor do we engage in any conscious interaction with it. Just the reverse holds for economics. People do hold beliefs and entertain hunches about economics, but much of them are systematically misguided. This book will document lay beliefs about economics and try to expose their sources.

Why is this important? Because people's economic views have practical consequences. Whereas what you think about your spleen doesn't affect it in any way, economic beliefs guide people's behavior (think of inflation expectations) and figure in economic models. Further, the general public's beliefs also affect public policy, especially in democratic regimes. The authorities ignore the views of the public at their peril, and if the policy measures they put forward are misunderstood or disliked, they may be difficult or impossible to implement. It is therefore extremely important to map the public's understanding of economics, and to consider what it implies for public policy. A recent poll (IGM Forum, 2017) asked two panels of respected economists in the US and in Europe whether "Insights from psychology about individual behavior – examples of which include limited rationality, low self-control, or a taste for fairness – predict several important types of observed market outcomes that fully-rational economic models do not." All the US

2 Introduction: folk-economic beliefs

experts and 88% of the European ones agreed that this is the case. George Stigler (1970, p. 61), who was awarded the Nobel Prize (inter alia) for highlighting the importance of information, turned his attention to economic knowledge:

> Why should people be economically literate, rather than musically literate, or historically literate? ... The citizen of a democracy is called upon to judge public policy in a thousand directions – military, educational, medical, economic, and recreational, for example – and he will make better decisions if he is well-informed.

Understanding by the public is of particular importance for Central Banks, who rely on transparency to convince the public that they will control inflation and are committed to their targets, and to that end routinely make all relevant information and considerations public. Ben Bernanke, then Chairman of the Federal Reserve's Board of Governors, was well aware of this:

> The Federal Reserve's mission of conducting monetary policy and maintaining a stable financial system depends upon the participation and support of an educated public. As the Fed pursues the monetary policy objectives ... it is essential that the public understand our objectives and our actions. Educating the public about the reasoning behind our decisions helps build confidence in our economic system.
>
> *(Bernanke, 2006)*

This is not just a matter of knowledge or ignorance: misunderstanding exerts its toll. Alan Blinder, an economist with major experience in both the Federal Reserve System and the US administration, discussed how the simplistic views of the general public raise difficulties for running delicate policies:

> There is apparently something in the American character that rejects any remedy too complex to be emblazoned on a T-shirt. ... this leads to simplistic solutions. Sometimes those are from the left, sometimes those are from the right. ... Too many American kids are brought up without any basic literacy in economics. I don't mean knowledge of fancy economic theory, I mean fairly elementary things like "demand curves usually slope down" ... if you are in the political arena, you can't ignore T-shirt attitudes as easily as you can when you are in an apolitical arena.
>
> *(Blinder, interviewed in Erickson, 1994)*

Psychology and economics have been fruitfully engaging for decades. Extensive work has taken place in Behavioral Economics, mostly concerning decision making by individuals. We will refrain from recapitulating the most important insights of behavioral economics, and refer the reader to existing surveys (Ariely & Jones, 2008;

Camerer, Loewenstein, & Rabin, 2011; Kahneman, 2011). Countless studies document the type of mistakes people make, both errors of omission and of commission. These findings have inspired research into helping people avoid mistakes. Best known are the attempts to "nudge" individuals to take a recommended course of action without downright imposing it (Sunstein & Thaler, 2008; Thaler, 2015). The newfound insights are widely being used in the attempt to develop "behavioral public finance." This embryonic field holds promise to expand the set of available policy instruments by relying on realistic psychological foundations, but also opens up the possibility of *evaluating* welfare with respect to a psychologically realistic model of decision making and so provide a sounder foundation for public policy (Congdon, Kling, & Mullainathan, 2011; OECD, 2017). Richard Thaler, the 2017 Nobel Laureate who ranks amongst the most prominent behavioral economists, wishes macroeconomics too were psychologically informed, and laments this isn't taking place to any great extent.

Compared to that extensive body of work, strikingly little is known about how people *think* in the economics domain, as opposed to how they *decide*. This neglect of lay economic understanding is a serious lacuna. As humanity expands its environment, it becomes increasingly important to investigate how our existing cognitive and psychological endowment is deployed in understanding this broader environment.

Psychology traditionally wasn't interested in the question. Cognitive psychologists mostly concentrate on the processing of limited quantities of information, such as can be encompassed in very few sentences at most, whereas the study of how entire domains are comprehended is relatively undeveloped (Friedkin, Proskurnikov, Tempo, & Parsegov, 2016). There are research traditions, originating with the work of Carey (1985) and Keil (1989, 1992), who study the development of understanding in fundamental domains such as the natural (fire, liquids, weather), biological (health and disease, organisms), physical (material objects, forces), and psychological/interpersonal realms of life, all domains where cognitive preparedness developed to benefit our forebears (Pinker, 2003; Shtulman, 2015). But, as Pinker notes, economics as it developed over the last centuries never benefited from such preparedness, and perhaps for this reason, the psychology of economic understanding wasn't considered an interesting psychological question. Recently Boyer and Petersen (in press) upended this insight to great benefit. These authors take domain-specific systems identified by evolutionary psychology (such as cheater detection, ownership intuitions, or coalitional psychology) and that evolved to the benefit of our evolutionary ancestors to enable coordination between them, and then trace how those play out in our current environment, leading to biases in folk-economics. We take a complementary perspective, and relate misunderstanding to the limited cognitive resources available to individuals who struggle to make sense of the modern economic environment. Much of this book involves relating the cognitive and psychological features of humans to characteristics of economic thinking, in an attempt to account for how ordinary people cope with it.

4 Introduction: folk-economic beliefs

And the fact is, they cope very poorly. Economists, frustrated by the failure of the public to grasp what they see as obvious economic realities, sometimes try to speak to the public and to explain what they are doing and why, only to be met with incomprehension or suspicion.

They typically do not realize the magnitude of the obstacle. Blinder also remarked: "I think the economists, with some exceptions, don't help a lot in that they spend precious little time talking – and I guess that means through the media – to ordinary people in ways that ordinary people can understand" (Blinder, interviewed in Erickson, 1994). Apparently, he believed that if only economists were to take the trouble to explain matters to the public, things would go much more smoothly. That naïve hope was shared by Valery Giscard d'Estaing. On February 10, 1972, while France's Finance Minister, he invited himself onto a talk show[1] because, as he put it: "I am responsible for the French tax system. I would like everyone to understand our tax system, and to a certain extent, approve it." Whereupon he stepped up to a flip board and explained the arcane principles of the now defunct "*l'avoir fiscal*" concept (tax credits linked to dividends paid to shareholders of French companies subject to corporate tax).[2]

A little fireside chat with the public will accomplish nothing, because members of the public understand economic matters very differently than economists do, and the mismatch is deeply rooted in our cognitive abilities. The coming chapters discuss this mismatch in detail, and show why numerous specific tensions arise.

But this covers only half our purpose. Failing to understand economic concepts and reasoning does not paralyze the public. On the contrary, a conspicuous feature of lay discourse about economics (the proverbial bloke in the pub) is that people speak confidently of policies and economic events. How can this be? Later chapters will discuss several means that enable them to be both confident and uninformed.

Economics is not a theoretical discipline that concerns academics only. There are social pressures on individuals to have economic views. Because the issues affect people so much, they are often debated in social settings, and everyone who is anyone *should* have a view. For the same reason, economic issues are frequently discussed in the media. News pieces on the current state of the economy, the consequences of policy changes or the goals pursued by those who formulate them, are routinely addressed to the general public, implicitly conveying to its members that they are expected to grasp them. Newscasts and the written press will discuss whether the present time is a good time to buy a house and why, the reasoning behind the latest decisions by the central bank governor and their likely consequences, or the economic significance of "Brexit" (UK withdrawal from the European Union). This state of affairs is unlike that observed in other domains: news programs do not invite civil engineers to talk about the precise technical mishap that caused a bridge to collapse, as no one expects laypeople to be able to follow the explanation. But in the economic domain, the corresponding information *is* conveyed to the public. Here is a curtailed example at random, taken from the *Orange County News*, entitled "What a Fed rate increase could mean for you" (www.nerdwallet.com/blog/finance/what-a-fed-rate-increase-could-mean-for-you/)

Home sales

Rising interest rates generally put downward pressure on the demand for homes and home prices, at least in the short term. So if the Fed raises rates, you may not see very many "For Sale" signs in front yards for a while.

This might make you nervous if you're planning to sell your home soon. …

Bonds

Interest rates and bond prices move in opposite directions. When interest rates go up, bond prices go down. If you're thinking about selling your bonds before they mature, higher interest rates will work against you. …

Stocks

The effect of rising interest rates on stock prices is a little murkier than its effect on bonds. Stock prices generally decrease when interest rates go up, but that's not always the case. If we're in an economic expansion when rates rise, more often than not, stocks go up. …

Hiring and income

By keeping rates low, the Fed hoped to encourage economic growth, which is often measured by employment numbers. If the Fed does raise rates, it would be a signal that employment is recovering, and firms are hiring.

The author, Jeff Bogart, tries to accomplish what the title announces, and spells out how a rate increase by the Fed affects ordinary people, their savings, and their jobs. By publishing such a column, the newspaper implies that its readers are expected to grasp it, and the readers to conclude that they ought to understand this stuff.

Can they really, though? Bogart's text is typical of such columns: it includes some intelligible claims (a rising rate means that firms are hiring), but these are interspersed with statements such as "Stock prices generally decrease when interest rates go up. If we're in an economic expansion when rates rise, more often than not, stocks go up." Non-economists cannot understand such connections properly. Indeed, although this is a topic that has not been studied, preliminary work we've done strongly suggests that most people don't quite know what the Fed does or what interest rates are involved. Understanding of the banking system is extremely defective and as far as the public is concerned, the Fed moves in mysterious ways its wonders to perform.

How to understand what you cannot?

Laypeople, who are faced with the assumption that they can – and ought to – understand those issues, try to make sense of them the best they can. And when they don't succeed, they often feel guilty. In a new and as yet published study involving

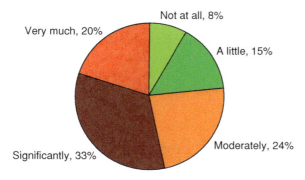

FIGURE 1.1 Do you feel guilty you don't understand more?

a nationally representative sample in Israel, we asked participants whether they felt guilty for not understanding the pension system better. Only a quarter of them reported experiencing little or no guilt (see Figure 1.1).

Retirement savings are a complex issue that featured extensively in the news over the last few years, and people were constantly warned that they must watch their savings to make sure they will be adequate.

In other domains, they don't always feel bad. Indeed, sometimes they think it is all very simple. In late 2015, Yánis Varoufákis, the former Greek Finance Minister, participated in the popular TV program *Question Time*.[3] One member of the public declared he could not understand why politicians complicate things unnecessarily. "Economics is really simple," he claimed: if he were to spend more than he earns, he would soon get into serious financial difficulty, and the same holds for the state. "It's not difficult, guys."

This is a wonderful example of the Dunning–Kruger effect (Dunning, Heath, & Suls, 2004; Ehrlinger, Johnson, Banner, Dunning, & Kruger, 2008; Kruger & Dunning, 2009). Poor performers grossly overestimate their performances because their incompetence deprives them of the skills needed to recognize their deficits. In this case, the man in the audience had no understanding of the difference between the budget of a household and the state's budget, and was blissfully unaware of the complexity of the topic. Varoufákis' answer was that the two cannot be compared because "in a country, total expenditure equals total income." This is a fundamental equation, indeed a tautology to the economically trained, but one that left the questioner more than a little befuddled.

People are but rarely countered by a trained economist. What, then, determines their views when knowledge is lacking? How can people pronounce themselves about economic issues that they understand so poorly? There are a number of ways to do so, some of which we will cover in the coming pages. One way economic opinions are determined is by inner, psychological factors. That opinions don't require detailed knowledge in order to be held can be illustrated by a recent study. Leiser, Duani, and Wagner-Egger (2017) presented about 300 laypeople in

Introduction: folk-economic beliefs **7**

TABLE 1.1 Various takes on the stock market

Stock markets …

1) … are a necessary tool, a mechanism that allows for sophisticated financial activity which is an indispensable component of modern economies (*"Economics 101"*)
2) … have evolved uncontrollably in the past decades and the government is not acting vigorously enough to regulate their activity (*government malfunction*)
3) … are easily manipulated by the select few who can influence them via speculation, causing many small players and individuals to lose a great deal of money (the conspiracy explanation)
4) … are an effective way for businesses to develop but they also allow wealthy individuals more power over the economy and over the development of other businesses (*the "bad" invisible hand*)

Switzerland, Israel, and the US with possible accounts for a wide range of economic concepts (the business sector, stock markets, globalization, etc.). The study involved four types of accounts for economic phenomena. Each such account represents a consistent tendency to explain economic matters in a certain way: (1) the liberal economics textbook explanation; (2) government malfunction – the government is to blame; (3) the conspiracy explanation – destructive outcomes are due to sinister forces who manipulate the system; and (4) the "bad" invisible hand (uncontrolled emergent processes sometimes lead to undesirable outcomes). Those views are not mutually exclusive, as it is perfectly reasonable to consider that stock markets are an indispensable component of modern economies (see Table 1.1), but also that the government is not regulating them properly and that some unscrupulous parties manipulate them. Accordingly, participants were not required to pick one correct answer, but rather to rate the extent of their agreement with each statement.

Figure 1.2 portrays the correlation between any two answers (combination of topic and view). The closer two combinations appear in the figure, the stronger the correlation between them. To illustrate, people who agreed with the Economic 101 view on the question about Unemployment (*UnemplA*) tended to agree to a similar extent with this view on the issue of Centralization (*CentralizationA*). Strikingly, the extent to which individuals endorsed each of the account types was consistent across domains. This may be seen from the way the questions cluster by view: the A's, B's, C's, and D's tend to cluster together. People who tend to accuse the government, or to endorse the economic textbook account, do so across issues, while those who explain economic phenomena by appeal to occult forces do so across the board.

Further, each type of account is associated with specific psycho-social variables. For instance, *Econ101* is positively correlated with self-reported Satisfaction with Life (SWL), Right-Wing Authoritarianism, and with the feeling of being in control of their lives. Economic conspiratorial thinking stands apart for its links with acceptance of non-economic conspirational beliefs (such as the allegedly fake Apollo moon landing and the claims of foul play regarding the death of Lady Diana) and

8 Introduction: folk-economic beliefs

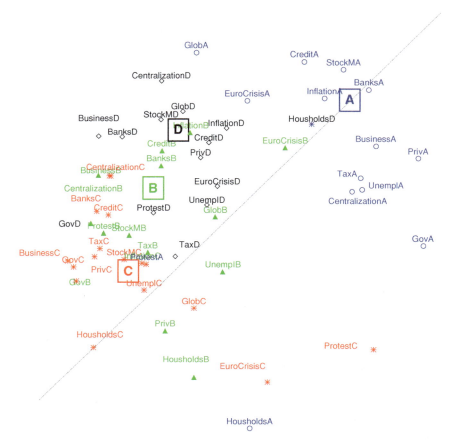

FIGURE 1.2 Multidimensional scaling – clustering of accounts across all topics (a. Economics 101; b. government malfunction; c. the conspiracy explanation; d. the "bad" invisible hand).

with the endorsement of paranormal beliefs (divination, astrology, and premonitory dreams).

It isn't knowledge that drives their opinions. They are moved to answer by broader attitudes that are not specifically related to economic issues, such as how they view politicians, their political orientation, and, with reference to the conspiratorial view, the trait called "truthiness" by Stephen Colbert: "the belief in what you feel to be true rather that what the facts will support" (Colbert, 2005).

This suggests an insight into one of the ways ordinary people assess economic views and explains how they can be confident of their views in the absence of knowledge and understanding of the issues: their judgments may express their personality rather than testify to their comprehension.

In coming chapters, we offer additional perspectives on how people handle economic questions. All serve the same purpose: the public is made to feel that it

Introduction: folk-economic beliefs **9**

FIGURE 1.3 On the point of having an opinion.
Source: Dilbert © 2015 Scott Adams. Used by permission of Andrew McMeel Syndication. All rights reserved.

should understand economics, and manages to "tolerate complexity by failing to recognize it" (Sloman & Fernbach, 2017). In Chapter 7, we discuss ideologies as a packaged set of socially coherent views, endorsed wholesale, which facilitates no end the need to have some opinion. In particular, we discuss how ideologies and personality traits interact (spoiler: ideology trumps psychology, but does not neutralize it altogether). Metaphors (Chapter 6) are another way for people to handle the complexities of the economic world, by assimilating an intractable issue to a familiar domain whose structure is better understood (Holyoak & Thagard, 1989). Yet another way to cognitively assimilate economic discourse is by using some cognitive heuristic to bypass the rich and complex interactions of large sets of variables that economic models strive to master, and reduce them to a much-simplified and tractable pattern (Chapter 5).

The following two chapters examine the roots of the difficulty to understand economics. We will then survey how people bridge the gap in the ways we just alluded to. In a final chapter, we will open a discussion of the consequences of this material for public policy.

Notes

1. www.ina.fr/video/CAF88003653.
2. The specific topic VGE chose to discuss was hardly fortuitous. It was central to the question whether the French President Jacques Chaban-Delmas had evaded or avoided taxes. He failed to be re-elected and was replaced by … his former Minister of Finance.
3. www.youtube.com/watch?v=YZNwdcESn90.

2

WHY IS ECONOMICS SO HARD?

> The Theory of Economics does not furnish a body of settled conclusions immediately applicable to policy. It is a method rather than a doctrine, an apparatus of the mind, a technique of thinking, which helps its possessor to draw correct conclusions.
>
> *(John Maynard Keynes, 1922, p. v)*

Why is it so difficult for non-economists to understand the principles of economics? Part of the difficulty has nothing to do with economics per se: people have a poor understanding of causal theories in *any* domain (Shtulman, 2015). "Laypeople's explanatory understandings are remarkably coarse, full of gaps, and often full of inconsistencies." (Keil, 2010, p. 826; see also Keil, 2003 and Leiser, 2001). Moreover, people are unaware of the extent of their ignorance. "We have very little idea of how little we know. We're not designed to know how little we know" (Kahneman, 2011, p. 24). People will readily answer questions about economic matters which they demonstrably understand poorly, just as they do in other domains (Cimpian, 2015; Leiser & Aroch, 2009; Sloman & Fernbach, 2017).

But understanding economics is uniquely difficult, as a result of particular and acute mismatches between the distinctive complexities of economics on the one hand and the constraints of the human cognitive system on the other.

What is it about economic explanations that make them so unintuitive? We will discuss four interrelated features of economic accounts that raise difficulties for laypeople:

1. the difficulties of thinking of the effects of the *aggregation* of intelligible transactions on a market or the national economy;

Why is economics so hard? **11**

2. the difficulty of thinking beyond direct effects, considering *indirect and feedback effects*, and integrating them into a systemic account;
3. the challenge of explanations relying on static and dynamic *equilibria*; and
4. the spontaneous tendency to think about economic matters as entwined with *moral considerations*. Economic theory separates between economic laws and moral tenets.

Economists focus on the aggregate; non-economists think of individuals

There are two modes to apprehend the economy, the systemic and the individual. The systemic mode focuses on *aggregate* values abstracted away from individual actors and their myriad transactions. It treats the economy as an integrated whole, albeit a whole that is comprised of and built up by individuals. Laypeople apprehend economic activity in terms of individual transactions, the actors involved in those transactions, and their particular motivations (see also Shiller, 2017; van Bavel & Gaskell, 2004) who contrast systemic and narrative modes).

This disparity leads to/produces significantly different views. A good example of the distinction between the systemic and individual approach is afforded by unemployment, which we discuss more fully in a later chapter. The systemic mode sees the causes of unemployment in the workings of the system: the economy is not growing fast enough; not enough jobs are being created for the overall number of people joining the job market at a given moment and the like. The narrative mode of thought, on the other hand, with its focus on people, seeks explanations of unemployment in the unemployed themselves, their actions and their traits, which makes almost as little sense as explaining a traffic jam by the characteristics of the drivers involved.

Another everyday example highlights the contrast between naïve and economic explanations. Suppose an ice cream cone at a given location costs five dollars. The most straightforward account is that the price is five dollars because the seller decided that's what they wanted to get for it. The evidence seems to be right there: he or she put up a sign to that effect.

But economists and laypeople differ on what they assume lies *behind* a given price. Adults are aware that sellers do not set the price capriciously. The price of an item is something related to the item, such as the cost of supply or some unexamined notion of how much it is truly worth, or is a reflection of consumers' willingness to pay (Leiser & Beth Halachmi, 2006; Leiser, Sevon, & Levy, 1990; Pang & Marton, 2005).

Economists look at the market as a whole. The simplest and best-known economic account for why the price is as it is, is the "law" of supply and demand, and it involves all the potential clients and all potential producers of a given good. All else being equal, the higher the price of a good, the less people will want it and therefore the lower the overall quantity demanded. The amount of a good that

12 Why is economics so hard?

buyers purchase at a higher price decreases because, as the price of a good goes up, buying the product will force them to forego the consumption of something else they value more. Conversely, producers supply more – not less – at a higher price, because they expect that selling more at a higher price will increase their revenues, which attracts capital from less profitable ventures. Nonetheless, the market will tend to reach an equilibrium, as *both* producers and consumers adjust their outlay of capital in and out of that particular market. If prices are set too high, above the market price, consumers unwilling to pay that price will use their money for something else, while if the price is too low, producers will take their capital to a more profitable product. Such changes will take place until the market price is reached, that of five dollars in our example. The law of supply and demand is how the "hidden hand" operates. Buyers and sellers are self-interested, and don't consider the effect of their actions on prices. There is no hidden mind that controls the hand with the intention to settle on a particular price. The price just emerges at the end of the process.

This conception is hard to grasp. Out of a group of 169 gifted Hong Kong high school students who studied economics as a school subject, only one correctly referred to changes in both supply and demand in answering the following question:

> In 1997, a new bird flu virus, H5N1, was found in humans in Hong Kong. Eighteen cases were reported and six people died. To stop the spread of the bird flu, the government immediately killed about 1.2 million live chickens in the territory. However, it was surprising to find that after this move, the price of live chickens in the market did not go up but fell. Why? Please explain.

And here is that student's answer:

> Because the government killed 1.2 million live chickens, the supply of live chicken decreased, but on the other hand, people in Hong Kong were unwilling to buy chickens because they were afraid of having the virus H5N1, therefore the demand and supply both decreased. In this case, we need to see what decreased more. Although the supply decreased, the demand decreased more, therefore the price of live chickens did not go up but fell.
>
> *(Pang & Marton, 2005, p. 176)*

We noted above the centrality of aggregation to the systemic approach in economics. Economists don't worry about individual transactions or decisions, but combine them in general measures, such as the rate of unemployment, household consumption, overall investment, and government expenditure. They then proceed to analyze how changes in some of these affect the others. For economists, the scope of aggregation matters greatly, and they distinguish microeconomics from macroeconomics. Microeconomics focuses on how specific markets evolve through supply and demand, as in the ice cream example, whereas macroeconomics is concerned with aggregation across markets, as with unemployment. Aggregate demand, for instance, encompasses the purchases of all consumers, businesses, the government, and foreign trade in an entire domestic economy. The relation between the two levels, micro and macro, is a matter of debate amongst professional economists. From our perspective, however, centered on what causes difficulties for laypeople, this distinction is unimportant. For those untutored in economics, there is one focal level, that of the individual. Aggregation beyond that is mostly ignored.

On the "willful agent" account, someone is responsible for the price. That someone sets the price with reference to the cost or some other reference such as historical prices. If the seller takes only little more – he is fair or generous. If he takes too much, he is greedy. If the decision strikes us as unfair, we know whom to blame (Kahneman, Knetsch, & Thaler, 1986; Malle, Guglielmo, & Monroe, 2014).

Attributing price setting to a decision by some willful agent has two additional cognitive pluses. First, causation is felt to be focal, rather than diffuse. It can be traced to a single cause rather than a cascade or system of interrelated variables which together produce the outcome. Second, the decision comes at a definable point in time, rather than evolving over time. Next to this simple account, explaining the price in terms of how an interlocking system of causal links produces an emergent outcome is unnatural and convoluted. There is no smoking gun, no one to pull the trigger, no trigger is ever pulled, only a diffuse generation of the outcome.

Pitching explanations at the level of individual elements is a general impediment to understanding a class of phenomena including heat flow, osmosis, diffusion, and natural selection. These are all instances of emergent processes, where the interactions of a collection of elements jointly cause the observable outcome. Emergent processes, in any domain where they occur, are cognitively challenging (see Chi, Roscoe, Slotta, Roy, & Chase, 2012) and typically lead to robust misconceptions, robust in the sense that they are difficult to eradicate (for the difficulty of grasping evolutionary theory due to these factors, for instance, see Ferrari & Chi, 1998; Grotzer, Kamarainen, Tutwiler, Metcalf, & Dede, 2013). In these cases, whether involving people, other organisms such as termites, or mere molecules, some outcome is observed at the "aggregate" level as the result of the interplay of elements constitutive of the lower level (Resnick, 1997).

Nothing fundamental is changed when the elements in question have volition, as in the example of how supply and demand jointly determine a market price. As Adam Smith (1776/2000, Book IV, ch. 2, para. 9) already observed, by pursuing profits, the businessman is "led by an invisible hand to promote an end which was no part of his intention." As individuals, customers and producers pursue their private and varied goals; the overall outcome of all their activity is separate from their particular intentions. The ultimate market price was not aimed for by any individual, just as the national level of unemployment is the outcome of countless decisions by individual employers and work seekers.

Whence this focus on the individual in seeking explanations? According to Carey and her collaborators (Carey, 2009; Carey, Zaitchik, & Bascandziev, 2015),

14 Why is economics so hard?

the human capacity for conceptual understanding and efficient reasoning relies on a small set of framework theories, which developed in humans in a specific evolutionary context (Pinker, 2005, 2006). Humans had to master the mechanics of their physical environment, to navigate the social world, and to negotiate the moral aspects of their social relationships. When people have to deal with matters for which humans are not cognitively equipped, they tend to assimilate them into one of these basic cognitive domains. Economic thought is mostly articulated with the help of a conceptual apparatus unavailable to laypeople, one that was developed in recent historical times by the deliberate and persistent efforts of dedicated thinkers. Even students who are explicitly taught those novel ways of thinking about economic issues experience persistent difficulties (Bice et al., 2014; Busom & Lopez-Mayan, 2015; Goffe, 2013; Sarnikar, 2015). Members of the public struggle to follow arguments expressed with concepts outside their conceptual repertoire. As Shtulman (2017, p. 5) put it, in a parallel discussion of lay understanding of natural phenomena:

> To get the world right, we need to do more than just change our beliefs; we need to change the very concepts that articulate those beliefs. To get the world right, we cannot simply refine our intuitive theories; we must dismantle them and rebuild them from their foundations. There are many, many truths that are not easy to understand, because they defy our earliest-developing and most easily accessed ideas about how the world works.

Let us specify what the hurdle is in our case. By dint of being human, people do have the cognitive wherewithal to understand other people (Shahaeian, Peterson, Slaughter, & Wellman, 2011; Wellman, Fang, & Peterson, 2011). Unless mentally disabled, suffering for example from autism, they readily grasp the fundamental elements of such an account, called "folk psychology," whose bedrock consists in the notions of beliefs and desires (Wellman, 1990). By this account, an actor performs an action if the actor both wants an outcome and believes that the outcome can be obtained by performing the action. Beliefs and desires do not immediately cause action; rather, intention is thought to mediate the causal link between belief–desire and action. People readily use the notions of beliefs, desires, and intentions to understand, predict, and explain human action, and do so from an early age (Kashima, McKintyre, & Clifford, 1998; Liu, Wellman, Tardif, & Sabbagh, 2008). This means they can appreciate the knowledge and motivations underlying actions by individuals involved in economic situations and transactions. But they are ill-equipped to predict their aggregate effect and, alas, this is precisely what is required to understand economics.

A story, probably apocryphal, is told of an economist who visited China under Mao Zedong. Seeing hundreds of workers building a dam with shovels, he asks: "Why don't they use a mechanical digger?" "That would put people out of work," replies the foreman. "Oh," says the economist, "I thought you were making a dam. If it's jobs you want, take away their shovels and give them spoons" (Kallaugher,

2007). For individuals to prosper, jobs are needed, even contrived ones. To those who think of the entire economy in the same way, "make work" policies will be held to bring prosperity to those who need it. For the nation as a whole, however, what matters is not whether people have jobs, but how much they produce: the more they produce, the greater the nation's prosperity. Distributing spoons won't increase production.

Direct and indirect effects

The French economist Frederic Bastiat observed in 1848:

> In the economic sphere an act, a habit, an institution, a law produces not only one effect, but a series of effects. Of these effects, the first alone is immediate; it appears simultaneously with its cause; it is seen. The other effects emerge only subsequently; they are not seen; we are fortunate if we foresee them. There is only one difference between a bad economist and a good one: the bad economist confines himself to the visible effect; the good economist takes into account both the effect that can be seen and those effects that must be foreseen. Yet this difference is tremendous; for it almost always happens that when the immediate consequence is favorable, the later consequences are disastrous, and vice versa. Whence it follows that the bad economist pursues a small present good that will be followed by a great evil to come, while the good economist pursues a great good to come, at the risk of a small present evil.
>
> *(Ch. 1, para. 1.3)*

People are remarkably poor at combining causal links into a system (Grotzer, 2012; Perkins & Grotzer, 2005). Causality is primarily seen as some factor A causing an effect B. Kicking a ball will set it rolling. Anything that goes beyond this simple schema is already more difficult to entertain, as are for instance domino effects (if A affects B while B affects C, A affects C too). People also tend to overlook feedback effects, whether direct (B affects A in return) or cyclic (A affects B that affects C that, in turn, affects A). The upshot is that the scope of their mental models and explanations tends to involve too few factors and aspects.

Why do people have such a limited horizon? As we develop in the next chapter, this follows from the principles of knowledge activation in memory. People come up with explanations by retrieving information that comes to mind easily, and use this information to construct their answer. Salience influences which stored knowledge units are likely to be activated in the immediate situation (Higgins, 1996). In thinking of the effect of some factors, laypeople give excessive weight to information easily brought to mind (Cimpian & Salomon, 2014a, 2014b), and this makes them very poor economists. People may be curious to hear about such indirect effects, and are sometimes delighted when those are pointed out to them, as attested by the remarkable success of *Freakonomics*, a book where an economist promises to

16 Why is economics so hard?

FIGURE 2.1 Population fluctuation cycles in two populations.

reveal "the hidden side of everything" (Levitt & Dubner, 2005). But there's the rub, someone else has to point them out.

Later chapters will feature several economic instances of the challenge posed by such complexities. For now, we will illustrate the issue with a classic example from ecology. To illustrate the difference between the direct and hidden, indirect effects, consider the following simple predator–prey system: an island hosting exactly two populations, rabbits and foxes (grass is abundant). Left unchecked, rabbits will multiply exponentially. Foxes, for their part, eat rabbits, and multiply. Therefore, as times goes on, there will be more and more rabbits, allowing foxes to multiply. This increase comes with some delay, as little fox cubs need to grow up. This part of the scenario is readily understood by everyone, but the story is not yet over. As foxes multiply, they will decimate the rabbit population, which in turn means that the large fox population will become unsustainable. Their numbers will dwindle, allowing the rabbit population to increase yet again, and the whole scenario is played anew. The size of both populations fluctuates, with the peaks of the fox population trailing that of the rabbits (see Figure 2.1).

Depending on various obvious parameters, such as the birth rate of each population, the age at which a female can produce offspring, and the rate of culling of the prey by the predators, it is possible to predict the sizes of the population, and also whether the ecosystem is sustainable. This scenario, when formalized by a set of differential equations, is called the Lotke–Volterra predator–prey model, and has a long history of use in economic theory (Samuelson, 1971).

A somewhat more complex model involves three populations, as when the fate of grass is included in the model, in addition to that of rabbits and foxes. An increase in grass leads to an increase in rabbits, which in turns leads to both less grass and more foxes, and so forth. People find such problems intractable, and experience difficulty in understanding ecosystems where such analyses are essential (Green, 1997; Grotzer & Basca, 2003). According to Green (1997), although many systems in our world (economic, human relationships) involve complex chains of cause and effect encompassing two-way causal processes, people tend to construct one-way linear chains when explaining them. Barman, Griffiths, and Okebukola (1995) found that students probed as to what would happen to an ecosystem if the fox population was reduced or the rabbit population doubled, their responses revealed a lack of understanding of the relationships that occur within a food web.

The failure to understand this kind of causality explains an interesting urban legend. The lemming suicide myth is a widely shared tale (Woodford, 2003), according to which the little arctic furry creatures commit mass suicide when their numbers become too large. In the words of the 1958 Disney *White Wilderness* movie narrator, Winston Hibbler: "A kind of compulsion seizes each tiny rodent and, carried along by an unreasoning hysteria, each falls into step for a march that will take them to a strange destiny." That destiny, it later becomes clear, consists in jumping to their death into the freezing ocean. Now it is true that the size of the lemming population fluctuates widely, and this would be very striking to any observer. But those fluctuations are not due to herds of lemmings intentionally or instinctively killing themselves. The *White Wilderness* footage was later revealed to be a fabrication. What is important for our purposes is to see how our cognitive inclinations and limitations may have given rise to this particular fable.

Neither food nor space limits lemming population growth. The scientific explanation of the fluctuation is to be found in the dynamics of a complex system implicating four predators with different characteristics, rather than the two, foxes and rabbits, in our example (Gilg, Hanski, & Sittler, 2003). It involves a one-year delay in the effect of increased numbers of lemmings on the size of the stoat population, while the dynamics is stabilized by density-dependent predation by three other predators (the arctic fox, the snowy owl, and the long-tailed skua, if you must know). The marked population fluctuation and abrupt drop in population size is entirely due to population dynamics – a notion that transcends individuals and lies outside the conceptual repertoire of untrained people, who are therefore left to grope for a different kind of cause, such as gratuitously postulating a suicidal urge that seizes individual animals.

This striking illustration is highly suggestive, and generalizes well: when the proper explanation lies outside their repertoire, laypeople will seek other accounts that belong to it. We will see many more examples of this.

Equilibrium as an explanation

A dominant methodology in macroeconomics is known as the DSGE approach, which stands for the *Dynamic Stochastic General Equilibrium* modeling of the economy. This fearsome string of words expresses some of the key aspects of economic thinking. That phrase also seems calculated to make most people's eyes glaze

18 Why is economics so hard?

over in shock and awe. In this section, we discuss equilibrium which is, according to Lazear (2000), one of the three factors that distinguish economics from other social sciences.[1]

One notable way to predict the equilibrium that the system variables will reach involves an important analytical move. Equilibria may be predicted by examining marginal returns and marginal costs for each incremental action, and performing an action if and only if marginal returns exceed marginal cost. Because marginal returns tend to diminish as one does more of an activity whereas marginal costs tend to increase, the marginal analysis will identify the point of equilibrium. This mode of reasoning coordinates individual decisions by reconstructing them artificially as sequential, using analysis at the micro level as a powerful tool to derive implications at the group or macro level. Only trained economists manage to assimilate it and "think at the margin."

The way equilibration of aggregate variables functions in economic thinking is nicely illustrated by the *MONIAC Hydraulic Computer*, designed by William Phillips in 1949 (see Figure 2.2). This is a physical model of the economy in which flows of consumption, savings, investment, and other economic forces are represented by liquid moving through tubes and pipes as monetary and fiscal variables vary, and the whole system still can be observed as it comes to an equilibrium. Separate water tanks represent households, business, government, exporting, and importing sectors of the economy. Colored water pumped around the system measures income, spending, and GDP. The system is capable of solving several simultaneous

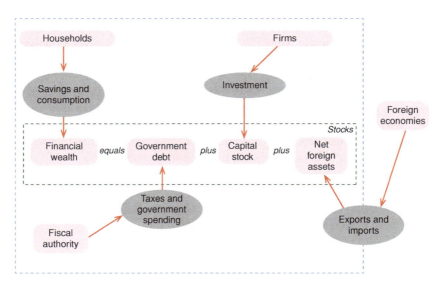

FIGURE 2.2 Stocks and flows as represented in the Forecasting and Policy subsystem of the MONIAC.

Source: Reserve Bank of New Zealand: *Bulletin*, Vol. 70, No. 4, December 2007. Used with permission of the Reserve Bank of New Zealand.

Why is economics so hard?   **19**

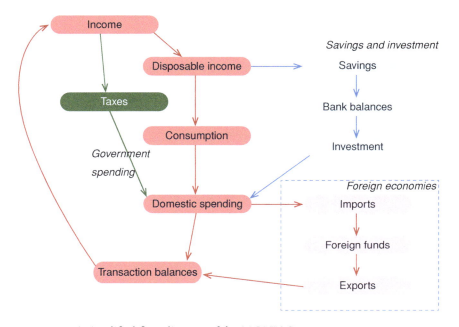

FIGURE 2.3 A simplified flow diagram of the MONIAC.

Source: Reserve Bank of New Zealand: *Bulletin*, Vol. 70, No. 4, December 2007. Used with permission of the Reserve Bank of New Zealand.

equations in response to a change of the parameters, to reach a new equilibrium (Ng & Wright, 2007). Seeing the model in action makes the spectator aware of the dynamics linking the variables, and the familiar dynamics of water in tubes at work in the physical implementation of an abstract model makes the system more intelligible.

Patterns of spending, income, and production are seen as flows of some liquid through different sets of pipes (see Figure 2.3). Categories of actors in the economy – the set of all businesses, or the government, or the set of all households – are seen as containers, into and out of which the fluid of purchasing power (i.e., money) flows. The economy is represented as consisting of ongoing, continuous patterns of activity exchange and transformation of flows of purchasing. Phillips based the relationships represented in the MONIAC on Keynesian and classical economic principles, showing the circular flow of income, expressed by the equation $Y = C + I + G + (X-M)$ (where Y = total income; C = household consumption; I = overall investment; G = government expenditure; X = exports, and M = imports). Crucially, individual transactions are nowhere to be seen. MONIAC's components are aggregate values that abstract away from the level of individual transactions, while the hydraulic causality involved in the links between those values makes it easier to conceive of the economy as a whole, a complex system that reaches equilibrium. The system implements quite literally the most

20 Why is economics so hard?

frequently encountered metaphor in economics, that of the *circular flow* of economic activity.[2]

Not only does this way of conceiving the economy integrate across and abstracts away from individual transactions, it also abstracts away from *human* agency by presenting aggregate "economic agents" (firms, individuals, households, governments, etc.) as the containers where those actions start from or reach (Alejo, 2010), rather as the agents active in the economy. There is no initial state, no decision maker, no decision, just a set of causal relations that run their course iteratively.

The central role of equilibrium follows from the resolute way in which economics strives to model the interplay of variables. Psychology students are taught to distinguish independent variables from dependent ones, and they learn how to investigate how the former affect the latter. Psychologists will also try to identify how additional variables mediate the relations between the two (or modulate them).

Economists do not like variables to remain independent, or "exogenous" relatively to their models. They want, as far as possible, to include all variables in the model: ideally, all should be endogenous, at least in principle. Once this is done, and the model is described mathematically, they can sit back and watch the developments of the system.

Amongst these developments, two varieties are especially worth mentioning. The first is that the behavior of the system may be cyclical. This is the case we illustrated above with the population dynamics of the foxes and the rabbits, and the mysterious case of the plummeting lemming population. The other is that the behavior of the system may change over time. One mode of activity gives way to another, as the system gradually settles down to some equilibrium. In such a case, analysis of the effect of a perturbation to the system needs to distinguish between the short and the long term. The challenges these essential components of economic analysis present to laypeople are obvious.

Morality

The type of explanation embodied in the MONIAC is heartless. Water will flow according to physical causality, and so too does the flow of income have its causality, captured in equations that relate aggregate quantities and in which individual actors, let alone their wishes and feelings, do not appear. This isolation of economic causality is one of the strengths of economic models. *Uber* rising its prices (algorithmically) when there has been a terrorist attack is perceived by many as heartless. While it is only natural to share this sentiment, it remains true that the higher price will attract additional drivers to the area, and this in turn will help more people leave the scene rapidly. So too, the outcome of a public policy does not depend on the intended goals of its sponsors, however laudable, but on economic realities.

The notorious statement in *The Godfather* movie: "It's not personal, it's strictly business" (as the henchman advises his soon-to-be victim not to take his impending execution personally) strikes decent people as just the kind of thing a mafioso would say. To them, you cannot separate morality from economic dealings.

Furnham (1988) was among the first to point out that as laypeople debate economic issues, they integrate economic, political, and moral beliefs. We will see this in detail in later chapters (see Chapter 7). It is not the case that self-interest drives all economic actions, and even less true that a detached appraisal of self-interest drives judgments about economic actions. Considerations of fairness make it unacceptable, for instance, to exploit shifts in demand for goods or work by raising prices or cutting wages. And yet, it is deemed fair for a firm to raise prices or cut wages when profits are threatened. It is also considered fair to maintain prices even when costs to the seller diminish. In terms of economic theory, these rules seem paradoxical. They make perfect sense, though, once it is realized that for ordinary citizens, morality and economics are not disconnected.

What is considered (un)fair in such cases hinges on a conception of entitlement, which accounts for the asymmetry between the cases. It is unfair for firms to exploit excess demand because this violates the customer's entitlement to what they consider the normal price. Entitlements are not symmetrical: in the case of increased costs, sellers are allowed to increase prices to protect their regular profit, but when costs decline, sellers do not have an obligation to lower prices because the reference prices of the buyers are not threatened (Kahneman et al., 1986; Watson, 1996).

Morality is also attached to financial speculations, but some forms of speculation are viewed as more immoral than others. By rights, if the objection to speculation is that it is a kind of bet, it shouldn't matter whether some individual bets on a rising or a falling market. Yet Lotz and Fix (2013) found that laypeople judge speculative short-selling as decidedly more immoral than traditional investments in which one participates in rising markets (i.e., long positions). Moral judgments are increasingly recognized as products of intuition followed by rationalizations to justify the intuition (Baron, Scott, Fincher, & Metz, 2015). Moral psychology suggests that judgments about speculative short-selling are based on unexamined intuitions, rather than on examination of arguments.

A different manifestation of morality was observed by Corcos and Moati (2008) who observed that food trade constitutes an exception to the rules we just saw. Even when customers were aware that prices rose due to an increase in the cost of raw materials, they still thought that it is unfair to raise prices, because food is a fundamental necessity. Incidentally, this view is no doubt made easier by the widespread belief (Gielissen, Dutilh, & Graafland, 2008; Moati, 2009) that the profit margin in large supermarkets is about 30%, an overestimation of the true state of affairs by a factor of ten. This moral dimension affects economics. Companies do not want to incur the scorn and anger of their clients, and take the latter's moral intuitions into account when setting prices.

Nobel Laureate Al Roth (2007) documents how moral considerations and feelings of unease about various transactions can constrain markets (McGraw & Tetlock, 2005). The best-known of these issues is that surrounding organ transplants, and the possibility of paying the donors of body parts (Roth, 2015). Most people find this notion morally repugnant: body parts should not be for sale. Nor should there be a trade in people (slavery) or sexual intercourse (prostitution). In the case of

22 Why is economics so hard?

organs, his analysis led Roth to devise a practical solution: constructing an exchange market so that organs are exchanged for organs, albeit at times in a roundabout way. Crucially, no money changes hands in such markets, and everyone benefits.

Morality is only the most salient illustration of the different range of considerations brought to bear on economic thinking by members of the public, when compared to that of professional economists. In an extensive study of lay views on economics, Williamson and Wearing (1996) interviewed Australian residents in depth, documenting every link and element brought up by their respondents. They found that most of those elements wouldn't be found in standard economic models. More than 70% of the time, respondents described the economic situation by *evaluating* economic variables (such as "high prices"), or referring to non-economic variables ("coping"), or explaining situations ("Australia is rich in raw materials but does not manufacture them") or meanings ("tax avoidance" is really "white-collar crime"). Clearly the isolation of self-contained economic models where all the relevant variables are "endogenous" to the model is a far cry from the scope of considerations and the mode of apprehension brought to bear on economic realities by laypeople (Sandel, 2012).

We claimed at the outset that economics is misunderstood by the public because of the mismatch between central features of economic theory, and the human cognitive endowment. This chapter focused on the first of these. We described several interrelated traits of economic theorizing, and illustrated how these features are not readily accessible to those untutored in economics. We discussed the reliance on the *aggregation* of individual transactions, the establishment of complex models, integrating *indirect and feedback effects* in a systemic account, the use of explanations involving the concept of *equilibrium*, and the very scope of what is included, and more importantly excluded from such models, in particular the role of moral considerations. The following is devoted to the cognitive endowment itself, and its consequences.

Notes

1 The other two being a focus on efficiency, and the notion of rational utility-maximizing individuals.
2 Nothing in this argument hinges upon macroeconomic being hydraulic, e.g., that there exists a quantity which might be called "aggregate demand" and may be adjusted by pumping in fiscal and monetary expansion. The argument holds equally if causation at the lower level is driven by rational agents acting as rational utility maximizers. While economists strive to build their macroeconomic models on solid micro-foundations, there are a number of emergent phenomena that are still difficult to trace back to their precise micro origins. One of the most important such concepts is aggregate demand, which does not have a clear counterpart in microeconomics (Korinek, 2015).

3

COGNITIVE HURDLES

> Technocrats, those are the guys that, when you ask them a question, by the time they are finished answering, you don't understand the question you asked anymore.
>
> *(Coluche, 1989)*

There is a wonderful scene in *The Hitchhiker's Guide to the Galaxy* where Marvin, an android endowed with a brain "the size of a planet," reveals one of his many talents to Arthur Dent, a decidedly average human:

> "You mean," said Arthur, "you mean you can see into my mind?" "Yes," said Marvin. Arthur stared in astonishment. "And …?" he said. "It amazes me how you can manage to live in anything that small."
>
> *(Adams, 2010, ch. 20)*

Marvin's comment was spot on. As we shall see, our cognitive makeup seriously limits the scope of our thinking on subjects we are unfamiliar with. In particular, laypeople will talk about the economic issues that impinge on their lives, they may offer solutions and debate them, but their solutions almost invariably suffer from crippling flaws.

Consider the following situation. A group of friends discuss the high costs of finding where to live. Finding an affordable flat has become impossible. One of them exposes "the" solution. It is very simple, too. Let the authorities cap those prices, and make sure that rentals remain affordable. So simple, so obvious, why don't they take this step? The others snigger: What do you expect? "They" always side with the wealthy against the common man. Or take the following case. In some countries, the housing rental market is very small, and people try to buy their flat or house. But people keep flocking into the cities, where jobs are to be found. When

24 Cognitive hurdles

the supply of housing doesn't keep pace with that influx, house prices will climb and climb, and become out of reach for first-time buyers. Again, obvious solutions spring to mind. Why doesn't the government subsidize first-time buyers? Or establish government-owned subsidized housing?

What's wrong with these discussions? For starters, only obvious ideas are brought up, what we referred earlier as direct effects, while non-obvious aspects of the same issues are left unheeded. Second, once people have come up with one idea, they are satisfied, and make no effort to trace through more distant consequences.

These twin failings are responsible for what is sometimes called the *Law of Unintended Consequences*, or the *Cobra effect*, the perverse unanticipated effects of regulation (Norton, 2008). This "law" is of course not a curse – it merely points to the high incidence of unforeseen effects, or as Bastiat put it, of effects that cannot be seen but must be foreseen. Here are classic examples: people are outraged when they encounter a higher price for snow shovels during a storm, or high prices of plywood in areas devastated by hurricanes, and may call for price controls as a fair means to force people to do what is right. The advocacy of price controls is intended to keep the prices at their "normal" levels. And yet, a moment's reflection will show that this policy will lead to an unintended consequence, one that it is possible to foresee: potential suppliers of plywood from outside the region, who would have been willing and able to move supplies to the area quickly at the higher (market) price, will be less willing to do so at a government-controlled "fair" price, resulting in a shortage of shovels or plywood where they are acutely needed.

A more complex example of the Law of Unintended Consequences is provided by overfishing. A positive movement away from meat to fish in the short run increased the fish consumed, and was beneficial. However, the pressure on the world fish industry increased the prices so much that larger and technologically more advanced fishing boats joined the industry. This led to overfishing – a level of fishing so intense that it hampers the recovery of a fish stock – and created a risk to the continuance of the fish population. Meanwhile, traditional fishermen were driven out of their occupation, jeopardizing the economic basis of many communities. Finally, the increased price of fish was such that poorer folk could no longer afford to consume fish. Thus, the change in the fishing industry created unforeseen negative spillovers.

Economists would analyze this planning failure in terms of partial and general equilibrium. Partial equilibrium models assume that what happens on the market being analyzed has no effect on other markets. They consider the market for one good and assume that the price of every other good does not change. General equilibrium models consider that every market may have an effect on every other market, so that a satisfactory model must study all of them simultaneously. The limited scope of lay economic reasoning means that it usually falls far short of this ideal, and unintended consequences have to be faced time and again.

FIGURE 3.1 The law of unintended consequences.
Source: © 2011 SMBC by Zach Weinersmith. Reprinted with permission.

26 Cognitive hurdles

Cognitive structure: a flashlight in the basement

We observed that people tend to think of obvious ideas and to be content with those that first came to mind, while they don't trace more distant consequences that might diminish their appeal. These limitations are intrinsic to the human cognitive makeup. Cognitive psychologists distinguish between two mental components, called working memory (WM) and long-term memory (LTM). The former is involved in real-time cognitive activity and may roughly be likened to the RAM memory in a computer, that part of the system where currently open files and programs are made available. LTM is a vast store containing all the knowledge we have accumulated. It may be compared to the hard disk on a computer. Needless to say, we simplify the picture in the interest of relevance and brevity.

Thought is often likened to a flashlight. Suppose you need to fix a leak in the plumbing. You go into the basement to see if you can find something suitable. The basement is dark, and no one ever made the effort to organize it tidily. You did take a flashlight with you, but alas, that flashlight has a narrow beam, and it is pretty dim. Not willing to spend too much time down there, you pick up some rags that you noticed, and try to tie them around the leak, a stopgap measure. Now, there may have been more appropriate stuff in that basement. There could be duct tape, or useful tools, perhaps even a plan of the house plumbing that could have indicated the location of a faucet to close off the water in that broken pipe. But you will never know, if all you do is just rummage a bit where the flashlight happened to illuminate something, get out with something salient and accessible, and leave it at that.

Good flashlights can illuminate in a broad beam, and reach far into the distance. Human cognition, by contrast, fares poorly on both counts. It doesn't reach far, and is too narrowly focused. As we shall see, these two limitations relate to the two cognitive components: shortness of range is due to WM, narrowness of focus to LTM.

WM – short range

Working memory is a cognitive buffer, responsible for the transient holding, processing, and manipulation of information. This buffer is a mental store distinct from that required to merely hold in mind a number of items (Diamond, 2013) and its capacity is severely limited. The complexity of reasoning that can be handled mentally by a person is bounded by the number of items that can be kept active in working memory and the number of interrelationships between elements that can be kept active in reasoning. Quantifying these matters is complicated, but the values involved are minuscule, and do not exceed four distinct elements (Cowan, 2001; Halford, Wilson, & Phillips, 1998, 2010). Winnie-the-Pooh humbly recognized "I am a bear of very little brain." People are no better, but lack this admirable self-awareness.

Due to the limited capacity of WM, complex ideas are hard to entertain (Oberauer, 2009; Oberauer, Süß, Wilhelm, & Sander, 2007) and long chains of reasoning are difficult to handle. Hence the tendency to manifest short-range, "myopic" reasoning.

LTM – narrow scope

LTM suffers from a different failing. Sherlock Holmes believed that LTM too is limited by size: "Depend upon it, there comes a time when for every addition of knowledge you forget something that you knew before" (Doyle, 1903) and therefore strove to remember only such matters as could be useful for him and his work. In this Holmes was mistaken. It seems there is ample room for our knowledge in the LTM. The real challenge relates to retrieval: people routinely fail to use knowledge that they possess – especially when there is no clear specification of what might be relevant, no helpful retrieval cue.

Half a century ago, Artificial Intelligence pioneers (Moore & Newell, 1973) confronted the distinction between knowledge and understanding. Even back then, it had become clear that you can store vast quantities of knowledge on a computer, and it seemed appropriate to say that the computer "knows" that stored information. But when is it fitting to say that it also *understands* that information? Moore and Newell offered the following criterion: "A system understands knowledge to the extent it uses it whenever it is appropriate" (p. 202). By that standard, there is little we truly understand for, amongst our many limitations, our knowledge is scattered (Leiser, 2001). Even when we possess pieces of relevant knowledge, we often fail to connect them with one another when appropriate. Typically, we don't access all the relevant knowledge that might be brought to bear on the issues that concern us.[1]

The classic illustration of this flaw was provided by Gick and Holyoak (1980). Participants in their experiments (also discussed from a different perspective in Chapter 6 on metaphors) were asked to solve several problems such as the following:

> A doctor needs to treat a patient with a tumor. The patient cannot be operated upon, but the doctor can use a particular type of ray to burn the tumor. However, the ray will also destroy healthy tissue. At a lower intensity, the rays would not damage the healthy tissue but would also not destroy the tumor. What can be done to destroy the tumor?

This problem is not trivial, and on average, only about 10% of people manage to come up with the solution (which will presently become clear). Gick and Holyoak then explored whether being exposed to a problem with a similar structure would help. The analogous story went as follows:

> A small country was ruled from a strong fortress by a dictator. The fortress was situated in the middle of the country, surrounded by farms and villages. Many roads led to the fortress through the countryside. A rebel general vowed to capture the fortress. The commander knew that an attack by his entire army

28 Cognitive hurdles

would capture the fortress. He gathered his army at the head of one of the roads, ready to launch a full-scale direct attack.

However, the commander then learned that the dictator had planted mines on each of the roads. The mines were set so that small bodies of men could pass over them safely, since the dictator needed to move his troops and workers to and from the fortress. However, any large force would detonate the mines. Not only would this blow up the road, but it would also destroy many neighboring villages. It therefore seemed impossible to capture the fortress.

However, the commander devised a simple plan. He divided his army into small groups and dispatched each group to the head of a different road. When all was ready he gave the signal and each group marched down a different road. Each group continued down its road to the fortress so that the entire army arrived together at the fortress at the same time. In this way, the commander conquered the fortress and overthrew the dictator.

Participants who read this story amongst several others had a somewhat higher success rate, of about 30%. But when they were given the hint that one of the previously read stories might be of use in solving the radiation problem, the solution rate jumped to 92%. The difficulty does not consist in working out how to adapt the solution of the commander problem to the radiation problem. It lies in thinking of its relevance in the first place.

The two flaws we described, the exiguity of WM and unreliable retrieval from LTM, interact with one another. Ideas and pieces of knowledge accumulate in LTM, but those bits often remain unrelated. Leiser (2001) argues that, since there is no process active in LTM to harmonize inconsistent parts, coordination between elements can only take place in working memory. And in view of its smallness, the scope of explanations is small too. Our mental makeup at birth and the mechanisms and conditions of knowledge acquisition therefore generate separate explanatory systems, and in the absence of general mechanisms responsible for spotting and improving coherence, coherence will remain local at best.

Limited knowledge, unavailability of many of the relevant economic concepts and variables, and restricted mental processing power mean that incoherencies are to be expected, and they are indeed found. One of the most egregious is the tendency, noted by Furnham and Lewis (1986) who examined findings from the US, the UK, France, Germany, and Denmark, to demand both reductions in taxation and increased public expenditure (especially on schools, the sick, and the old). You can of course see why people would rather pay less in taxes, and also that they prefer to benefit from more services, but it is still surprising how often the link between the two is ignored. This is only possible because, to most people, taxes and services are two unrelated mental concepts, sitting as it were in different parts of LTM, a case of narrow scoping, called by McCaffery and Baron (2006) in this context an "isolation effect."

In a differently structured experiment where subjects had to balance taxes and spending, they wanted to reduce both taxes and spending, preferring balanced budgets and even surpluses to deficits. Yet when asked about specific spending cuts, which emphasizes the loss of services, they were reluctant to make cuts, leading to large and persistent deficits (Baron & McCaffery, 2008).

As another example, consider Salter's 1986 thesis, which suggested that people hold large-scale overarching beliefs. Specifically, he claimed, on the basis of a very limited sample, that people can be classified by what they consider the fundamental force driving the economy: demand-siders (consumption is primary) or supply-siders (business activities are key). Bastounis, Leiser, and Roland-Levy (2004) ran an extensive survey on economic beliefs in several countries (Austria, France, Greece, Israel, New Zealand, Slovenia, Singapore, and Turkey) among nearly 2000 respondents, and studied the correlations between answers to the different questions. No such broad clustering of opinions as that predicted by Salter was in evidence. Instead, the data indicate that lay economic thinking is organized around circumscribed economic phenomena, such as inflation and unemployment, rather than by integrative theories. Simply put, knowing their answers about one question about inflation was a fair predictor of their answer to another, but was not predictive of their views regarding unemployment.

It gets worse. It is not just that local theories regarding different phenomena are often inconsistent. In the same way as we may be adult, fair, rational, and poised people, yet may revert to childish behavior when sitting on a plane next to someone who tries to steal some room on our armchair, people can also hold conflicting views on a single phenomenon, the one naïve, the other more sophisticated. When they reach a novel understanding and the newly adopted view conflicts with the previous one, the new one does not simply override the other (Chi, 1992; Shtulman & Harrington, 2016; Shtulman & Lombrozo, 2016; Shtulman & Valcarcel, 2012). The new insight grows alongside the older conception, without eradicating it. Individual intellectual individual history leaves its mark on our later functioning.

Clinging to primitive notions even when more advanced ones have been achieved is ubiquitous. Returning to the economic domain, consider how we conceive of monetary value. We may hold a mature conception: the price of an object is determined by the intersection of the demand and supply curves, and if seller and buyer agree on a price, that is the object's price. But a more primitive, absolutist view coexists alongside the first, and sometimes makes itself felt. This is the view, dominant in childhood, that every object has its inherent value (Cimpian & Salomon, 2014a; Cimpian & Steinberg, 2014; Leiser & Beth Halachmi, 2006), or that the proper price is derived from the cost of supplying it. The notion implies that whoever charges extra is overcharging. It is due to this conception that we deem unfair the higher prices charged by the small vendor on a remote track, since a cold drink is so much cheaper at the local supermarket, or to use another of our examples, that changing the price for plywood or snow shovels just when they are most needed is shameful.

Thinking, fast and slow

Cognitive psychologists have long identified two modes of cognitive functioning (Sloman, 1996; Sloman & Fernbach, 2017), intuition and deliberation. One of their contrasting properties gave its name to Kahneman (2011)'s book: *Thinking, Fast and Slow*, a work that brought this dichotomy to the attention of a wide public. The fast, intuitive thinking mode, sometimes called Type 1 or System 1, is the default. It is associative, effortless, spontaneous, and its product is often experienced as intuitively certain. The slow mode (Type 2 or System 2), by contrast, is deliberative and analytic. It involves controlled and deliberate efforts. People are cognitively lazy, and rely on the fast mode as much as possible, without bothering to check its conclusions, which are often correct anyway (Gigerenzer, 2007). Under certain circumstances, such as when they detect a conflict (Pennycook, Fugelsang, & Koehler, 2015) or sense a disfluency in coming up with an answer (Thompson et al., 2013), people may engage in the more taxing Type 2 mode of functioning.

The slow, analytic mode of thinking involves WM, whereas the fast mode relies on associative processing in LTM. Ziv and Leiser (2013) examined whether, when laypeople reason about several everyday domains, including economics, they do so using a slow, serial, deliberate process or an autonomous, effortless, associative process (Stanovich & Toplak, 2012). They concluded that the inference questions in the economic domain (and most other ones as well) were mainly processed by the associative systems in LTM. This was derived from the fact that the inference process is unaffected by a concurrent secondary task that taxes WM. We conclude that Type 1 appears to be the thinking mode of choice when answering inference questions in economics.

The intentionality bias

Intentional and teleological accounts come intuitively to people. "Whenever we see a well ordered arrangement of things or men, we instinctively assume that someone has intentionally placed them in that way" (Polanyi, 1951). By default, people see actions as deliberate. Faced with sentences such as "she broke the vase" or "he set the house on fire," people tend to interpret the action as intentional, an implicit "agency theory." The events depicted in such studies were perceived by most to have occurred because of somebody's willful action, in order to fulfill some purpose, and this phenomenon was observed in many contexts: among children, among adults suffering from dementia, and among healthy adults choosing under time pressure (Donovan & Kelemen, 2011; Kelemen & Rosset, 2009; Kelemen, Rottman, & Seston, 2013; Leiser & Beth Halachmi, 2006; Lombrozo, Kelemen, & Zaitchik, 2007; Rosset, 2008). The intentionality bias appears to be related to the limited functioning of Type 1 thinking. In a recent study (Tardiff, Bascandziev, Sandor, Carey, & Zaitchik, 2017) it was found that the healthy elderly rely on the agency theory pervasively, and careful experimentation established that this was caused by the difficulties they experienced in deploying a different and more accurate explicit theory. Such studies strongly suggest that Type 1, the fast and intuitive cognitive mode, interprets causes and events as intentional, and that this constitutes the default, unthinking account. Other types of causality are invoked only by more advanced thinkers functioning under favorable conditions.

This conclusion has serious consequences for lay understanding: the public is poorly prepared to think of how the interaction of a large number of actors leads to outcomes neither intended nor anticipated by any of them (aggregation and equilibrium) and it is partial to accounts based on an identifiable actor who makes decisions in accordance with his goal and beliefs. This leads it to personalize economic matters, and to look for someone responsible for any given state of affairs (Williamson & Wearing, 1996). The tendency to see occult and conspiratorial causes behind economic events (Leiser et al., 2017), constitutes an extreme expression of the intentionality bias, but the phenomenon may also be observed in accounts of the economic crisis studied by Leiser, Benita, and Bourgeois-Gironde, 2016 and Leiser, Bourgeois-Gironde, and Benita, 2010 where a majority of respondents attributed the crisis to intentional and moral factors such as economic actors' stupidity, negligence, and greed, rather than to any systemic malfunction.

Economic theory relies on aggregate variables that integrate across different actors and circumstances, and are not necessarily reducible to belief-desire analysis. Even when they are, the derivation is complicated. The complexities of the interactive, multi-level emergent accounts combine with the partiality to intentional accounts to generate explanations very different from those entertained by professional economists.

Consequences

How does all this play out when looking for a solution to a problem, such as that of devising a policy that will result in affordable housing? Lay solutions will exhibit three traits:

1. *Directness (short range)*: People will look for simple, direct solutions – they don't allow for indirect and feedback effects, because keeping track of complex reasoning steps in WM is too taxing.
2. *Narrow scope*: People don't trawl their vast knowledge store to include all potentially relevant variables and consider consequences further afield, even when they do have the knowledge or the ability to infer them. Retrieval from LTM is fairly bungling.
3. *Uncritical*: The first ideas that come easily to mind are implicitly considered as the best option, and the search for solutions will stop.

One popular solution is capping rental prices. It isn't difficult to work out that artificially low prices will make renting out flats unattractive, and that the rental market will suffer. Fewer people will build and rent out flats, or maintain and upgrade ones they own, if their capital will be more productive in other sectors. This will tighten

32 Cognitive hurdles

the market even more. Further, people will also pay under the table above the permitted rate. For its part, a public housing solution can entail problems of mobility, as people will resist moving to a place where work is available in order to preserve their entitlement to public housing.

This is not to say that the idea is necessarily wrongheaded. There are places where rental caps are in place and the rental market functions well, allowing landlords to make enough to stay in the market, while protecting tenants from excessive prices. But what is lacking is a critical perspective. The considerations we listed, despite being readily intelligible to laypeople, don't come to mind unaided. Granted, to bring up such arguments is more demanding than the example of the puzzles about the general and the physician, where only retrieval was needed. Here, novel arguments must be mounted. But the inference required to predict, e.g., that unofficial payments will proliferate is pretty obvious, and people do recognize the objection as valid as soon as they are prompted to entertain its possibility. Yet they usually won't do so unprompted.

Direct solutions might work, or they might not, but if you first think of a direct consequence and never examine it critically, this restricts the range of alternatives. A single solution, the one that comes naturally to the mind of the bloke in the pub, will be felt to be the natural one, its alternatives ignored, its consequences unexplored, while better but less obvious ones will go unexamined. And the pubgoers will likely want to know why the administration turns its back on the one solution worth pursuing.

Discussing simplistic solutions and the reason they are supported in the same spirit, Chris Dillow (2016) lists many examples of direct links in his well-regarded and psychologically informed *Stumble and Mumble* economics blog: American voters who believe cheap imports have depressed domestic wages support the introduction of tariffs. People who believe that immigration has depressed wages favor immigration controls. Voters over-rated the direct benefit of Brexit. "We are giving £20 billion a year or £350 million a week to Brussels" was a famous statement by the then Mayor of London in favor of Britain leaving the European Union and under-rated the indirect cost, that Brexit would weaken the economy and hence the public finances. If your thinking doesn't encompass the relevant variables and their interactions, you can do no better than come up with a simplistic perspective, one that pushes in the opposite direction to the presenting symptom. Higher import prices become "the" solution to cheap imports; higher minimum wages "the" solution to low pay; monetary, rather than fiscal, policy is to blame for low interest rates, and so on.

This is the time to remember the Dunning–Kruger effect mentioned above, the observation that the incompetent are ill-suited to recognize their incompetence. We saw that people tend to rely on the intuitive Type 1 reasoning, and it is only when they are dissatisfied with their experience that they engage in the more demanding Type 2. Pennycook, Ross, Koehler, and Fugelsang (2017) showed that the less analytic you are, the less you are aware of the fact and the less likely you are

Opportunity cost neglect

We now turn to discuss several manifestations of the cognitive traits and limitations we just described.

The tendency to focus on one issue to the neglect of all others is responsible for a pervasive and extremely serious flaw: opportunity cost neglect. It is common to contrast incurred expenses ("out-of-pocket" costs) and "opportunity costs," which refer to the absence of a potential income or foregone alternative purchase. Prior to choosing an option, a rational decision maker would consider its opportunity costs. The difficulty arises because, to properly consider the opportunity costs of a purchase or a policy, the decision maker must mentally generate the alternatives that it would displace. People seldom think this way. Instead of considering missed alternatives, they restrict their attention to the focal option and don't think about opportunity costs, unless those costs are salient in the context in which the decision is made. Opportunity costs are not merely underweighted relative to out-of-pocket costs (Thaler, 1980, 2015); they tend to be neglected altogether.

Although opportunity cost is routinely presented in economics textbooks as a fundamental principle of market economies (see, e.g., Principle 2 in Mankiw, 2014), there are precious few studies about how the topic is understood by laymen, or even by economics students (see Collett-Schmitt, Guest, & Davies, 2015; Davies, 2011). Frederick and his colleagues (Frederick, Novemsky, Wang, Dhar, & Nowlis, 2009) presented their subjects with a choice between a $1000 stereo and a $700 stereo, and recorded their reasoning for choosing either. In the absence of a cue prompting them to do so, only 13% of subjects mentioned outside goods (e.g., "I'll have $300 left over for shopping for clothes") as a factor influencing their decision. Similarly, Brown (2005) found that less than 10% of his study participants referred to outside goods when asked to describe how they determined their willingness to pay for certain items.

Opportunity cost neglect has consequences for how the general public judges public policy (Lucas Jr., 2015). We saw that people favor spending more money on most government services, but dislike taxes and do not want them raised (Furnham & Lewis, 1986). The Pew Research Center periodically asks the public whether spending on certain government programs should increase, decrease, or stay the same. They consistently find that large majorities support maintaining or increasing spending on nearly all major government programs, including social security, health care, national defense, education, combating crime, environmental protection, and aid to the needy. Mentioning the possibility of a tax increase dramatically reduces support for additional spending, and the majority support for additional funding of any of those programs disappears (Faricy & Ellis, 2014; Mueller, 1963). Plainly, if additional taxes are not levied, any funding for a program will come at the expense

34 Cognitive hurdles

of the funding of others. Funding would therefore have to be apportioned based on priorities. But this is not how voters think. Instead, people support funding of programs solely on the basis of the programs' perceived worthiness *considered in isolation*, and their deliberation does not cover possible alternative uses of the resources spent on the program under consideration.

Aggregate effects

More difficulties arise because people don't consider aggregate effects, as we saw in the previous chapter. Considering aggregate effects requires a mental maneuver for which our intuitive mode of thinking is ill-prepared: going from the well-understood activities of separate individuals to what happens when all individuals behave in the same way.

This is brought out by an example that is well-known to all economists and central to Keynesian economics, the "paradox of thrift." It runs as follows: if members of the public save more, they spend less. Collectively, this means less aggregate demand. If people stop going to restaurants to save the money, there will obviously be less demand for restaurants; if they go longer before renewing their clothing, demand for clothing will drop, and so forth. As a result, workers in the restaurants, entertainment, and clothing businesses will earn less. And so will their suppliers. Some workers may even be made redundant. All those people affected will be able to save less from their reduced income. Overall, then, an increase in savings due to bad times will make matters worse, and yet worse, in a downward spiral. This is why economists recommend finding ways to stimulate the economy in times of downturn, encouraging people to save less and consume more, which is the exact opposite of the rational behavior of any one individual in that situation.

Without the benefit of a broader perspective, this is a paradox, since total savings *decrease* due to individuals' attempts to *increase* their saving. The assumption that what is true of the parts (increased savings) must be true of the whole is sometimes called the *fallacy of composition*. The assumption sounds reasonable, and for those unable to navigate the broader context, that claim is compelling.

The account we just sketched is a wholly un-mysterious case of emergence, where the whole possesses properties at variance with those of its parts. But the notion to encourage people to save less in a downturn sounds perverse to non-economists who struggle to combine causal links into a system. Negative interest rates, in particular, seem insane. "Selling" such policies to the public is a challenge.

Ignoring the equilibrium

Aggregate effects and equilibrium effects are the very opposite from direct consequences. The tendency to suffer from "tunnel vision" and look only for direct effects, while under-appreciating equilibrium effects was demonstrated experimentally in the context of policy preference. Certain ill-thought policies may set up a social dilemma in which individual and collective interests are in conflict.

Dal Bó, Dal Bó, and Eyster (2017) ran a lab experiment illustrating this. Participants had to select between two games. One of the games was a version of the Prisoner's Game, the best-known game of strategy in social science, that centers around a dilemma of coordination:

> Police have arrested two suspects, and interrogate them in separate rooms. Each can either confess, thereby implicating the other, or keep silent. No matter what the other suspect does, each can improve his own position by confessing. If the other confesses, then one had better do the same to avoid an even harsher sentence. If the other keeps silent, then one can obtain the favorable treatment accorded a state's witness by confessing. Each will therefore end up confessing, although, when both confess, the outcome is worse for both than if they had both kept silent.

The alternative game involved no such dilemma. Participants played several rounds of the Prisoner's Game, to ensure that they felt the brunt of the twisted logic of the game, that consistently causes both players to lose out because each has an incentive to defect. As is normally the case in such experiments, participants usually defected. In a second phase, they were introduced to the variant on the game, the Harmony Game, which fundamentally modifies the payoffs. In that game, a "tax" is added on each outcome, such that gains are all lower but, crucially, the newly inflicted taxes render cooperation more worthwhile than defection.

Participants who analyze the games correctly can see that the Harmony Game yields better outcomes for all, since cooperation is to everyone's interest and therefore constitutes the (Nash) equilibrium. They realize that the higher gains theoretically achievable in the Prisoner's Game are illusory, as each participant will end up defecting, an outcome that is the equilibrium for this game. Dal Bó and colleagues report that people select the Prisoner's Game over the Harmony Game nonetheless.

Applying this to the real world, they suggest that voters are biased against policies that impose direct costs (the equivalent of the tax in the Harmony Game) even if they will induce larger benefits through adaptation of new behavior by the public. Conversely, they support policies that, while producing direct benefits, create social dilemmas and ultimately hurt welfare.

Uni-dimensionality and the halo effect

The tendency to oversimplify complex judgments is also manifest in the "halo" effect. In misty weather, light sources are perceived as surrounded by a radiant halo. So too, knowing a few positive traits of a person leads us to attribute additional positive traits to them. This phenomenon was first described by Thorndike almost a century ago: "the estimates of the same man in a number of different traits such as intelligence, industry, technical skill, reliability, etc., were very highly correlated and very evenly correlated" (Thorndike, 1920, p. 25). Thorndike suggested the following underlying mechanism: when information is meager, specific perceptions

36 Cognitive hurdles

and judgments are derived from global internal attitudes: "Ratings were apparently affected by a marked tendency to think of the person in general as rather good or rather inferior, and to color the judgments of the qualities by this general feeling" (p. 27). The halo effect comes from the tendency to rely on global affect, instead of discriminating among conceptually distinct and potentially independent attributes.

This bias is unfortunate enough by itself, as it leads to the unwarranted attribution of traits to individuals. But it becomes even more pernicious when it blinds people to the possibility of tradeoffs, where two of the features are inversely correlated. To handle a tradeoff situation rationally, it is essential to disentangle the attributes, and to realize that if one increases the other decreases. When contemplating an investment, for instance, a person must decide whether to invest in stocks (riskier, but with a greater potential return) or in bonds (safer, but offering lower potential returns). Why not go for the best of both worlds – and buy a safe investment that also yields high returns? Because no such gems are on offer. A basic rule in investment pricing is that risk and return are inversely related, and for a good reason. If you sell an asset that is risky, people will want to pay less than for an otherwise comparable asset that is risk-free. Conversely, safer investments are more attractive and command a higher price. Treasury bonds illustrate this well. Those emitted by, say, the Greek national bank offer a high rate of return, because of the perceived lingering risk that they will not be honored. And because the risk of the US Federal Bank defaulting is so small, the Fed can sell bonds that pay a low interest, and still find willing buyers. Indeed, the return on bonds in a given time and place is taken as an index of the stability of the economy at that time and place.

Strikingly, this relation is systematically violated when people are asked for an independent evaluation of their risk perception and return expectations. Shefrin (2002) asked portfolio managers, analysts, and MBA students for such assessments, and found, to his surprise, that expected return correlates *inversely* with perceived risk. Respondents appear to expect that riskier stocks will also produce lower returns than safer stocks. This was confirmed experimentally by Ganzach (2000). In the simplest of his several experiments, participants received a list of (unfamiliar) international stock markets. One group of participants was asked to judge the expected return of the market portfolio of these stock markets, and the other was asked to judge the level of risk associated with investing in these portfolios. The experiment was straightforward: for both perceived risk and return, participants were asked to directly rate these concepts on a numerical scale. The relationship between judgments of risk and judgments of expected return, across the financial assets evaluated, was large and negative (Pearson $r = -0.55$). Ganzach interprets this finding as showing that both perceived risk and expected return are derived from a global preference. If an asset is perceived as good, it will be judged to have both high return and low risk, whereas if it is perceived as bad, it will be judged to have both low return and high risk. This explains the negative relationship between the judgments of risk and of return for unfamiliar assets (for familiar assets, the respondents would be aware of the risk and return of the asset, and the halo effect

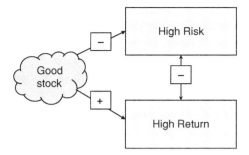

FIGURE 3.2 Good stocks are good through and through.

would not obtain). Unfamiliar assets are perceived on a continuum ranging from "good" to "bad," and judgments of risk and returns are both derived from this one-dimensional attitudinal continuum.

The denial of tradeoffs

In his collection of essays on Russian thinkers, Sir Isaiah Berlin criticizes the Russian revolutionary anarchist, Mikhail Bakunin (1814–1876), for assuming that all desired goals are compatible, indeed, for presuming that they are mutually reinforcing.

> Bakunin lumps all the virtues together into one vast undifferentiated amalgam: justice, humanity, goodness, freedom, equality ("the liberty of each through the equality of all" is another of his empty incantations), science, reason, good sense, hatred of privilege and of monopoly, of oppression and exploitation, of stupidity and poverty, of weakness, inequality, injustice, snobbery – all these are represented as somehow forming one single, lucid, concrete ideal, for which the means would be only too ready to hand if only men were not too blind or too wicked to make use of them. Liberty will reign in "a new heaven and a new earth, a new enchanting world in which all the dissonances will flow into one harmonious whole – the democratic and universal Church of human freedom.
>
> *(Berlin, 1978)*

Berlin is right, of course. "The liberty of each through the equality of all" is an absurdity. Equality may be enforced at the cost of liberty; conversely, if liberty is granted, equality will most likely be reduced. A hard choice cannot be avoided. Winter (2013) lists the constitutive steps of public policy analysis: identify tradeoffs, measure tradeoffs, and recommend policy (to which defining the policy objective must of course be added). Refusing to countenance and analyze tradeoffs, as was Bakunin's stance, guarantees irrelevance to the real world, and is likely to usher in problematic policies.

38 Cognitive hurdles

Unfortunately, naïve thinking tends to be unaware of the necessity to manage tradeoffs. Consider higher minimum wages as a solution to low pay. To the public, politicians who hold those views are the only moral, socially aware ones. In reality, there is an ongoing debate in public policy circles over whether raising the minimum wage causes job losses, and on the potential magnitude of those losses. Recent research shows conflicting evidence, and suggests that it is appropriate to weigh the cost of potential job losses from a higher minimum wage against the benefits of wage increases for other workers (Manning, 2016; Neumark, 2015). Beilharz and Gersbach (2016) explain how unawareness of complex economic links ("general equilibrium effects") may lead the public to support minimum wages above market ones, and argue that voters' obliviousness may give rise to economic policies that eventually lead to a crisis.

People avoid agonizing about tradeoffs, and this makes life easier for them. Suppose you contemplate taking advice about a financial matter of great import. In an experiment (Barnett White, 2005) involving this situation, participants could choose between indifferent experts and benevolent advisors whose expertise was markedly lower. They turned to advice from the experts when the decision was not emotionally stressful, but preferred benevolent advisors when having to make emotionally difficult choices. This might be described as a tradeoff, yet participants did not experience it as such. Instead, they convinced themselves that the benevolent advisers' advice would be no less accurate.

In real life, tradeoffs are ubiquitous. "People face tradeoffs" is the first of the Ten Principles of Economics offered by Mankiw (2014), and is a central feature of policy making. Both inflation and unemployment make people unhappy. If they are in a tradeoff relation, you need to decide which is worse, or work out the most tolerable mix (Blanchflower, Bell, Montagnoli, & Moro, 2014). Similarly, you may have to decide whether to go for economic development or for equality – sharing the pie (Rubin, 2003) (usually the public's demand) or enlarging it (the economists' bias).

Matters are even less transparent with trilemmas. Whereas a dilemma forces you to choose between its two horns, A and B (or find an intermediate middle ground trading one off against the other), trilemmas involve three variables, A, B, and C, such that you can pursue any two, but then must renounce the third.

The best-known economic trilemma is that to which monetary regimes are subject. A country can accomplish only two out of the following three policy goals: a fixed exchange rate, the free movement of capital, or monetary independence, but it cannot aim for all three. By pursuing any two of these policy goals, it necessarily closes off the third. Another such trilemma, called "the Trump trilemma" by *The Economist*, states that you cannot have tax cuts, an investment boom, and a smaller trade deficit. Since those are three central goals of the Trump administration, their overall policy is self-defeating (The Economist, 2017). Yet another one, that involves economics and politics, was expounded by Dani Rodrik in *The Globalization Paradox* (see Figure 3.3). The eponymous trilemma consists of the following observation: a country cannot simultaneously pursue democracy, national self-determination, and economic globalization. It could combine democracy and globalization if people

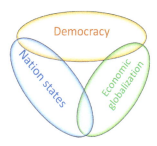

FIGURE 3.3 Sample trilemma: the globalization paradox. You can pick any two out of the three, but the intersection of all three is empty.

were willing to give up the nation state. But accepting globalization means that some rules will be set internationally, even if this means running roughshod over the citizens' stated wishes (Rodrik, 2011). A similar tension is currently troubling the European Union project.

The unwillingness of laypeople to acknowledge the need to balance between conflicting goals is one more obstacle to conveying public policy to the public, and it needs to be studied in order to seek ways to overcome this reluctance.

In the previous two chapters, we discussed the roots of the difficulty experienced by non-economists in their encounters with economics. We looked at central features of economic theory and of human cognitive endowment, and illustrated a range of consequences. The following chapter will discuss how those limitations manifest themselves in their views about two major phenomena, unemployment and inflation.

Note

1 McCaffery and Baron (2006) call more or less the same effect an "isolation effect," a phrase that also carries other, irrelevant meanings in psychology. Mullainathan and Shafir (2013) refer to "tunneling." By this term they mean focusing on what is essential and actively ignoring anything outside the focus, but the state they refer to by this also impairs executive control and inhibits cognitive capacities, and these aspects are not intended here. We call the effect "narrow scoping." Our choice of term is neutral: our normal mental makeup simply has its limitations. Our use of the term also recalls the related "narrow framing" in decision making (e.g., James, Lahti, & Thaler, 2006).

4
UNEMPLOYMENT AND INFLATION

Unemployment and inflation are the most important macroeconomic variables that non-economists care about. Other variables, such as growth and the Gross National Product of course concern economists greatly but their significance is unclear to the general public (Drews & van den Bergh, 2016). Unemployment and inflation affect individuals directly and significantly. They are of great consequence for politicians too: voters hold their government accountable for economic performance in their country, especially with regard to unemployment and inflation, and this "retrospective voting" affects the incumbent's vote share and popularity (Bischoff & Siemers, 2013).

Increases in either are disliked by members of the public, who believe that the authorities should fight them both. Unemployment is of course awful for people who cannot earn a living and those who depend on them, and bad for the economy at large, so there is little need to explain why it is disliked. But – contrary to most economists – the public objects to inflation too. Shiller (1997), interviewed laypeople in the United States and Germany about inflation, and found that the primary reason people cite for opposing non-zero inflation is that they think it makes them poorer. Mankiw, the director of the Monetary Economics Program of the National Bureau of Economic Research, commented on Shiller's results:

> (1) People widely believe what might be called the inflation fallacy – the view that inflation per se erodes living standards. (2) People have largely similar views of inflation in different countries with substantially different inflation experiences. People of different ages also have largely similar views of inflation. ... Put simply, people are people. (3) Economists aren't people. To be more precise, economists view inflation very differently than laymen do.
>
> *(Mankiw, 1997, p. 65)*

Not only do members of the public hold different views on inflation than the experts, they are often off-the-mark in evaluating current levels. Many economic psychology studies have examined the evaluation of these variables by members of the public, and probed what causes the often substantial discrepancies between evaluation and official statistics (Brachinger, 2008; Bruine de Bruin et al., 2010; Malmendier & Nagel, 2016; Ranyard, Missier, Bonini, Duxbury, & Summers, 2008). This is important because evaluations and expectations regarding inflation and unemployment affect people's economic behavior and are incorporated in economic models. Psychological inflationary expectations figure into the inflation-generating process itself. When labor unions negotiate wage contracts, for instance, or when firms enter into contracts to deliver their goods at some future date, contract pricing is influenced by the level of prices expected to prevail over the course of the contract. So too, estimations and expectations regarding unemployment affect the negotiating stances of work-seekers and those of their prospective employers. Evaluations of present inflation are derived from several sources of information: prior expectations, personal experience of price changes (which are biased by frequency of purchase and salience), media reports (which amplify such biases), and official statistics. The formation of expectations of future inflation involves the same sources, along with expert forecasts (when available) and lay mental models of the economy (Ranyard, Missier, Bonini, & Pietroni, 2017).

Our focus in this chapter will be on those lay models, as we discuss how people understand the causes of inflation and unemployment. The topic hasn't been studied much, but it is possible to derive some useful insights from the existing work.

Unemployment

We begin by presenting some findings that emerged from a large-scale international study, the Adult Economic Values and Economic Models Study (AEVEMS). That study involved close to 2000 respondents, ranging from 19 to 65 years, and surveyed eight nations:[1] Austria, France, Greece, Israel, New Zealand, Singapore, Slovenia, and Turkey from all levels of the population. All the questions required the participants to select one out of several options. The first relates to how they think the government should tackle unemployment (Table 4.1).

TABLE 4.1 Tackling unemployment (in percentage)

In order to solve the problem of unemployment in (this country), what should the government do, in your opinion:	
Encourage people to buy more	4
Encourage initiatives in the industry	62
Begin infrastructure projects that have been postponed for a long time	26
Bring about an increase in the salaries of salaried people	8

42 Unemployment and inflation

The two most popular solutions manifest a feature of lay thinking that we discussed in previous chapters: people don't think of indirect causation. Since unemployment means that there are too few jobs, the solution that naturally suggests itself is to encourage employers to generate more of them. The second most popular recommendation obeys the same logic, except that this time it is the government that would generate the jobs. This is rather less popular, because this implies that the government would be spending money, whereas the cost is more transparent in the case of the industry. The difference between these two is instructive. "Encouraging" industry cannot be limited to exhortation, if it is to have any effect. Some economic incentive would be required. But as this is not explicit in the alternative as presented, the need for an incentive is not salient, and therefore less daunting. Strikingly, encouraging people to buy more – the natural choice for a modern economist – is simply not perceived as a policy relevant to the issue of employment.

A second question asked about how personal economic actions might help (Table 4.2).

TABLE 4.2 Citizens' contribution (in percentage)

As a citizen in this country, you can contribute to lower the rate of unemployment. What conduct will most strongly reduce unemployment?	
If I buy only national products, there will be fewer unemployed	40
If I save less and invest more in my own economic stability by increasing my personal wealth, I will help lower the unemployment rate	9
Investment in the stock exchange and in industrial firms will contribute to a lower rate of unemployment	13
If I expand my own business activity, I will contribute to a lower unemployment rate	38

The same principles are at work here too. Only obvious, direct links are endorsed. The employer can help reduce unemployment by offering work. The consumer too can insist on local products, and so more local workers will have a job. But the small step to investment in existing business is not made. With more money investment in them, existing businesses could expand and employ more people.

The last question concerns the effect of savings on unemployment (Table 4.3). When the economy is sluggish, saving less and spending more can invigorate the market and decrease unemployment. Setting of negative interest rates on savings is the extreme form of pushing people to consume, thus increasing demand and the need for labor. Yet the first statement, that expresses this relationship, is also the least popular. Instead, options 2 and 3 (which are basically identical) are the popular ones. They state that more savings would lead to less unemployment. This may be another manifestation of the "good begets good" heuristic: increased savings, higher investment, diminished unemployment are all "good things," and "therefore" more savings imply lower unemployment.

Unemployment and inflation **43**

TABLE 4.3 The effect of savings upon unemployment (in percentage)

How do you think that the level of personal savings affects unemployment?	
An increase in personal savings means less consumption. This leads to lower production, and therefore to more unemployment.	19
The more personal savings there are, the more money is available for lending by the banks. This means more investment and therefore less unemployment.	28
When people save more, investment increase, and there is therefore less unemployment.	29
The level of personal savings does not significantly affect unemployment.	24

Three causes for individual unemployment

Furnham (1982; Furnham & Lewis, 1986) asked a representative sample of British adults for their explanations of unemployment, and classified the explanations as belonging to one of three categories:

- *Individualistic factors*, attributing unemployment to personal dispositions (will-power, effort, ability) – an attribution sometimes characterized as "blame the victim." Such explanations follow the inherence heuristic (Cimpian, 2015) according to which explanations should be sought in the properties of the object or person affected;
- *societal factors*, attributing unemployment to governmental policies (later modified to include lack of education and qualifications as provided by the state);
- *fatalistic*, attributing unemployment to uncontrollable parameters (cycles, luck, chance).

This tripartite classification was recently confirmed in a study involving about 1700 participants from eight countries (Brazil, Greece, Poland, Romania, Turkey, Spain, the UK, and the US). The three categories constitute a fair description of the dimensions of causation spontaneously invoked by non-economists (Mylonas et al., 2016).

Furnham (1982) also examined the differences in the perception of the causes of unemployment according to political affiliation, and found that political affiliation is related to the importance attributed to the three factors. Specifically, Conservatives emphasized individualistic causes whereas Labour supporters focused upon societal causes.

This difference was investigated in much greater depth in the United Kingdom by Peter Lunt (1989), who did not merely examine the degree of importance ascribed to each factor, but also probed the participants' perception of the links between them. One key question was whether the categories of answers were felt to be mutually exclusive. Lunt had his participants assess the causal relationship between pairs of factors derived from the work of Furnham (1982). Here is the list of factors he used:

44 Unemployment and inflation

TABLE 4.4 Factors involved in explaining unemployment in the Lunt study

---

- Unemployed people can earn more on social security
- Lack of effort, laziness among unemployed people
- Unwillingness of the unemployed to move to work
- Lack of intelligence or ability among the unemployed
- Poor education and qualifications among the unemployed
- Weak trade unions that do not fight to keep jobs
- Incompetent industrial management with poor planning
- The introduction of widespread automation
- World-wide recession and inflation
- Policies and strategies of the present government
- Bad luck
- The policies and strategies of previous governments

All possible pairings of factors were presented in the questionnaires, and participants rated the likelihood that one of the factors affected the other in the direction indicated. The main links affirmed by voters of the two main parties, the Labour Party and the Conservative Party, are presented in Figures 4.1 and 4.2. To illustrate, both Conservative and Labour voters believe that incompetent management was responsible for recession, which brought about governmental policies. But Labour voters believe that those policies are responsible for a poorly educated workforce, whereas Conservative do not make this connection.

There are important and systematic differences between these two patterns. Comparing Figure 4.1 and Figure 4.2, one sees that key arrows have switched directions. For instance, the Conservatives assert that it is the laziness of the unemployed that leads to their poor education, and to existing governmental policies. This kind of explanation means that the unemployed are ultimately responsible for their status. Such an account fits the inherence heuristic of Cimpian and Salomon (2014a) discussed earlier. Conversely, Labour voters endorse the opposite view. The governmental polities are responsible for the lack of effort and the poor education of the unemployed.

Labour supporters hold that social and political causes are more basic than personal causes of unemployment, and that the personal motivations and abilities of the unemployed to obtain work are the outcome of social and political forces. These beliefs are reflected in their party's policies on reducing unemployment. Conservative supporters perceive government policy as a reaction to the lack of motivation of the unemployed. Labour supporters' beliefs are also in harmony with their party's policies. They see direct government intervention as economic, industrial, and social pressure as having the potential to affect the motivations of the unemployed.

There are also differences in the relative complexity of these two accounts. Conservatives perceive multiple interconnections *among* the internal factors, whereas the Labour supporters perceive more complexity among the external ones.

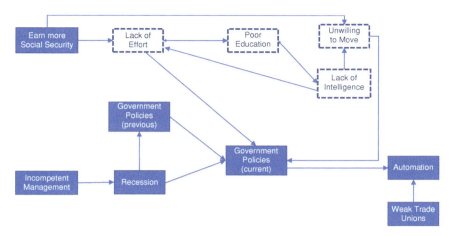

FIGURE 4.1 Conservative voters' perceived causal structure of unemployment. Internal causes have a dashed border and a clear background; external causes have a blue background.

Source: Lunt, Peter K. "The Perceived Causal Structure of Unemployment." In: Grunert, K.G. and Ölander, F. (eds.) *Understanding Economic Behaviour*. Theory and Decision Library (Series A: Philosophy and Methodology of the Social Sciences), vol 11. Springer, Dordrecht. © 1989 Springer. Used with permission.

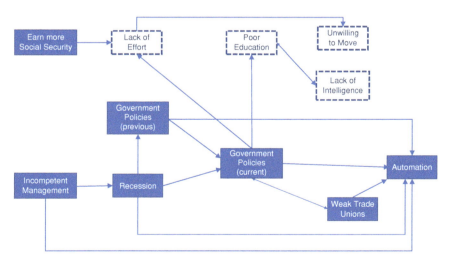

FIGURE 4.2 Labour voters' perceived causal structure of unemployment. Internal causes have a dashed border and a clear background; external causes have a blue background.

Source: Lunt, Peter K. "The Perceived Causal Structure of Unemployment." In: Grunert, K.G. and Ölander, F. (eds.) *Understanding Economic Behaviour*. Theory and Decision Library (Series A: Philosophy and Methodology of the Social Sciences), vol 11. Springer, Dordrecht. © 1989 Springer. Used with permission.

46 Unemployment and inflation

These ideas were taken up by Green, McManus, and Derrick (1998), who used the same factors as the earlier study by Lunt, but required students to construct diagrams of the causal interconnections as they perceived them to be and, crucially, to rate the strengths of each of the paths in their diagram. A composite diagram was prepared by examining each separate path between any pair of factors for each participant and including paths represented by at least 10% of them. The complexity of the resulting map is much reduced compared to that found in Lunt's work. When people are prompted to consider all the possible links and to express their view on whether any two are linked, all manner of rich patterns emerge. But when they are invited to indicate the links that occur to them spontaneously, the resulting composite map consists for the most part of simple links between each factor and unemployment, even with the very low criterion for entry used (10% of the participants). Remove the "unemployment" box, and scarcely anything remains, a striking illustration of short-range thinking.

As might be expected, the causes that people endorse as responsible for unemployment relate to the solutions they support. Murray and Millar (1992) investigated this relation between lay explanations of and solutions to unemployment in an area of high unemployment at the time, Northern Ireland. The participants rated the importance of 20 explanations of unemployment identified by Furnham (the now familiar trio of individualistic, societal/managerial, and fatalistic/uncontrollable) and also 20 solutions to unemployment, as identified by Heaven (1990). Those had been found to cluster into three categories which were labelled punitive, opportunity creation, and resource management. It was found that the policy supported corresponded to the cause identified. Endorsers of individualistic factors support a tough-minded, punitive approach to unemployment, whereas those who saw the unemployed as victims of incompetence or bad luck supported increased government spending and similar solutions.

It is worth noting an important common trait in the Furnham–Lunt–Green approach. While unemployment is undoubtedly a macroeconomic variable, the focus of the questions asked relates to individuals: How come *a certain person* is unemployed? Is that person responsible, or is it the socio-economic system (or indeed, is it just his/her fate)? That question is distinct from the macroeconomic, aggregate one: How did we reach the present level of unemployment, and how shall we go about improving it? We already mentioned the work by Shiller (2017) and van Bavel and Gaskell (2004) who contrast *systemic* and *narrative* modes of understanding economics. The systemic mode looks at aggregate values and focuses on the economy as a whole. In the narrative mode of economic thinking (the one tapped by the question asked), the individual is the figure and the economic system remains in the background. To be sure, the Furnham tradition also references factors beyond the individual, but the *explanandum* is the state of individuals, not the system. The type of explanations that economists can offer to the question of "the causes of unemployment" lie largely outside the scope of these studies.

Our pilot studies suggest that when asked what might the state do to reduce unemployment, people suggest that the state could hire more people, or launch requests for tenders to perform work that will ultimately lead to more people being employed. This is the direct route again: not enough jobs → create jobs. The notion that the economy might be so regulated that more jobs will be created doesn't occur to the untutored.

Lay views about unemployment conform to the cognitive principles outlined in Chapters 2 and 3. When people consider what produces unemployment, they come up with simple and direct causes. Invited to rate several possible remedies to employment, the solutions they favor involve direct causation. Finally, when forced to rate all possible links between relevant variables, each group considers direction of causation, either from the system to the individual or conversely. The direction endorsed is in keeping with each group's worldview, as we will discuss in depth in Chapter 7 devoted to capitalism.

Inflation

Attention to the psychology of inflation has been around for a while. That work started with George Katona who, in the 1930s, studied hyperinflation in Germany and looked at how economic expectations influence consumer spending, saving, and borrowing. This led him, after World War II, to quantify changes in consumer sentiment (Katona, 1960). The outcome was the famous Index of Consumer Sentiment survey (University of Michigan) which interviews about 500 individuals each month about their present financial conditions and current and future buying plans, and whose findings are one of the inputs to economic models.

Most later work on the psychology of inflation continued to focus on perceptions and expectations (Armantier, Bruine de Bruin, Topa, Klaauw, & Zafar, 2015; Batchelor, 1986; Ranyard et al., 2017), seeing as they affect confidence and saving behavior (e.g., Warneryd, 1986, 1999; Warneryd & Wahlund, 1985). Perceptions and expectations are especially important because the behavior resulting from them sometimes leads a life of its own; even after government sharply cuts back or stops inflating, consumers may persevere with low cash holdings or sellers may go on raising prices, in the expectation of being justified by more inflation.

The psychology of inflation goes beyond the inflation predictions and their expected effects. Savadori, Nicotra, Rumiati, and Tamborini (2001) who studied the content and structure of mental representation of economic crises in Italy, showed that inflation is considered by people to be a prime symptom of economic crisis, despite the fact that persistent inflation tends to become the normal state of affairs in an economy. So too, the introduction of the euro has routinely been held responsible for producing price inflation, and this colored many Europeans' negative view of the euro (de Rosa, Jesuino, & Gioiosa, 2003), whereas careful studies concur that the alleged link is unsupported by evidence (Angelini & Lippi, 2008; Del Giovane & Sabbatini, 2008).

Our own focus will again be on folk-economic conceptions, on how the public understands inflation and its causes. There are even fewer studies on this topic than concerning unemployment. Leiser and Drori (2005) examined lay beliefs about

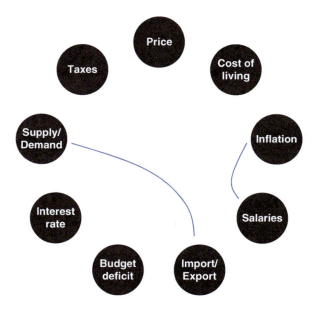

FIGURE 4.3 Linking economic concepts.

inflation. Domains such as economics that have substantial practical or social importance are structured by society at large, resulting in "social representations," defined as socially shared ideas, opinions, attitudes, and theories (Moscovici, 1981, 1984; see Abric, 2005a; Ernst-Vintila, Delouvee, & Rouquette, 2010; Flament & Rouquette, 2003; Vergès, 1989, 1992; Vergès & Bastounis, 2001; Vergès & Ryba, 2012). For instance, we saw above how Labour and Conservative party voters have contrasting social representations of how factors responsible for unemployment are interrelated.

Leiser and Drori analyzed and compared the social representations of inflation among various groups of people with no economic training. Participants were shown the layout of economic terms (as presented in Figure 4.3) and were requested to draw a line between those that they considered most closely related. They then explained why they had drawn each link. The number of participants selecting a given link between two concepts was taken as a measure of their "proximity." The resulting table was subjected to a mapping procedure known as multidimensional scaling (Clémence, 2005).

A striking phenomenon is the general willingness of respondents to indicate links between concepts, even though, when questioned about them, they could not say much of significance on the nature of those links. More than 80% of the explanations for the links proposed by the respondents were either very superficial or downright vacuous, as also observed by Williamson and Wearing (1996).

Interesting differences in the organization of the concepts were found when the strength of the links was analyzed by group. For price setters such as shopkeepers, inflation is a central concept associated with increases in their operating costs (mainly to higher interest payments on debt) and to lower demand. Prices too are central, as shopkeepers are of course preoccupied with prices in the day-to-day. The topic of salaries, central to teachers, is peripheral to them, as it is not relevant to them. In contrast, people receiving a salary (state-employed teachers) fear that in an inflationary episode, updates of (nominal) wages will lag behind increases of the consumer price index. To them, salaries are central, and the concept linked to taxes and inflation, the two perceived threats on their salaries. Finally, for university students (non-economist majors or minors) neither salaries nor inflation are central. Students usually work in temporary little jobs and linking their wages inflation (cost of living index) is not an issue, as they don't expect to remain with the same employer after they graduate. No single organizing concept appears in the middle of their map.

Summarizing, the place of inflation in the mental map of people reflects their different economic circumstances (Vergès, 1989; Vergès & Ryba, 2012) and constitutes another manifestation of narrow scope retrieval. Concepts that come to mind are triggered by personal, and therefore highly salient, circumstances. Those that are less relevant to them do not come up as relevant at all.

The central psychological core of "inflation"

Not all elements of representations have the same importance. Some are essential, others are important, yet others are secondary. A social representation is a socio-cognitive system with a specific organization: it is organized around and by a central core consisting of a very limited number of elements which gives it its meaning and determines the relations between its elements. The theory of the core has an essential methodological consequence: to study a social representation requires to look for the constituents of its core (Abric, 2005b; Ernst-Vintila et al., 2010; Flament & Rouquette, 2003; Moliner, 1996).

In another part of the study by Leiser and Drori, participants were asked to write down a list of terms or short phrases that they considered to be related to inflation. These terms were later content-analyzed and regrouped into a number of more general concepts. Two obvious criteria for assessing the importance of a concept are the average *rank* it occupies in the respondents' lists, and how *frequently* it is mentioned across respondents. We used these two criteria to detect the "central core" of inflation representations: concepts that were mentioned both frequently and early on in participants' lists were taken to constitute the central conceptual core (Abric, 2005b; Vergès, 1994). Figure 4.4 plots frequency against mean position across all 200 participants. As is generally found, the two criteria go together in an orderly fashion, and no concept occurs early on that is not also frequent, as concepts that are strongly associated to inflation are popular and spring to mind early on.

The central core, clearly identifiable in the bottom-right quadrant, includes the following concepts: money, price increases, the cost of living index (COL), and devaluation. To the economically naïve individual, inflation is perceived as

50 Unemployment and inflation

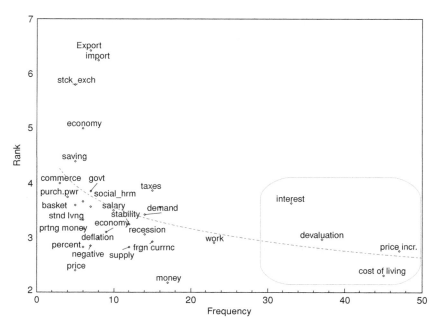

FIGURE 4.4 Core and peripheral concepts evoked by the prompt "inflation."

something bad that befalls prices and money: money is worth less, and prices are higher. Tellingly, whereas devaluation is salient, imports and exports are rarely mentioned and don't feature among the early associates. This is because inflation is thought of as something that happens to money. Money loses its value, whilst devaluation only expresses that fact. Once again we may see how lay thinking takes only one tiny step forward in the causal sequence, making the consequences of inflation for trade and currency virtually invisible (i.e., short-range reasoning). There are other glaring omissions: absent from this account are wages and salaries, unemployment, the government, the central bank, foreign trade, savings, and indeed, any reference to economics as a system.

This conception could not be more different from Milton Friedman's famous helicopter image. "When we economists hear the term 'inflation'," writes Mankiw in reference to that image, "we naturally start thinking about helicopters dropping money over the countryside. We imagine a continuing change in the unit of account that alters all nominal magnitudes proportionately" (Mankiw, 1997, p. 66). As we discuss in Chapter 9 on financial literacy, non-economists have huge difficulties with the corresponding question, that about the money illusion: "Suppose that in the year 2010, your income has doubled and prices of all goods have doubled too. In 2010, how much will you be able to buy with your income? (more/less/same)." In a representative sample of the Dutch population, only 22% of the respondents answered the question correctly (Van Rooij, Lusardi, & Alessie, 2011). Akerlof and Shiller rightly point out that "Money illusion is another cornerstone of our theory.

The public is confused by inflation and deflation and does not reason through its effects" (Akerlof & Shiller, 2010, p. 61).

Little wonder, then, that contrary to most economists, non-economists are categorically averse to inflation. To them, zero inflation is best. Katona (1975) showed long ago that at least 80% of people complain about being hurt by inflation – the poor more so than the rich. They believe it should not and need not happen. Later studies confirmed Katona's findings. Recall that when Robert Shiller (1997) interviewed laypeople and asked them why they so dislike inflation, one cause stood out: they believe that inflation makes them poorer. His respondents do cite various inconveniences associated with inflation such as making it harder to judge whether a price is advantageous and to plan for the future. They have other concerns too, such as the perception that inflation provides the opportunity for some economic agents to take advantage of others. Some mentioned that inflation is misleading and weakens the country's currency, damages its national prestige, and increases political instability (the direction of causation they identify going from inflation to instability). Still, the supposed direct effect of inflation on the standard of living is their overriding concern (Scheve, 2003; Shiller, 1997).

Having looked at inflation and unemployment in isolation, we now turn to the relation between the two and to other economic variables.

Note

1 We thank the following colleagues for their assistance with data collection: Erich Kichler and Katja Meier (Austria), Marko Polić (Slovenia), Marian Bastounis (Greece), Ronit Briskman (Israel), Christine Roland-Levy (France), Jale Minbas (Turkey), Ng Seok Hui (Singapore). Allen, Ng, and Leiser (2005) and Bastounis et al. (2004) are based on this survey, but the data presented here were not previously published. The questionnaire itself was developed by Briskman-Mazliach (1998).

5

THE "GOOD BEGETS GOOD" HEURISTIC

The relations between macroeconomic variables

Economic theory explains that, in the short run, there is a tradeoff between inflation and unemployment, as can readily be seen from the following argument. When unemployment is high, there are many more people willing to work than there are jobs available. Employers can therefore offer low wages, and have no motivation to offer more. Wages will remain stagnant, and there will be no wage inflation. Conversely, it is when unemployment is low that employers will offer higher wages to attract employees, which leads to rising wage inflation. Recent years have not always followed this theory, but discussing the reasons for this is outside the scope of this work.

To determine whether the perceptions of inflation and unemployment are related, Orland (2013) asked a sample of 2000 students to estimate unemployment and inflation: "Please state or guess (up to one decimal place) the current yearly inflation rate in % ___; and the current unemployment rate in % ___." He found that individuals who overestimate/underestimate one variable tended to overestimate/underestimate the other too. This suggests that both variables have a common core, that may be interpreted as the health of the economy, just as to the uninformed, some stocks are good, and sport both low risk and high returns. Those who believe that the economy is in good shape will judge both inflation and unemployment rates to be low. Those who see the economy as going through difficult times will report both high inflation and high unemployment.

Matters become more complicated when predictions are elicited. Expectations of inflation are the beliefs held by the public about the likely path of inflation in the future. The Phillips curve states that there is a tradeoff between the rate of unemployment and the rate of inflation in an economy. (More precisely, it is believed by many that unemployment varies with *unanticipated* inflation.) This relation held for a long time and the reasoning behind it is a standard component of economics courses, though in recent years its slope has substantially declined (Blanchard, 2016).

The public does not believe in the Phillips curve. In fact, it believes its opposite, and this demands an explanation. Dixon, Griffiths, and Lim (2014) analyzed a long-running survey (Melbourne, 1995–2011) comprising over 220,000 observations of consumers' views about the expected state of the economy. The questionnaire included many questions, out of which we will be concerned with two: the one on inflation: *Thinking about the prices of things you buy, <u>by this time next year</u>, do you think they'll have gone: (1) up, (2) down, or (3) stayed the same? (4) don't know*, the other on unemployment: *Now about people being out of work <u>during the coming 12 months</u>, do you think there'll be (1) more unemployment, (2) about the same/some more some less, (3) less unemployment, (4) don't know*. Analyzing the pattern of answers to these two questions, Dixon et al. (2014) show that (except for rare special cases such as during the financial crisis) the evaluations of future inflation and unemployment rates correlate positively, as did the assessments of their current values. Similar findings were reported by Dräger, Lamla, and Pfajfar (2016) who exploited the data accumulated over the years by the University of Michigan Survey of Consumers, which collects consumers' expectations regarding the main macroeconomics variables on a monthly basis.

In all those cases, the underlying logic appears to be the same as what we saw earlier regarding the evaluation of stocks. "Good" stocks are good through and through: they sport high returns *and* low risk. Similarly, if the economy is ticking along nicely, both inflation and unemployment must be low. The same relation holds for expectations, which is merely an assessment of the state of the economy in the future: if the economy is predicted to be in good shape a year hence, both indicators will be low. If bad times are ahead, both are expected to be high. Those links are purely associative, and economic reasoning plays no role in them.

The "good begets good" heuristic

The studies just summarized relate to participants' assessment of levels of economic activity and how they expect them to evolve. We now turn to people's explicit beliefs about how such variables are related. People typically think in terms of links between two variables at a time, not more. This is one more manifestation of the narrow scope of lay reasoning: it will consider two variables and hold views about how changes in one would affect the other, but mostly does not countenance more complex relations that involve three.

To illustrate, in one early study of economic understanding, Rubin (2001) provided participants with index cards carrying the name of 36 economic variables, such as the rate of economic growth, inflation rate, and the savings rate. Participants tried to identify as many causal pairs as possible, where an increase in one of the variables causes either an increase or a decrease in the other. For example, a subject might judge that an increase in income would provoke an increase in consumption and in savings. If a participant believed that generous unemployment benefits reduce the motivation of the unemployed to seek jobs, she will select cards 32 and 12 (see Figure 5.1) and indicate that a negative relation links the two. She may

54 Relations between macroeconomic variables

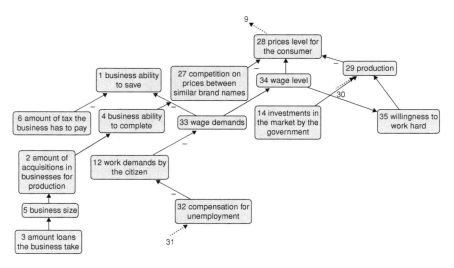

FIGURE 5.1 Fragment of the conceptual map of one participant.

further judge that increased demand for jobs will lower the demands for higher wages, and select cards 12 and 33, again with a negative link between the two. But the same participant may remain unaware of the link between generous unemployment compensation and higher wages.

When binary relations are combined into a map, patterns emerge, but these often strike as novel the very people who provided the binary relations. Several investigators have commented on how rare it is for subjects to mention features of the overall structure of their understanding, such as loops (Ackermann, Cropper, Eden, & Cook, 1991; Eden & Spender, 1998; Weick & Bougon, 1986; White, 1995). Williamson and Wearing (1996), for instance, mapped painstakingly the economic cognition of their subjects and concluded that, whereas there exists an overall cognitive map that includes all the links mentioned by at least some respondents, individuals mentions only a small subset of that overall map, and none were aware of the whole. Knowledge tends to remain fragmented (DiSessa, 2006, 2009; Vosniadou & Skopeliti, 2014). Researchers and other practitioners who engage in mapping cognitions find directed graphs useful to help people reflect upon their knowledge (Axelrod, 1976; Laukkanen, 1996; Sevón, 1984), and there exists a class of commercial software meant to assist such "mind-mapping", or "cognitive mapping". The relative popularity of mind-mapping is attributable to their providing an overview of the local links that the users have knowledge of, which helps them consolidate their own knowledge (Chiou, 2008; Horton et al., 1993; Nesbit & Adesope, 2006).

While participants may be unable to combine their individual insights into a system unaided (Barbas & Psillos, 1997; Grotzer, 2012; Leiser, 2001; Lundholm & Davies, 2013; Perkins & Grotzer, 2005), there is a pattern to their understanding, and that pattern was elucidated by the following study.

Relations between macroeconomic variables 55

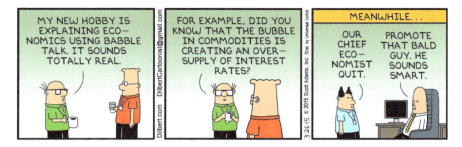

FIGURE 5.2 Eco-babble is easy.
Source: Dilbert © 2012 Scott Adams. Used by permission of Andrew McMeel Syndication. All rights reserved.

Leiser and Aroch (2009) presented some 19 macroeconomic variables to participants. These included measures of aggregate economic activity (like the GNP), the rate of economic growth, corporate profits, wages, private spending, private investments on the stock market, the rate of inflation, the rate of unemployment. For every pair of variables, they were asked to judge explicitly whether they were causally related and if so, how.

The questions followed a fixed format:

> If *VARIABLE A* increases, how will this affect *VARIABLE B*?
> e.g.: If the *unemployment rate* increases, how will this affect *the inflation rate*?

For every pair of variables A and B, participants were asked: *If variable A increases, how will this affect variable B?* They had to select one out of four possible answers: B will increase; B will decrease; B will not be affected; "don't know."

We learn about how comfortable participants felt answering questions on causal connections between variables from the prevalence of substantive answers. The average rate of "don't know" was 27%. In other words, on average, the participants felt confident enough to answer three times out of four. This is startling, considering how little people understand. How do they presume to decide how an increased money supply impacts corporate profits, the national credit rating, or the GNP, seeing that they don't have any clear concept of what an increased money supply even means?

To answer this, we had to look for a pattern. The first step is to determine which factors the participants consider to be causally linked, by counting the proportion of participants who judged that if A goes up, B goes up (or down), or conversely, or both. The more such positive links between A and B, the closer they are.

Armed with this information, we ran a (k-means) clustering procedure, that grouped the 19 variables into two clusters (see Table 5.1), on the basis of how closely linked they are. Looking at the resulting clusters, one is struck by how neatly they divide into two groups: a cluster of "good" developments and a cluster

56 Relations between macroeconomic variables

TABLE 5.1 "Good" and "bad" increases in economic variables

Positive cluster	Negative cluster
GNP	Government expenditures
National credit rating	Rate of inflation
Corporate profits	Income tax rate
Investment by the public in stock market	Interest rate on loans
Average net salary	Unemployment rate
Consumption rate	Consumer debt
Money supply	Depth of recession
Rate of economic growth	Government welfare expenditures
Competitiveness of the market	
Preference for local products	
Personal savings rate	

of "bad" ones. On the left side are items such as national credit rating, corporate profits, average net salary, and the like. On the right side, items such as tax rate, inflation, and unemployment.[1]

That is to say, our participants categorized changes in economic variables as either good or bad, and this provides the participants with the (dubious) ground for their answers. We saw they seldom admit they don't know how one variable affects the other. Non-economists manage to muster answers thanks to this simple yet powerful trick. In their view, the economic world functions in either a virtuous or a vicious circle. An increase in one good variable always increases the values of other good variables, and decreases those of bad variables, and conversely. When asked about some A and B, all they need to do is check to see in what cluster each belongs: if both belong to a same cluster (good or bad), a raise in one will raise the other. If they belong to opposite poles, an increase in one causes the other to drop. This heuristic we called the *good-begets-good (GBG) heuristic*. It explains how people manage to answer so readily how two variables affect one another, without a clue about the mechanism responsible for this influence, and without even thinking about how more than two variables might be involved in accounting for their mutual influence.

The GBG heuristic isn't cut off from reality. Professional economists too commonly look at the economy as being in good or bad shape, and even devised economic indices to suggest an overall evaluation of the state of the economy. Note that in Table 5.1, increases in both inflation and in unemployment are in the negative column. The original "misery index," introduced by Okun in the Lyndon Johnson years, is simply the unemployment rate added to the inflation rate, to which the "augmented misery index" adds the change in housing prices. Merrill Lynch's economists later devised a broader index (The Economist, 2006) that adds unemployment and inflation rates, interest rates, and the budget and current-account balances, and subtracts GDP growth. Its rationale is that high unemployment, inflation, and interest rates are bad, whereas positive budget and current account balances and a high GDP growth rate are good.

Macroeconomic consequences of the GBG heuristic

Dräger et al. (2014) analyzed the microdata of the Michigan Survey to evaluate whether US consumers form macroeconomic expectations "consistent" with the economic concepts we discussed here: the Phillips curve, linking inflation and unemployment rates; the Taylor rule (linking employment and price stability); and the Income Fisher equation, linking inflation with nominal and real interest rates (or income). This is an objective distinct from judging whether public expectations accurately predict inflation or unemployment, a cardinal question in its own right. But the Dräger et al. study fits our purpose, by putting side by side the predictions of the GBG heuristic and well-known relations between economic variables often posited in the literature. That study found that 50% of the surveyed population have expectations consistent with the Income Fisher equation, 46% consistent with the Taylor rule, and only 34% are in line with the Phillips curve. Note that these figures certainly overestimate what laypeople understand, inasmuch as the analyses rely on correlations between predictions and people may have got the direction right without understanding. Moreover, only 6% of consumers form theory–consistent expectations with respect to all three concepts. Unsurprisingly, those relatively few consumers with theory-consistent expectations also tend to have lower absolute inflation forecast errors, and are closer to professionals' inflation forecasts, suggesting that they follow economic news rather closely, which suggests strongly that they belong to a select group of informed citizens.

Predictions become harder when the economy becomes unstable. Dräger et al. (2014) observe that consumers are even less consistent with the Phillips curve and the Taylor rule during recessions and when inflation exceeds 2%. From the perspective of the central bank, stabilizing the economy and leading it to growth becomes more of a challenge. In addition to the economic complexities involved, the laypeople's model plays a role. GBG implies that rising actual and expected rates of inflation ("negative" developments) are predicted to lead to lower actual and future economic growth, higher unemployment, and lower corporate profits. As the expected rate of inflation increases, individuals become more pessimist about the future prospects of the whole economy. In times of crisis, this lessens the chances of recovery. It is well known that the concept of overall sentiment about the economy has a large psychological component (Bovi, 2009; Resende & Zeidan, 2015) and the GBG explains in part how this component functions in a self-reinforcing circle.

We saw above that Dixon et al. (2014) showed (in their analysis of expectations of economic change) that lay predictions of inflation and unemployment conform to the GBG heuristic, and are at variance with the Phillips curve. Gaffeo and Canzian (2011) further showed that the GBG heuristic has real world economic consequences, and in particular that it complicates the task of the central banks. The Taylor rule is a monetary-policy rule that stipulates how much the

58 Relations between macroeconomic variables

central bank should change the nominal interest rate in response to changes in inflation, output, or other economic conditions. The GBG heuristic means that the public perceives the economic situation simplistically, as improving or deteriorating, and this generates waves of optimism or pessimism. A wave of sentiment among the public can trigger a corresponding change in aggregate demand. "Such waves triggered by inflation dynamics but also governed by the GBG heuristic enhance the effectiveness of monetary policy when the volatility of the public's sentiment is relatively low, but act as a destabilizing device when intense" (p. 666). The authors conclude that controlling the system by means of monetary policy is a much tougher task than predicted by the received wisdom on the stabilizing properties of the Taylor principle.

GBG has been applied to additional domains. Drews and van den Bergh (2016) investigated the Spanish public opinion about the relation between economic growth, prosperity, and environmental sustainability. To this end, they ran an online questionnaire survey on a representative sample of 1008 citizens. Analyzing the data, they found a strong belief that economic growth delivers, or is even a prerequisite for, jobs, happiness, public services, and economic stability. And what might bring economic growth to an end? Here the answers pointed to a range of bad things: about 30% of the respondents saw "growing income inequality" as the main reason for an end to economic growth, followed by "high public debt" with 23%, and "aging population" with 12%.

It is interesting to reflect about that disposition to brand economic variables as either good or bad.

The tendency to make binary distinction is one of numerous "human universals" found in all culture, according to the list compiled by anthropologist D. E. Brown (1991). Henri Wallon (1945) observed its prevalence amongst children and discusses it as a primitive mode of intellectual functioning, available to children starting around age six. Adults too exhibit this tendency.

Up to this point, we presented the GBG heuristic as some sort of clever trick that allows non-economists to respond to questions about how variables relate, without any knowledge of the causal link between them. But this is only the surface of the story.

We discussed earlier the two central modes of thinking, fast and slow (Evans 2010; Kahneman, 2011; Stanovich & Toplak, 2012; Stanovich, West, & Toplak, 2011). The fast and associative thinking mode is the default. The slow and analytic mode requires effort, and since people are cognitively lazy, they are reluctant to engage in it. Thinking in terms of good and bad and using the GBG heuristic finesses the analytic approach, which would involve working out how one variable affects another, that is, a proper economic analysis. As we stressed throughout, laypeople are incapable of engaging in this type of analysis. The depth of explanation of economic concepts is low in all segments of the population (Leiser & Drori, 2005). Indeed, a lack of explanatory depth is a general feature of human understanding (Ackermann et al., 1991; Leiser, 2001; Leiser & Ackerman, 2010; Rozenblit & Keil, 2002; Sloman & Fernbach, 2017). GBG explains how opinions are formed despite the absence of a non-trivial understanding of economics. They are formed by a fast, associative, and superficial mode of thinking, that relies on a convenient human universal to come up with some answer: using the good/bad dichotomy.

A century ago, educational books for children in Europe would classify animals in a similar way. Some animals were described as useful, others as harmful pests. The dichotomy was grounded in an agrarian context, where interest in wild animals was practical – which are the pests that will ruin the crops, which are useful and should be protected. Reasonable as the dichotomy is, it hardly forms the basis for a proper understanding of the ecosystem in which those animals participate. What the GBG heuristic tells us is that the economic world is viewed by the public as a largely undifferentiated whole, one that can be in more or less good shape, more or less healthy. To the economist, the assorted variables featuring in the experiment are elements in a complex model, where for instance the link between inflation and monetary mass may be modulated by the rate of unemployment. To the laypeople, those variables are just manifestations of the overall health, or otherwise, of "the economy." This is a deep-seated difference in outlook.

Note

1 For those interested in technicalities, the relation is even stronger than just a classification as good or bad. The *degree* of goodness/badness is highly significant. A one-dimensional multidimensional scaling of the variables, placing them on one line according to how much they are judged to affect one another, is almost perfectly predicted by how good or bad an increase in each variable is judged to be (Pearson r correlation between the position on the MDS and judged goodness/badness according to a control group is a whopping 0.93) (Leiser & Aroch, 2009).

6

WHAT IS THE ECONOMY LIKE?

How metaphors shape our understanding of economics

Commenting on the metaphors used to frame policy debates in the aftermath of the 2008 financial crisis, economist Paul Krugman wrote:

> I say block those metaphors. America's economy isn't a stalled car, nor is it an invalid who will soon return to health if he gets a bit more rest. Our problems are longer-term than either metaphor implies. And bad metaphors make for bad policy. The idea that the economic engine is going to catch or the patient rise from his sickbed any day now encourages policy makers to settle for sloppy, short-term measures when the economy really needs well-designed, sustained support.
>
> *(Krugman, 2015)*

For many, *the economy* conjures up a rather hazy and far-away image. By any account, it is an immense and intricate system, in which we are at once active participant and powerless observer. We all buy and consume goods; we have bank accounts and credit cards; some of us invest in stocks, take loans, and purchase retirement plans. To be sure, we *live* the economy. But do we *understand* it? How does raising the minimum wage affect unemployment? How does inflation modulate interest rates? How is it OK for a country to be trillions of dollars in debt? And who lent it so much money in the first place? The economic world can be overwhelmingly complex, involving countless variables that interact over time and space, and which operate by principles unintuitive and foreign to everyday thought (Chapters 2 and 3). In want of formal training, sufficient time and energy to verse oneself in these matters, or the cognitive wherewithal, how do we come to grips with the workings of the economy?

To grapple with the novel and complex phenomena we encounter daily in the modern world, humans fall back on a cognitive toolbox of rough-and-ready

What is the economy like? **61**

instruments crafted by evolution to guide understanding and action. A subset of these has been termed "heuristics"; simple rules of thumb that work (sometimes) (Gigerenzer & Gaissmaier, 2011). The *good-begets-good* heuristic in economic reasoning (Chapter 5) submits that whenever something "good" occurs (employment goes up), other good things will follow suit (GDP will grow). The corollaries maintain that GOOD↑BAD↓; GOOD↓BAD↑; BAD↑GOOD↓; and BAD↓GOOD↑. A simple rule of thumb, the good-begets-good heuristic enables people to generate countless inferences with confidence going on precious little to begin with.

Another such tool is metaphor. Far from a mere "device of the poetic imagination and the rhetorical flourish," metaphor is a matter of thought and action no less than it is of words (Lakoff & Johnson, 1980). "Love is a journey"; "a classroom is a garden"; "life is a marathon"; these figures of speech stand testimony to the way we think – or at least are invited to think – about the issues in question. Metaphors allow us to understand and reason about novel phenomena by recourse to prior experience in seemingly unrelated domains. They provide structure for fluid reality, clothing the abstract in familiar terms and making the chaotic seem more tractable. For if love is a journey, a few bumps along the road are all but expected; if a classroom is a garden, then it must be tended with care and patience; and if life is a marathon, one would be wise to think long-term and avoid burning out.

In economics, metaphors allow us to trudge the abstract and technical field with newfound ease and confidence. They trade treacherous territory for a simple map, cutting through the complexities and leaving the details by the wayside. They afford mental crutches to the uninitiated; explanatory and suasory powers to the adept. Metaphors are useful, deceptively so.

In earlier pages, we encountered one particularly stubborn metaphor: *the state budget is like a household budget*. Remember the chap from the Introduction who lamented how politicians complicate things unnecessarily? "Economics is really simple," he declared; if he were to spend more than he earned, he would soon run into serious financial difficulty, and the same holds for the state. This logic, while straightforward, is invalid.

In the household, income and expenditure are independent. While households' spending usually flows *outwards* from the family unit (taxed by the government or spent on food, clothing etc.), national expenditure mostly flows *inwards* (Clark, 2015). If the state were to run a surplus in a given year, that would mean a net flow of money going from the public, in the form of tax revenue, to the government (Keen, 2015). In other words, government earning would exceed government spending on its citizens, in the form of infrastructure investments, employment, education, and social services. If this were sustained over time, it would result in a downward spiral for the economy: the public would run down their savings, leading to decreased demands, and therefore lower overall economic activity, in a vicious, self-reinforcing deflationary circle. Ultimately the government would collect fewer taxes, and find itself at a *worse* position to pay down its debt. Government spending in such cases can prevent recessions. The purpose of spending by the government is not to cover "its" needs but to adjust economic activity. Conversely, when the

62 What is the economy like?

economy is "over-heating" (another common metaphor), the government may reduce its expenses.

State and household budget differ in yet other respects. For example, states can create money "out of thin air" via their central banks, with an eye to increased future productivity; households cannot (Smith, 2014). And while states raise money by selling bonds with diminutive interest rates, enabled by their trustworthiness and longevity, families depend on loans to be repaid at much higher interest rates (Olen, 2013).

In spite of this, to many, the household metaphor is compelling. After all, the two units – family and state – are ostensibly parallel: the governing body corresponds to the parent and the citizens to its children (Lakoff, 2010). We know that a household cannot spend more than it earns; that would be irresponsible and could be catastrophic. How the government could get away with such behavior, let alone, how it could constitute sound economic policy, is baffling. How could the answer to debt be *yet more debt?*

Yet the responsibility for economic misconception can hardly be heaped on the public and its cognitive makeup. "Your family has to operate on a budget, so why doesn't the federal government have to do the same?" was the slogan of the Republican Romney campaign in the US presidential elections of 2012 (The Rachel Maddow Show, 2013). Later it was echoed by former President Barack Obama of the Democratic Party: "Families across this country understand what it takes to manage a budget … Well, it's time Washington acted as responsibly as our families do" (Craighead, 2011).

A recent BBC News article laments the many metaphorical forms that the UK's exit from the European union (Brexit) has taken on (Landale, 2017).

> Since Britain voted to leave the European Union, politicians and commentators have deployed everything from cakes, cherries, cats, even golf clubs to try to explain what it might all mean … The head of the UK's public spending watchdog, Sir Amyas Morse, compares Brexit to "a chocolate orange" that might fall apart at the first tap. The Tory MP Charlie Elphicke fears a "Hotel California" Brexit where "you can check out any time you like, but you can never leave." … Brexit was compared to marital separation because it allowed people to distinguish between Britain's immediate exit from the EU – the "divorce" – and its longer-term trading relations … There was also the small problem that in this divorce one side was made up of 27 different nations. Is "Mutti" Merkel the mother in this metaphor and the other 26 countries her children? … The prime minister told MPs in March she did not like the "divorce" metaphor. "I prefer not to use that term with regard to the European Union because often, when people get divorced, they do not have a good relationship afterwards."

Indeed, metaphors pervade economic discourse. Politicians use them to drive their points to audiences (Boeynaems, Burgers, Konijn, & Steen, 2017; Gibbs Jr.,

2015). Journalists pepper them generously in news reports (Krennmayr, 2015). Even professional economists indulge in metaphorical language (Klamer & Leonard, 1994; McCloskey, 1983). Time and again we hear of stocks shooting up, sliding down, bouncing and rebounding; businesses slashing prices; markets shaken to their foundations; investors subject to rough seas; companies jumping corporate loopholes; predatory lenders; ravenous investors; jobs fleeing; inflation roaring; unemployment soaring; toxic loans; start-ups taking root and green shoots signaling recovery. Non-economists get most of their information about the economy from these sources.

In the fall of 2008, the world experienced one of its most devastating financial crises to date. The crisis, having been triggered by the collapse of the US housing bubble, went on to cascade through the interconnected web comprising the global financial system (Financial Crisis Inquiry Commission, 2011). Many have tried to identify the causes that precipitated the crisis and those that blew it to its colossal proportions (in trillions lost).

One prominent metaphorical theme elaborated at the time was *the financial crisis is a tsunami* (Cheng & Ho, 2015; Pühringer & Hirte, 2013). The propagators of this metaphor were alluding to the deadly events of the 2004 Indian Ocean tsunami; an undersea earthquake off the coast of Indonesia that was caused by a subduction of tectonic plates, displacing massive amounts of water and provoking a train of tidal waves (i.e., tsunamis). The tsunamis hit the landmasses bordering on the Indian Ocean, killing hundreds of thousands and destroying infrastructure in 14 countries.

The metaphor is compelling, but what does it amount to psychologically? Leaving aside the undoubted emotional impact, how does the metaphor affect our *understanding* of the crisis, to the extent that it does?

To answer this question, let us get a better grasp of what metaphors are and how they work at the cognitive level.

Metaphors as structure mapping

Cognitive psychologists explain that metaphors have two "sides": a *source* and a *target*, with information flowing from the former to the latter (Bowdle & Gentner, 2005; Gentner, Bowdle, Wolf, & Boronat, 2001). In the metaphor *the financial crisis is a tsunami*, *a tsunami* serves as the source of the metaphor and *the financial crisis* the target. The source is what we already know, it tends to be more concrete and familiar. The target is that which we are trying to comprehend or cast in a new light, it is unfamiliar, and does not admit of a clear conceptual structure (Lakoff & Johnson, 1980).

When novel metaphors are encountered, they set off a process called structure mapping (Bowdle & Gentner, 2005; Gentner et al., 2001). In the first stage of structure mapping, features common to both source and target are identified and cross-linked, pulling the two concepts closer together in alignment – a kind of conceptual overlapping. In our case, the features common to both a tsunami and the financial crisis are: being *powerful*, *sudden*, *destructive*, and *difficult to foresee*,

64 What is the economy like?

having a *center* from which *shocks emanate* and exert *far-reaching effects*. What is pertinent to structure mapping is not superficial semblance, but deep relational similarity; tsunamis are tall and wet, but these characteristics are irrelevant in the metaphor context. By contrast, in a tsunami the strength of the quake at the epicenter implies the forcefulness of the waves and the extent of the damage wrought on shore. For the financial crisis, a similar relation obtains between the size of the housing bubble, the severity of its crash, and its destructive downstream effects in other parts of the world. The more similar the two concepts are found to be in terms of underlying conceptual structure – that is, the more neatly they map onto one another – the more apt a metaphor will seem, and the more likely that a transfer of information will occur.

The next stage is a filling-in process, in which properties *unique* to the source are projected onto the target. This is the stage where new knowledge is created. Tsunamis are *transient*; they can be expected to go just as fast as they had come. They are brought about by *natural* and *uncontrollable* forces; there is little to do about them except *take cover or flee*. These pieces of information, previously attached to tsunamis alone (i.e., naturalness, transience, uncontrollability, hide/flee strategy), can now serve to inform our mental representation of financial crises. Note that an entirely different set of inferences would have spawned from the metaphor *the financial crisis is a disease plaguing the economy*. In the latter case, candidate inferences might have involved crisis agents (corresponding to pathogens), malfunctioning components of the system (corresponding to organs), and the possibility of correcting the system (corresponding to a remedy).

Essentially the same mechanism underlies the process of analogical reasoning and problem solving. Consider the following scenario: a doctor is trying to treat a patient with a tumor in his stomach. The tumor is so situated that if high intensity rays were to be passed through to it, they would inevitably damage the surrounding tissue and kill the patient. Weaker intensity rays would spare healthy tissue, but be insufficient to destroy the tumor. How does the doctor treat the patient? In a classic study that put this puzzle to participants, only 10–20% mustered a valid solution (Gick & Holyoak, 1983). However, fully 90% managed to solve the puzzle once they were encouraged to consider the applicability of an analogous story they had read earlier in the study: a military commander is trying to capture a fortress, but all roads leading to it are mined with explosives. If a large force were to pass on one of the roads, the mines would detonate. Small groups of soldiers could pass through unharmed, but they would be insufficient in force to overtake the fortress. The commander decides to divide his army up into small groups and send them across several paths simultaneously to converge at the fortress.

Once the participants likened the two situations, the problem's corresponding elements clicked into place, and a "convergence" solution could be projected from the familiar to the novel problem: irradiate the tumor with weak intensity rays from several angles simultaneously.

In Chapter 3 we discussed this study to demonstrate that we often do not draw on the knowledge we possess unless explicitly prompted. Metaphors do just this;

they point out precisely the knowledge that we should bring to bear when trying to understand a novel phenomenon.

Therefore, metaphors carry no small benefit. By exploiting structure mapping they afford us purchase on subjects we previously knew nothing about. Not only do they illuminate current states of affairs, they may also imply how they came to be and can be expected to unfold.

But herein also lies a heavy cost. For metaphors highlight and hide, they lead but can also mislead. Each metaphor brings into focus only certain aspects of its target, effectively obscuring the rest. Thinking that the government is like a household, for instance, we might unwittingly infer that the federal budget should be run like a family one, and neglect to appreciate the crucial ways in which they differ. Under the impression of a persuasive metaphor, people are conducted to incomplete views of the issues at best, and to false beliefs and wrongheaded decisions at worst. Exacerbating this situation still, metaphors imbue complicated topics with a sense of familiarity, which can easily be confounded with genuine understanding and inspire undue confidence (Landau, Keefer, & Rothschild, 2014).

When are metaphors most influential?

In Chapter 2 we introduced the features of economics that make it so difficult to comprehend: the intellectual challenge of aggregating effects over time, the cumbrous task of integrating indirect links and feedback loops into a systematic account, and the foreignness of static and dynamic equilibria. All of these features, being so alien to everyday thought, make economics a prime target for "metaphorizing." Recall that a defining feature of metaphorical targets is that they do not admit of a clear conceptual structure (Lakoff & Johnson, 1980).

Our deficient knowledge of the workings of the economy leaves economic concepts wide open to metaphoric interpretations. Generally speaking, the less you know about a subject, and the more uncertain you feel about that knowledge, the more vulnerable you will be to the thrust of a metaphor (Landau et al., 2014, Study 2; Robins & Mayer, 2000; Williams, 2013).

Another factor that drives people to seize on metaphors is when they're highly motivated to gain an understanding of the target. These are issues in which poor decisions and false judgments on their part could lead to harmful consequences (Landau et al., 2014).

Economics satisfies both these criteria: it is puzzling, yet important.

Metaphors in problem solving and decision making

Let us now go over some examples of how the process of structure mapping, elicited by metaphors, unfolds in everyday comprehension and decision-making scenarios (for reviews see Keefer & Landau, 2016; Thibodeau, Hendricks, & Boroditsky, 2017). The following experiments simulate everyday situations in which people encounter economic metaphors; reading the paper or watching the news.

66 What is the economy like?

Landau et al. (2014) presented participants with a text passage describing the bankruptcy of a fictitious company. Half the participants read a version of the text that framed the company's failure as an automobile accident, the other half read a neutral version of the text. Later, the researchers measured the degree to which the participants assigned blame to the CEO for the company's failure. The authors found that participants who read the metaphorical passage were indeed more likely to blame the CEO, but only to the extent that they blamed *drivers for car accidents*. Those who did not share these a priori assumptions were unswayed by the metaphor. In other words, the metaphor prompted participants to transfer their knowledge about car accidents to their understanding of corporate failure.

In a complement to this study, Williams (2013) had participants read a fabricated news story about a company that filed for bankruptcy, metaphorically framing it as a medical condition culminating in death. It varied on a literal passage by substituting metaphorical terms for literal expressions: instead of "filing for bankruptcy," the company was arriving "at death's doorstep"; instead of "a possible prelude to closing down completely," the company tried "a last ditch effort to avoid financial death." And instead of the manufacturers being characterized as "soon to be bankrupt," it said they were "ailing." The respondents indicated to what extent they held different factors accountable for the company's failure: the government, the economy, the management, and the consumers. As expected, those who read the disease metaphor attributed more responsibility to the three situational factors: the government, economy, and consumers, than those who read the literal passage. Disease and death are natural and inevitable processes not usually caused or desired by their objects; likening a failing business to an ailing patient disposed the respondents to see the causes of the company's demise as external and uncontrollable.

Metaphorical language affects stock market forecasting too. Morris, Sheldon, Ames, and Young (2007) presented participants in their study with the intra-day fluctuations of the Nasdaq index on six sample days. They then read commentary on the market's movement which featured either animate, mechanical, or non-metaphorical expressions. For instance:

TABLE 6.1

	Mechanical	*Animate*	*Non-metaphorical*
Upwards	This afternoon, the Nasdaq was swept upward	This afternoon, the Nasdaq started climbing upwards	This afternoon the Nasdaq index posted a gain
Downwards	Today the Nasdaq drifted lower	Today the Nasdaq leaped and bounded lower	After volatility in the morning the Nasdaq index ended lower

Next, the participants indicated for each sample day how they thought the market would perform in the next. Participant responses revealed that, in general, they expected that the trends from the current day would persist into the next; a so-called *continuance bias*. Furthermore, describing stock market fluctuations in animate terms (climb, leap, bound, head), rather than in mechanical or non-metaphorical terms, produced an even greater continuance bias. That is, animate metaphors disposed the respondents to expect that the present-day trend would persist *and amplify* in the next, presumably because animals are goal-driven and pursue their goal with some consistency. A simple manipulation of wording changed the participants' expectations because it caused them to assume a different logic behind the market's movements.

Economic metaphors in the media

What are the major economic metaphors prevailing in the media, and presumably in people's minds? To uncover the popular metaphors of economics, *discourse analysis* studies comb through reams of text from the news media in search of metaphorical expressions suspect of carrying extra conceptual load. Once exposed, the expressions are analyzed and traced back to their roots (Charteris-Black & Ennis, 2001; Krennmayr, 2015). Discourse analysis studies take the premise that our language is a record of the metaphors that dominate our thinking (Lakoff & Johnson, 1980). Consider the import of the following sentences on how we think and act with regard to the matters in question:

1. Your claims are *indefensible*.
2. His criticisms were *right on target*.
3. He *attacked* every weak point in my argument.

The italicized metaphorical expressions bespeak a lurking metaphor: *argument is war*. Just so,

4. Look how *far* we've come.
5. We're at a *crossroads*.
6. We'll just have to *go our separate ways*.

These metaphorical expressions attest to the underlying metaphor *love is a journey* (Lakoff & Johnson, 1980).

To identify economic metaphors, the discourse analysis literature has cast its net far and wide, collecting data from many countries, cultures, and languages around the world, spanning the past few decades of economic reporting. Following is a short discussion of two of the most prevalent metaphors: *the economy is an organism* and *the economy is a machine*.

68 What is the economy like?

The economy is an organism

Silaški and Đurović (2010) followed news reports of the 2008 financial crisis in English and Serbian. They uncovered, in both languages, expressions hinting at the underlying metaphor *the economy is an organism*. For example:

1. The financial sector is the *life blood* of any economy. (*Financial Times*, July 6, 2009)
2. History has shown that a vibrant, dynamic financial system is *at the heart* of a vibrant, dynamic economy. (*Financial Times*, February 8, 2009)
3. They struck at our military and economic *nerve centers*. (*Financial Times*, December 2, 2009)

Such expressions are not merely interspersed in economic reporting, they are systematic. So called *extended metaphors* elaborate upon a key metaphorical theme (e.g., *the economy is an organism*) by cross-linking various elements in the source (*organism*) and target (*the economy*).

Sentences 1–3 draw a set of mappings from the *anatomy* of an organism to the *structure* of the economic system. Further probing reveals that analogies are also to be found between states of *health and disease* and states of economic *function*. From Silaški and Đurović (2010):

1. Dubai's recent economic *malaise has spread* to its smaller neighbour. (*Financial Times*, November 17, 2009)
2. When global financial market turmoil first erupted in August last year, a common view was that while the US economy would *catch flu*, continental Europe might escape with *just a cold*. (*Financial Times*, October 10, 2008)
3. The *patient* is not responding. Liquidity infusions, co-ordinated rate cuts, state sponsored bank bail-outs – nothing seems to be working. The London market is in *cardiac arrest*. (*Financial Times*, October 11, 2008)

This pattern suggests that the organism-metaphorical expressions strewn throughout economic discourse are not the result of journalists' poetical whim, but rather of a systematic appeal found in their sources – organisms. Indeed, corpus-based studies have revealed metaphorical mappings from organisms to the economy as regards the lifecycle (White, 2003); bodily movement (Chow, 2014); health and disease (Boers & Demecheleer, 1997); metabolism (Vukićević-Đorđević, 2014); and up the entire organism domain (Charteris-Black & Ennis, 2001; Domaradzki, 2016). By studying corpora from various times and places, these studies show that the organism metaphor is ubiquitous.

The economy is a machine

Another prominent metaphor in media discourse likens the economy to a grand machine, complete with receptacles, pipes, and pumps, where money circulates as liquid throughout the system (in the 1950s this metaphor was literally embodied in the Phillips Machine, see Chapter 2). On this metaphor, economic processes abide by the laws of physics; what goes up must come down; movement proceeds along a set and foreseeable trajectory; cause and effect are strictly and predictably linked, and so on. If we were to manipulate this system by changing the size of the receptacles or the rate of liquid exchange, the results would follow determinately. Like any machine, the system is susceptible to malfunction, but also can be fixed.

Traces of this metaphor were recorded in a discourse analysis exploring the conceptualization of money in English and Japanese (Takahashi, 2010):

1. Instead, the banking sector has carried on *trickling out* money to companies that should have folded; the government has kept the banks alive; and the economy has been kept *above water* with *huge fiscal injections*. (*Financial Times*, March 2, 2003)
2. At the previous policy board meeting, the bank raised the maximum level of the liquidity target by 2 trillion yen ($18 billion) from 30 trillion yen ($276 billion). *Flooding* the system with cash helps *lift* the economy by making it easier for commercial banks to dole out loans to companies. (Associated Press, November 1, 2003)
3. Separately, financial regulators said that they would study a proposal to permit the government to *inject* public money into struggling banks without waiting for them to formally declare that they are short of capital. (*The New York Times*, May 21, 2003)

O'Mara-Shimek, Guillén-Parra, and Ortega-Larrea (2015, p. 116) reconstructed the extended machine metaphor from US news reporting of the financial crisis of 2008:

> The [*New York Times*] displayed understandings of the stock market as a machine with "burnout," as when a machine is pushed beyond its limits and ceases to function, or when it "crashes," or when market "engineering" needs "fixing" or "tinkering" with after its "gyrations" "grind down." The [*Wall Street Journal*] had similar ways of expressing the problem in terms of a "breakdown," or when the stock market "falls apart." [*The Washington Times*] expressed similar sensibilities as when the stock market "go[es] to pieces," or even when a "meltdown" occurs or the stock market is "shattered."

Media metaphors don't only target the economy as a whole, but also its constituent phenomena, events, and processes. Economic metaphors have been applied to inflation (Hu & Liu, 2016); money (Charteris-Black & Musolff, 2003; Semino, 2002; Takahashi, 2010); the stock market (Smith, 1995); and the financial crisis (Awab & Norazit, 2013; de los Ríos, 2010).

70 What is the economy like?

The most common economic metaphors

Taking a bird's-eye view on the discourse analysis literature reveals a remarkable feature of economic metaphors: they consistently draw upon a concise list of source domains ever-present and ever-important in human life. In one large-scale study, Arrese & Vara-Miguel (2016) reviewed the corpus-based literature on the euro sovereignty debt crisis between the years 2008 and 2014. They found that across nationality and language, the most commonly invoked source domains included: (1) health and disease; (2) natural events and disasters; (3) events around artifacts and constructions (i.e., mechanical metaphors); (4) wars and clashes; (5) sports, games, and entertainment; and (6) actions and situations of living beings. These categories were confirmed in the authors' own corpus-based analysis including data from six European countries with four representative newspapers per country.

In another large-scale study, Hu and Chen (2015) analyzed inflation metaphors within the Corpus of Contemporary American English, including 450 million words from fiction, popular magazines, newspapers, academic texts, and spoken language recorded between 1990 and 2012. Using a computer algorithm, the authors identified the words that most commonly accompanied the term "inflation." They then constructed categories which best accounted for the metaphorical source domains from which these words were taken. Here are some of the most common metaphorical sources for inflation:

1. *Fire*: spark, ignite, kindle, stoke, fuel, flare-up, dampen, choke off
2. *Liquids*: erode, surge, simmer, ebb, dilute
3. *Animal*: roaring, taming, monster, galloping, rampant, rein, creep
4. *Disease*: plague, benign, virulent
5. *War*: besieged, injured, threat, subdue, beat, ravage
6. *Sports/*competition: pace, outstrip, lag, surpass, outrun
7. *Machine*: accelerate, control, trigger, skyrocket, heat, escalate, decelerate

If we were to trim away some of the details from the above lists, we would end up with the following major source domains for economic metaphors: the natural (fire, liquids, weather, events and disasters), biological (health and disease, organisms), physical (machines, forces), and psychological/interpersonal (competition, war, goals, actions) realms of life.

Looked at from the perspective of cognitive science, this list tells us as much about the human mind as it does about the economy.

Intuitive theories: the source of metaphorical sources

Metaphors are more than convenient explanatory clutches. Their roots are to be found in the very structure of our cognitive system. Throughout evolutionary history, humans have accrued a specialized set of skills to cope with the natural and social environments in which our species had evolved. While plants and animals rely on chemical and locomotive strategies to cope with their surroundings, humans have evolved altogether different skills, cognitive in nature, to help extract the environmental resources needed for their survival (Pinker, 2010). To overcome the defenses of the organisms sharing their environments, humans capitalized on cause-and-effect reasoning and inference. Hunter-gatherers designed and fashioned sophisticated tools to capture and kill animals, and devised methods such as cooking and fermenting to process their prey and forage into food. To inform these efforts our forebears drew on an evolved set of intuitive "theories" of the physical and biological worlds they inhabited (Pinker, 2010). An intuitive appreciation of physics involves the ability to distinguish independent worldly objects and the physical laws by which they abide. Intuitive biology involves the understanding of the logic that governs plant and animal life; their taxonomy, anatomy, physiology, and survival mechanisms (Pinker, 2010).

Another important force shaping people's cognitive toolkit was their social environment. Humans evolved in small bands, where social skills and cooperation were of the essence (Boyer & Petersen, in press). Supporting the negotiation of social interactions was our faculty for intuitive psychology; the ability to contemplate the contents of other people's minds: their beliefs, desires, intentions, and motives (Pinker, 2010; Wellman & Gelman, 1998).[1]

These three major domains – physics, biology, and psychology – are distinguishable in terms of their postulated ontology, the logic that governs their operation, and the observable and unobservable forces that impinge on their entities:

> The ball moves if driven by some external force transmitted directly to it (e.g. another ball striking it), evidencing characteristic mechanical motion. The butterfly is self-propelled; it moves because of an inner biological "engine," evidencing characteristic biomechanical movements. A human engages in intentional action based on psychological reasons; the act of voting, for example, based on the belief that one candidate is best and on the desire to see him or her elected.
>
> *(Wellman & Gelman, 1992, pp. 342–343)*

Intuitive or "framework" theories "impose order on the evidence" (Gelman & Legare, 2011). They imply a causal structure for observed events, enabling their wielders to extrapolate from the observed also their hidden causes and potential consequences (Pinker, 1999, 2010; Wellman & Gelman, 1998).

So deeply ingrained are these modes of thinking that despite the extraordinary changes that human environments have undergone since evolutionary times, they still prevail in the everyday. Cognitive scientist Steven Pinker neatly summed up this idea:

> According to a saying that is well known among psychologists, if you give a boy a hammer, the whole world becomes a nail. The saying is usually aimed at overreaching theoreticians, but it seems to be appropriate to *Homo sapiens* in

72 What is the economy like?

> general. If you give a species an elementary grasp of psychology, biology, and mechanics, then for better and for worse, the whole world becomes a society, a zoo, and a machine.
>
> *(Pinker, 1997, p. 45)*

This holds in particular in economics, where the objects of understanding are so foreign and abstruse. Metaphors usher in our intuitive theories, bringing them to bear on economic actors and processes. Not only do they serve to draw analogies between sources and targets, metaphors co-opt our intuitive framework theories in the service of economic reasoning.

Each framework theory brings into focus the aspects it was "designed" to deal with, introducing its own unique biases along the way. Once our faculty for intuitive psychology is invoked, we start to see intentions behind events, and the motivations and beliefs of independent agents that drive them. We may impute individuals, groups, and institutions with beliefs, desires, and intentions, and weave emotion- and intention-laden stories to explain why events turned out the way they did. Alternately, if a metaphor activates our faculty for intuitive physics or mechanics, our knowledge of forces, trajectories, and flows comes to the fore. Modeling the economy in mechanical terms implies that events adhere to clear-cut cause-and-effect relationships and proceed in a determinate and predictable manner. An intuitive biology perspective introduces a degree of indeterminacy to economic events, an appreciation of the economy as an interrelated system, with cycles, needs, and conditions of health and disease. Applied to economic actors, we conceive of the birth, development, and demise of companies, of their appetites and struggles to survive.

Intuitive theories at work: folk-psychology

Enlisting our intuitive theories in the service of economic reasoning can have far-reaching effects. Several studies have documented how our tendency to *see intentions* – that is, our (ab)use of the faculty for intuitive psychology – can distort our perception of the economic reality. Intuitive psychology is the faculty for contemplating the contents of other people's minds – their beliefs, desires, and intentions. It serves us in dissecting the hidden causes that animate the events we observe out in the social world. In what follows we will present studies which show what happens when this faculty overreaches in the realm of economics. To date, little attention has been given to the operations of our other framework theories (of physics and biology) in economic reasoning. Such an undertaking is merited in the future.

Our cognitive system is exquisitely attuned to cues indicating the presence of mental states behind observed events. In a classic study, Heider and Simmel (1944) presented participants with a short clip depicting three small geometrical figures dancing around a scene. Importantly, the shapes weren't just moving about aimlessly, but seemed to be *interacting*. Their movements were related; they sometimes moved synchronously, other times gravitated towards each other, and yet other times moved away from one another, as if being repelled or pushed around (the original clip is available on YouTube[2]). Tellingly, when asked to recount what they had seen, the viewers almost invariably elaborated a rich emotion-laden drama between the geometrical figures, complete with heroes, villains, fear, and triumph. The little geometrical figures were endowed by the observers with intentions, personality traits, and even personal histories.

This "intention-seeking" bias is not limited to our perceptual faculty, but manifests broadly in cognition (Keil & Newman, 2015; Rosset, 2008). For instance, when people read sentences depicting ambiguous events (e.g.. "She broke the vase" or "He hit the man with his car") they are biased to interpret them as purposeful actions, despite the fact that they typically happen by accident.

In economics, the intention-seeking bias manifests itself, for instance, in people's intuitions about how prices are set. In one poll, when asked about the reasons for rises in gasoline prices, most Americans appealed to oil companies' desire to increase profits, as opposed to the law of supply and demand (an explanation preferred by economists, Caplan, 2011, p. 72). Leaving the nitty-gritty details of price setting to the background, an intention to increase profits emerges as a straightforward way to explain why prices go up (see Chapters 2 and 3).

Finally we know where conspiracies come from – an overactive faculty for intuitive psychology. Brotherton and French (2015) investigated the link between the tendency to see intentions behind events and belief in conspiracy theories. They presented participants with sentences ambiguous with respect to intent, such as "He set the house on fire" and "He dripped paint on the canvas." Participants then described the first image that came to their minds, and indicated whether they believed the events were accidental or intentional. In addition, the participants answered a questionnaire that measured their tendency to hold conspiracist beliefs, including sentences such as "New and advanced technology which would harm current industry is being suppressed" and "The power held by heads of state is second to that of small unknown groups who really control world politics." The authors found that people who spontaneously provided intentional rather than accidental interpretations of ambiguous events also tended to believe in conspiracy theories.

The intentionality bias is intertwined with economic reasoning in yet other ways. People spontaneously associate the intentional actions of agents with order rather than disorder (Keil & Newman, 2015). Intentional explanations dissipate the haze of uncertainty and randomness by supplying underlying causes for observed events. Conspiracy theories make intelligible the ambiguities of economics and politics by tying events together in a storyline where, typically, an agent or group of agents intentionally manipulate events in order to achieve their goals.

74 What is the economy like?

The tendency to explain economic events in intentional terms was documented in a study investigating lay perceptions of the causes of the 2008 financial crisis (Leiser et al., 2010). In this case the *dis-integration* of order, epitomized by the crisis, was mostly attributed to human failings, rather than to flaws in the financial system. Leiser et al. (2010) presented a worldwide sample of respondents with a range of possible explanations for the causes leading up to the economic crisis. The study found that a majority of respondents attributed the crisis to intentional and moral factors such as economic actors' stupidity, negligence, and greed.

Introducing intention and agency into our interpretation of events can also thwart an accurate perception of the economic reality we are trying to grasp. Ames and Fiske (2013) demonstrated this when they showed that individuals who perceive intentions behind harmful acts grossly overestimate their negative consequences. In one experiment (Study 4), participants read a story about a village that was suffering from a water shortage after a nearby river dried up. In one condition the participants were told that the river went dry due to a lack of rain; in another, that a man in a nearby village had diverted the stream. Participants were then shown the costs in dollars that the water shortage had inflicted, and asked to make an estimation of the total accumulated costs. Although both groups were presented with the exact same figures, it was found that those who thought the drought was naturally occurring gave accurate estimations of the total costs, whereas those who believed the shortage was the result of an intentional manipulation overestimated the cost almost 1.5-fold.

The perception of intentions behind events also dramatically alters the way we expect them to unfold. The "hot hand fallacy" is "the intuition that a short run of consistent, but statistically independent, events is likely to continue" (Caruso, Waytz, & Epley, 2010, p. 149). Originally it described people's intuition that a basketball player's streak of successful hoops would persist (Gilovich, Vallone, & Tversky, 1985). Caruso et al. (2010) explored the relationship between the perception of intentions and the tendency to endorse the hot hand account. They presented participants with a video clip of a person tossing a coin, and were told that the tosser was *trying* to flip heads. Some participants were instructed to focus on the man's intentions, while the others were instructed to concentrate on his physical movements. Having observed a streak of "heads" tosses, the group that focused on the person's intentions was more likely to predict that the streak would continue (the "hot hand fallacy"), while those that focused solely on bodily movements expected the streak to end (the "gambler's fallacy"). A simple manipulation of attention to what the tosser intended led to a profound change in their expectation of how events would turn out. Inasmuch as people adopt an intentional stance, they will tend to expect trends which they perceive to be intentionally driven to persist.

In this section we explored the implications of over-activating our faculty for intuitive psychology in the realm of economics. Metaphors induce these biases into economic reasoning when they trigger this faculty into action.

Concluding remarks

When it comes to economic understanding, people find themselves in a peculiar predicament: they must form sensible opinions and make wise decisions in a field they know little about. One way to cope with the problem would be to learn economics from the ground up, as one would any field of expertise. But the time and energy necessitated by such an enterprise makes it unfeasible for most.

In this chapter we looked at one way to circumvent the problem: reasoning by metaphor. By drawing analogies between familiar and novel concepts, metaphors allow us to carry over our existing knowledge and apply it to subject matter we know little about. What's more, metaphors engage our most basic ways of understanding the world, our intuitive theories of psychology, biology, and physics, bringing them to bear on economic actors and events. As we saw, each metaphor highlights particular aspects of its target while hiding the rest. And each intuitive theory makes us acutely aware of the logic and entities it was "designed" to deal while ignoring the rest. In this way, metaphors, while useful, can lead to profound economic misconceptions.

In the foregoing sections we concentrated mostly on how metaphors affect comprehension and decisions in real time, and in circumscribed problems. What we don't yet know is how pervasive and long-term such effects really are. Do metaphors linger in the mind? How do they figure in people's mental representations of economics at large?

As we have argued before (Chapter 3), economic knowledge – indeed knowledge in general – is piecemeal in nature. It accumulates over time from different sources and is distributed in the mind in the form of independent pieces of information that can, but need not, be reconciled (Leiser, 2001). Previously, we saw that people are constantly exposed to economic metaphors in the media, and that these metaphors are freely mixed in discourse. That is, conceptualizing some aspect of the economy in mechanical terms does not preclude conceptualizing others in organic or intentional ones. Therefore, it is unlikely that each and every metaphorical expression we encounter in the media re-shapes our understanding in its image.

Instead, to the extent that economic metaphors are internalized, they will not be integrated into a grand theory of economics. Rather, they can be invoked to reason about circumscribed problems at particular times, for instance, who's to blame when a company fails? How is this stock going to perform? And what is an effective policy to deal with a particular societal problem?

In this context, metaphor can be thought of as a kind of heuristic; a mental shortcut that helps us reach a conclusion in a state of uncertainty, with little to no deliberation (Gigerenzer & Gaissmaier, 2011). Metaphors offer a real boon to cognitive resource conservation: they save time, minimize effort, and dispel uncertainties, but they do so at a considerable cost to accuracy and comprehensiveness.

76 What is the economy like?

Notes

1 One major source domain we had identified for economic metaphors was natural events and disasters. However, no evolutionary psychology theory of intuitive conceptions has taken account of a "folk meteorology." For the remainder of the chapter, we will focus on findings pertaining to the other three major source domains and corresponding intuitive theories – intuitive physics, biology, and psychology.
2 For the original clip see: www.youtube.com/watch?v=VTNmLt7QX8E.

7

IDEOLOGY

Lay understanding of capitalism

In the course of the televised debates leading up to the 2016 US presidential elections, capitalism took center stage. Contender for the Democratic Party nomination, Bernie Sanders, was asked whether he identified as a capitalist. His reply:

> Do I consider myself part of the casino capitalist process, by which so few have so much and so many have so little, by which Wall Street's greed and recklessness wrecked this economy? No, I don't.

To which his opponent, Hillary Clinton, retorted:

> When I think about capitalism, I think about all the small businesses that were started because we have the opportunity and the freedom in our country for people to do that and make a good living for themselves and their families.

Casino, inequality, greed, recklessness … small businesses, opportunity, freedom, making a good living – could these two influential figures be talking about the very same economic system? How could capitalism mean such different things to different people?

And yet this exchange is typical of debates on the topic. Indeed, controversy over capitalism runs as deep as its roots (Plender, 2015). Critics have blamed capitalism for trampling workers' rights the world over, degrading the environment, and causing ever-growing levels of inequality and instability (Klein, 2014; Moore, 2009). Following the financial crisis of 2008, capitalism has received increasingly negative attention from the public (Kohut et al., 2012). Perceptions of growing inequality and irresponsibility of the business sector provided the impetus for the worldwide Occupy movement calling for social and economic justice (Van Gelder, 2011). Recent polls suggest a decline in support for capitalism alongside a climb in

78 Lay understanding of capitalism

support for socialism, particularly among the younger generation (Dahlgreen, 2015; Moore, 2015).

In spite of this, champions of capitalism are quick to point out that since the spread of capitalism around the world, more and more countries have been experiencing unprecedented economic growth, their citizens escaping poverty and enjoying longer, healthier lives (Smith, 2017; Worstall, 2016). Some have even suggested that the advent of capitalism may have played a role in establishing long-standing peace between nations (Pinker, 2012).

The public is on the receiving end of many and conflicting messages. In 2016 alone, more than 111,000 news articles were published online which mentioned "capitalism" ("News articles including 'capitalism'," 2016). And there are currently more than 25,000 clips on the video-sharing site YouTube bearing the term in their titles, which explain, explore, applaud, and condemn capitalism. Some article headlines include: "Does capitalism cause poverty?" [Project Syndicate]; "How capitalism is making poverty history" (Telegraph.co.uk); "Capitalism: morality and the money motive" (*Financial Times*); "Capitalism is moral, and it works" (CNBC); "Capitalism v the environment" (*The Guardian*); "Capitalism is the solution to climate change" (CNBC); "How capitalism turns love into addiction" (Reuters Blog); "Is capitalism dead?" (*The Guardian*); "U.S. capitalism isn't a 'free market'" (Reason.com); "Unbridled capitalism is the 'dung of the devil', says Pope Francis" (*The Guardian*); "Capitalism vs. 'smiley-faced socialism'" (*Forbes*); and "Scrap the rhetoric: There's no such thing as capitalism" (*The Independent*).

In recent years several popular movies have even taken up the subject, most of them drawing fire to capitalism (Michael Moore's *Capitalism: A Love Story* and Naomi Klein's *This Changes Everything: Capitalism vs. the Climate*).

Small wonder, then, that capitalism is on people's minds. In 2015, capitalism was among the top 1% most searched terms on the Online Merriam-Webster Dictionary ("capitalism," 2017). And while some of the economic concepts we have covered so far would seem arcane to most, capitalism is readily taken up in debate. With its moral, psychological, and cultural implications, capitalism is a perfect match for people's penchant for moral and intentional reasoning (Chapter 2).

Lay views of capitalism encompass attitudes with some of the most sweeping consequences for the economy at large. What are the virtues and vices of free markets? How does globalization affect the lives of citizens in developed and developing countries? What is the responsibility, if any, of companies towards their workers, to society, and to the environment? What is the role of government in regulating economic activity and protecting its citizens? These questions feed directly into policy considerations, such as whether wealth should be redistributed, and how? Who should be taxed, and in what form? Which functions of the government are privatized? Does the government hold price controls? And how strict is regulation of international trade?

Economists stand mostly united in preferring minimally regulated markets and free trade, seeing that they provide overall benefits in productivity, income, living standards, and consumption. They point to the public's anti-market biases, which

Lay understanding of capitalism **79**

blind them to their benefits (Caplan, 2011; Rubin, 2014). But what this focus does not sufficiently consider is that what people care about most is not efficiency, but *fairness* (Chapter 2).

For example, it is known that today's living standards are the highest that they have ever been. Global poverty is dropping, and people are vastly wealthier than their counterparts just a century ago. And yet, the 2017 Global Risks Report published by the World Economic Forum (2016) points to rising inequality as the leading challenge facing the world over the next decade. According to their analysis, the slow relative increase in real income among the middle class of advanced economies has bred discontent and anti-establishment sentiments, leading to the startling results of the 2016 US elections and the Brexit vote in the UK to leave the European Union.

While economists rack their brains over the anti-capitalist biases of the public, some political psychologists are grappling to understand why people are seemingly *too capitalistic* for their own good. Jost, Gaucher, and Stern (2015), for example, note that despite growing levels of inequality in the United States over the past few decades, roughly half of Americans still approve of the economic system as fair and legitimate, and prefer policies which go against their own material interests. To explain why it is that people don't revolt against the system, these scholars refer to *system justification* – a motivation to warp one's perception of reality so as to conform to their conception of the world as a just place.

Our approach to tackling this conundrum is to first map out what people really do think when they think about capitalism. For this, we will turn to social media and see how people freely express themselves on the matter. As a second step, we will identify the major points where opinions diverge, and try to pinpoint the underlying premises that give rise to these differences: What are the deeper moral-psychological nerves touched upon in the debate? Finally, using insights and concepts developed in economic and political psychology, we will try to explain why different people have such different sensitivities and come to hold polar views on the topic.

Contrasting views of capitalism

A recent project in our lab has been to map out the various beliefs and attitudes pertaining to capitalism in circulation among members of the public. To get an initial grasp on the matter, we turned to social media. We combed through thousands of reader responses to online news articles, comments posted on YouTube videos, and arguments made in open debate platform. For the most part, we found that beliefs about capitalism (and indeed those who held them) fell into one of two categories: pro-capitalist and anti-capitalist. Following is a summary of these beliefs as they constellate in the pro- and anti-capitalist camps, accompanied by a selection of the original comments from which they were derived.

Proponents of capitalism emphasize how life has transformed for the better in countries that have embraced free markets and opened to trade. They point to the

80 Lay understanding of capitalism

progress, improved standards of living, and longer and healthier lives enjoyed in these countries. In this respect, they contrast capitalism with socialism or communism. How could anyone be opposed to escaping poverty and improving one's conditions, they wonder?

Capitalism is the only political order that relieves suffering by creating more food, medicine, clothes, and other basic necessities so that more people can live better lives.	Well, let's see, it has resulted in the wealthiest, safest, and most free societies in human history where food is abundant and the biggest complaint is "I am bored" ... not to mention the fact that this video wouldn't exist without it. So no capitalism is not "bad" for you. In fact it's quite good for you. Socialism, on the other hand, IS bad for you ...	Socialists are beyond retarded... They come on here ranting about how capitalism is bad and evil. Yet they would have a heart attack the minute their cellphone, xbox, or favorite restaurant were removed.

Free market capitalism allows opportunity for even the poorest of people to obtain capital to grow business that people need.

FIGURE 7.1 Capitalism brings prosperity.

Critics emphasize the damage and injustice wrought by capitalism. Economic growth in one place, they say, often inflicts costs and claims victims in others. Examples include laborers exploited for meager wages in devastating working conditions, the ongoing degradation of the environment, and the erosion of cultural identity wreaked by industrialization, urbanization, and globalization. Progress is good, they may concede, but why must it come at someone else's expense?

The very basis of capitalism: unlimited growth, wealth inequality, wage labor exploitation, the predation of poor countries by rich countries, the military conflicts that arise out of attempts to obtain resources, rampant and vacuous consumerism, etc. just cannot last.	Make a list of all the environmental and social problems that today afflict us and our poor battered planet – not just the extinction of species and animals and plants ... the growth of mega-cities ... loss of arable land, desertification, famine, increasingly violent weather, the acidification of the oceans ... the loss of rain forest ... they all share an underlying cause ... intricately linked with capitalism.	Capitalism has metastasized into a predatory, megalomaniacal manifestation of enterprise that plays lip service to competition for the benefit of the consumer while pursuing predatory strategies of domination and consolidation wherever possible that kills competition and diminishes freedom of entry in too many cases.
The environment, the natural wealth of the earth, on which the economy is dependent, are all priced at zero but are finite and being destroyed or used up.		

FIGURE 7.2 Prosperity comes at an unbearable expense.

Pro-capitalists don't necessarily see economic inequality as a problem in and of itself. There is nothing immoral about some people having more than others, they say. Inequality gives people incentive to move up the social ladder by applying themselves to the production of something of value to their fellow men and women. In fact, the opportunity to climb the social ladder (i.e., "upwards social mobility") is seen as a core virtue of the system. Economic success is thought to derive from virtues such as a strong work ethic, ambition, creativity, ingenuity, and a willingness to take risks in business. Far from evoking condemnation, successful and rich people are seen as praiseworthy models to be emulated. Redistribution – the transfer of wealth resulting in a more equal wealth distribution – on the contrary, is deemed

Lay understanding of capitalism **81**

both unfair and counterproductive. It involves taking from people's hard-earned money and simply giving it to someone else. Even worse, providing welfare rewards laziness instead of endeavor, thus giving people no real reason to work, with the downstream consequence of burdening the economy and country in the long run.

Capitalism is the best system that there is. It allows people to make something of themselves if they have the drive to work hard towards their goal. No other system around does that.	in a capitalist society, those who deliver products and services that many consumers like and value get rewarded more than those who do not deliver these goods and services or do so to a lesser extent.	Fundamentally rewarding people for endeavor, effort, and risk via the pursuit of profit has brought the world to the point where we can have nice, comfortable first world debates and surveys about how we can improve the system we have.
The vice you should really be worried about is envy. That's where people can't bear to see someone else have more than they do, even if the other person worked hard their whole life to get it. That's when they cry out "wealth inequality." It's Socialism that caters to bad vices.	Capitalism is hard work ... it requires every person to work hard and take responsibility for their own actions and own results. Innovate, create, and don't expect the government to help you (regardless of how wonderful in your own way you are striving to be).	Capitalism is nothing more than bringing your talents to market. It allows you to strive to be better and create value for others to enjoy.

FIGURE 7.3 There is nothing wrong with inequality.

Critics perceive capitalism as a system that perpetuates inequality, a state which they deem to be unjust and in need of remediation. That someone should live a profligate and lavish life while others suffer and struggle over the very basics is morally repugnant to them. Critics suspect the integrity of those higher up the wealth distribution. Did they acquire their fortunes honestly? Do they deserve it more than others, who worked just as hard if not harder? Is it not the workers who generate the wealth, and if so, are they not entitled to a fair share of it? Critics disagree that capitalist economies afford equal opportunities for advancement, often voicing the opinion that "the system is rigged" in favor of some over others.

You call getting rich off another person's labor rewarding people for endeavor? A system where the boss slides off most of the cream from the top of the cake and leaves a thin layer to the one who produced it?	You don't need billions of dollars when children are starving, so if you have billion of dollars while children starve then you value money that you'll never even use over your concern of suffering children.
All wealth after all is generated by workers, hands not the hands of the boss, that is why we are called the working class, cos we are legally obliged to do all the work for those who do nothing yet own everything.	Poor supporting capitalism is like turkey voting for Christmas.
	It seems to me like an obese man would be a good metaphor for capitalism. He keeps eating more and more unhealthy food, while neglecting the organs' desperate call for healthy nutrition. The man doesn't want to change his diet ... His organs are protesting heavily, but he ignores it ...

FIGURE 7.4 Inequality is wrong.

Supporters of capitalism believe that the market has the ability to self-regulate. In addition, the success of players in the market is thought to indicate how well they

82 Lay understanding of capitalism

have done in catering to the needs and desires of their customers. An environment of open competition is believed to bring out virtuous qualities in people such as ambition, creativity, skill, and a sense for business, as these become essential to compete successfully. Not only the competitive, but also the cooperative aspects of the market are emphasized: in a free market, participation is voluntary, and therefore business and trade are mutually beneficial forms of cooperation almost by definition. Government involvement in the economy is objected to, as it is thought to distort the dynamic of the free market. Governments are seen as clumsy, inefficient, and self-interested (even corrupt). The government does not (and cannot) possess the knowledge necessary to direct the infinitely complex economy. Disproportionate power of market forces, such as big corporations and monopolies, is not desirable, but acceptable, so long as the free market system is in place. With time, it is believed, competition will rise to the challenge and change the status quo. Governments, on the other hand, are considered illegitimate wielders of excessive power.

The problem isn't companies, it's corruption. Those big established companies, if they are getting tax subsidies, or bailouts, they are not good companies, and not capitalist at all. The only way a monopoly can form in a true free market is if the customers love that company and the product. If that is the case, is that really so bad?	Government bureaucracy complicates things, raises the starting cost & maintenance fees. Unless you're a business genius, no starting company can survive such heavy burden on shallow pockets.	Capitalism is all about where the demand is. If there is demand for bad TV shows or Apple watches then who are you to say those things are useless? As long as there is demand for something, there will be entrepreneurs who will be willing to provide. Your solutions are totalitarian and unfree.
The only thing plaguing the system right now is the ability to use the government to provide themselves with economical advantage in the expense of other competitors.	In a real free market any time a business makes a product, another business can make a competing product, Only government use of force can prevent such things.	Is it the corporation's fault if it is forced to pay to play by powerful politicians? Or even if the corporation chooses to pay to play to increase profits? Or is pay to play the natural result of an all-powerful federal government? I think it's obvious that it's the latter.

FIGURE 7.5 The free market works.

The problem critics see in the free market is the inherent potential for unfair play. The free market favors players who have a better starting point, for example, more money or more connections. The free market legitimizes the law of the jungle in the name of profit; when concern for others is not profitable, companies will almost invariably sacrifice the well-being of their customers. Furthermore, putting natural and national resources in private profit-seeking hands, rather than governments who serve their citizens, generates conflicts of interest, where citizens inevitably find themselves on the losing side. Critics disapprove of business practices legitimized by the free market, such as raising prices on life-saving drugs people cannot afford not to buy ("price gouging"). They see the market as unstable and prone to bubbles and crashes, often citing the example of the 2008 financial crisis. Critics are also concerned with the corrupting potential of money in politics, with the rich buying influence over politicians to make policies go their way. Therefore, regulation of the economy is believed to be essential to protecting citizens and workers from special interests, promoting a fair market, restraining reckless market forces from running amok, and ensuring stability.

Capitalism does not care if people need the medicine, capitalism does not care if our citizens are educated and cultured. All capitalism does is give the ultra rich a moral reason to ship their manufacturing arm to Taiwan and pollute where it is cheaper. Capitalism has no sense of right and wrong, only profitable and non-profitable. If people die, but a profit is realized then great for capitalists, they don't have to care.	Why assume no legisation is better than legislation? Self-regulation led to the 2008 financial crisis.	Capitalism is only good when it's heavily regulated to prevent exploitation of others.
	When corporations get large and powerful, they often take shortcuts resulting in the pollution of the environment.	The problem with laissez-faire markets is they tend towards monopolies, collusion, and corruption, which destroys competition. This is why industrial countries run mixed economies.
	The most recent rounds of monopolizing began when governments stopped regulating competition.	

FIGURE 7.6 The free market breeds unfairness which the government must keep in check.

Moral-psychological roots of lay views of capitalism

Surveying the expressions above (Figures 7.1–7.6) one gets a clear sense that people's reasoning and perceptions regarding capitalism are strongly driven by moral and psychological considerations.

Self-interest

The first among these is the morality of the *profit motive* and how, psychologically, it affects those who pursue it. Anti-capitalists evince an almost visceral distrust in those trying to turn a profit, casting them as greedy, callous, and indulgent. The motivation to attain wealth is seen as a malign force that, once triggered, can cause people to lose their sense of right and wrong. And since people tend to judge actions by their intentions rather than their outcomes (Cushman, 2008; Young & Waytz, 2013), practices that are seen to be motivated by greed are likely to be judged negatively regardless of their effects. From this sentiment follows the anti-capitalist distrust in business, as well as the aversion to situations that pit corporate profit against people's welfare, such as the privatization of healthcare and natural resources.

Manifesting this attitude, the following exchange is taken from an interview between Naomi Klein and Michael Moore, two social activist filmmakers and prominent critics of capitalism (Klein, 2009).

> Naomi Klein: [T]his is something that I hear a lot – this idea that greed or corruption is somehow an aberration from the logic of capitalism, rather than the engine and the centerpiece of capitalism. And I think that that's probably something you're already hearing about the terrific sequence in the film about those corrupt Pennsylvania judges who were sending kids to private prison and getting kickbacks. I think people would say, "That's not capitalism, that's corruption." Why is it so hard to see the connection, and how are you responding to this?

84 Lay understanding of capitalism

> Michael Moore: Well, people want to believe that it's not the economic system that's at the core of all this. You know, it's just a few bad eggs. But the fact of the matter is that, as I said to Jay [Leno], capitalism is the legalization of this greed.

Pro-capitalists, on the other hand, feel much more comfortable with the notion of profit-seeking and self-interest. This can be unpacked in two ways. First, they think it arrogant to purport to know what is good or desirable for others; that is to be decided by each individual for him or herself. From this standpoint, top-down attempts by the government to tell people what to want and how to act are futile and perverse. Second, they see self-interest not so much as a topic for debate as a fact of life. People *are* self-interested, whether we like it or not. In this light we can understand the pro-capitalist disdain for economic systems that reject this fundamental, though fraught, aspect of human nature (for an in-depth exploration of the two competing visions of human nature and their ramification into politics, see Pinker, 2003).

In this, once again, pro-capitalists and economists are mostly united. Milton Friedman, Nobel Laureate economist and prominent advocate of capitalism, was asked once in an interview:

> Phil Donahue: When you see around the globe the mal-distribution of wealth, the desperate plight of millions of people in underdeveloped countries, when you see so few "haves" and so many "have-nots," when you see the greed and the concentration of power … did you ever have a moment of doubt about capitalism and whether greed is a good idea to run on?
> Milton Friedman: Well first of all, tell me, is there some society you know that doesn't run on greed? Do you think Russia doesn't run on greed? Do you think China doesn't run on greed? What is greed? … The world runs on individuals pursuing their separate interests. The great achievements of civilization have not come from government bureaus … In the only cases in which the masses have escaped from the kind of grinding poverty you're talking about … are where they have had capitalism and largely free trade … there is no alternative way, so far discovered, of improving the lot of the ordinary people that can hold a candle to the productive activities that are unleashed by the free enterprise system.
>
> *(Brkic, 2013)*

The question of how different attitudes to self-interest play out in conflicting views of capitalism has yet to be explored. But a few clues can be gleaned from the field of political psychology.

Social worldviews and economic ideology

In the field of political psychology, the pro- versus anti-capitalist divide is captured in the notion of *economic ideology*, which involves beliefs and attitudes regarding wealth inequality, perceptions of private enterprise, the free market, and the role of government in regulating the economy and redistributing wealth. *Economic conservatism* accords with pro-capitalist arguments, favoring private over government ownership of businesses, supporting the free market, and opposing government regulation and redistribution. *Economic liberalism* takes issue with the tenets of capitalism, favoring more regulation of markets and demanding redistribution and welfare to even out inequalities (Everett, 2013; Hiel & Kossowska, 2007; Zumbrunnen & Gangl, 2008).

To identify the sources from which spring divergent views of capitalism, let us look to the psychological-level correlates of economic ideology. An influential perspective in this respect has been the Dual-Process Model of ideology (Duckitt, 2001; Duckitt & Sibley, 2010; Perry & Sibley, 2013).

According to this model, beliefs and attitudes in the economic domain stem from an ideology supporting the maintenance of social hierarchies and opposing equality, termed Social Dominance Orientation (Pratto, Sidanius, Stallworth, & Malle, 1994). It is defined as "the extent to which one desires that one's group dominate and be superior to out-groups" (Pratto et al., 1994, p. 742). SDO has been found to be highly predictive of economic ideology and policy preferences: those who support social dominance are more likely to be economically conservative, opposing redistribution and welfare, preferring private over government ownership of business, and endorsing competitive free markets (Altemeyer, 1998b; Bobbio, Canova, & Manganelli, 2010; Duriez, Van Hiel, & Kossowska, 2005; Everett, 2013; Ho et al., 2012; Perry & Sibley, 2013).

But where does social dominance orientation come from? According to Duckitt (2001), SDO is rooted in people's perceptions of the social world: what are other people like? How do they treat each other? And how should they be responded to? A central feature of these models is the degree to which the social world is perceived to be essentially competitive versus cooperative in nature. In one extreme, the world is construed as a competitive jungle, dominated by "a ruthless, amoral struggle for resources and power in which might is right and winning is everything" (Perry, Sibley, & Duckitt, 2013, p. 125). On the other pole is the view of the world as a place of cooperative harmony in which "people care for, help, and share with each other" (Perry et al., 2013, p. 125). Recent studies have shown that a person's social dominance orientation can be predicted by their social view of the world. Those who believe the social world to be a competitive jungle tend to support social dominance, and those who believe the world is cooperative and harmonious in nature are likely to oppose it (Duckitt, Wagner, Du Plessis, & Birum, 2002; Perry et al., 2013; Sibley & Duckitt, 2013).

Notice how the different social worldviews mesh with different conceptions of the nature of human motivation. While the competitive worldview sees self-interest as the central driving force behind people's actions, the cooperative one emphasizes compassion as the more basic (and important) motive. Thus for those who believe the social world to be a place of compassion and harmony, the notion that people are inherently selfish, and the capitalist celebration of the profit motive

86 Lay understanding of capitalism

are undoubted threats. They are likely to take issue with these tenets of capitalism and demand policies that protect citizens from the forces of the market, extend help to the needy, and avoid pitting profit against welfare. But for those who accept self-interest as basic, a degree of social conflict over resources is inevitable. They are likely to support the idea of competitive, unregulated markets and accept that some win and some lose as a brute fact of life. They will prefer policies which acknowledge and even harness the power of self-interest to bring about desirable outcomes overall.

Fairness

The foregoing discussion revolved around the *means* for achieving desirable economic *ends* (self-interest or compassion?). But the two camps also differ on what those ends might be. What constitutes a just economy? How should wealth be distributed within society?

As we saw above, proponents of capitalism believe that economic rewards should be allotted based on inputs such as effort, talent, or liability. Rewarding laziness was considered by them both unfair and deleterious. That someone should get "something for nothing" (as in people on welfare) is wrong by their standards.

This notion of fairness was echoed in a speech by UK Prime Minister, Theresa May, where she posed the question: "[W]hat kind of country – what kind of society – do we want to be?" (May, 2016).

> I am clear about the answer. I want Britain to be the world's great meritocracy – a country where everyone has a fair chance to go as far as their talent and their hard work will allow … I want Britain to be a place where advantage is based on merit not privilege; where it's your talent and hard work that matter, not where you were born, who your parents are or what your accent sounds like.

Anti-capitalists, on the other hand, were relatively silent on the question of matching inputs to outcomes. Instead, they were preoccupied by the moral character of rich people and their business practices, and on whether they shared the wealth or kept it to themselves, depriving those down the social ladder. When surveying the social landscape, critics were disturbed by the appearance of clear winners and losers in the economic game, something that to them cries out unfairness.

Bernie Sanders – whose views of capitalism we encountered in the beginning of this chapter – gives voice to these sentiments ("The transcript of Bernie Sanders's victory speech," 2016):

> [O]ur great country was based on a simple principle, and that principle is fairness. Let me be very clear, it is not fair when we have more income and wealth inequality today than almost any major country on Earth. And when the top one-tenth of 1% now owns almost as much wealth as the bottom

90%, that's not fair. It is not fair when the 20 wealthiest people in this country now own more wealth than the bottom half of the American people.

Therefore, when we consider people's evaluations of the distribution of wealth in their society, we have to distinguish two competing notions of fairness: proportionality and egalitarianism (Haidt, 2013; Rasinski, 1987). The proportionality principle holds that outcomes should be matched to inputs. In economics, this manifests as the assertion that people should get rewarded based on their efforts and talents. The other principle, egalitarianism, implies an equality of outcomes. On this conception, the spoils of society should be widely shared and extended to those in need.

How can we explain why different people champion different intuitions about fairness? Some insights into this question come from research on "hypothetical societies" (Mitchell & Tetlock, 2009). In these studies, participants are shown the income distribution in a made-up society, and asked to judge between two policy alternatives that would modify it. After seeing the pairs of alternatives, the participants indicate which in their opinion is more fair. The experimenters control various features of the society: where the does the line of poverty run, what is the average income, and what is the initial level of inequality. Crucially, the experimenters also manipulate the degree of *meritocracy* within society, that is, the degree to which outcomes are determined by inputs (Mitchell & Tetlock, 2009).

These studies pull back the curtain on the inner conflicts and value tradeoffs people go through as they arrive at their final judgments of fairness. How important is it to minimize income inequality when it comes at the expense of overall prosperity (i.e., lower average incomes)? How far are people willing to go to increase a society's prosperity, when it means that some will be far worse off than others?

The authors found that overall, people were willing to tolerate considerable levels of inequality so long as they perceived the society to be highly meritocratic. And this tendency held across political ideology - whether liberal or conservative. That is, if someone came by his or her fortune by virtue of hard work and bringing their talents to market, they can keep it. And if someone else was not willing to put in the requisite efforts and in turn is worse off, they deserve their economic fate. These findings indicate that both liberals and conservatives care deeply about the principle of proportionality.

An additional finding in high-meritocracy societies was that most people still avoided situations that would cause others to slip beneath the poverty line, reflecting a universal concern for basic needs.

In societies that were not at all meritocratic, the situation was different; here people largely preferred distributions that bolstered the lower class, reflecting a concern for those who were struck by bad luck, even if it came at the expense of those who happen to be doing better. These tendencies held regardless of political orientation.

The most interesting results emerge under conditions of moderate-meritocracy, where inputs and outcomes are only loosely connected. These ambiguities most closely model judgments in the real world. And it is here that political ideology

88 Lay understanding of capitalism

comes to the fore. Liberals faced with these dilemmas tend to sacrifice prosperity to achieve equality, and conservatives to sacrifice equality to ensure prosperity (Mitchell & Tetlock, 2009; Mitchell, Tetlock, Mellers, & Ordonez, 1993).

Another way to frame it is that any decision to change the present distribution would thwart a different aspect of fairness, each dear to another ideological group. These dilemmas and value tradeoffs are part and parcel of policy discourse. Making society more equal (e.g., by taxing the rich) subverts the present meritocracy, and conservatives won't have it. But making it more prosperous (e.g., by giving tax cuts to the rich) will subvert the ideal of egalitarianism, and liberals cannot accept that. Put differently, liberals need to be fairly certain that a strong meritocracy is in place before they are willing to relax their egalitarian ideals, while conservatives are intent on safeguarding the existing meritocracy even when it is imperfect.

Indeed, in the real world, liberals and conservatives support different economic policies, and have different conceptions of fairness to back them up. In a study titled "What's fair is fair – or is it?," Rasinski (1987) found that liberals are more likely to endorse statements like "in America, everyone should be treated equally because we are all human beings," "Those who are well off in this country should help those who are less fortunate," "Compassion for others is the most important human value," and "It is not right for people to go hungry in our country." By contrast, conservatives were more likely to agree that "Many poor people just don't want to work hard," "There are too many people getting something for nothing in this society," "Anybody receiving welfare in this country should be made to work for the money they get," and "All things considered, most people get just what they deserve out of life."

Notice how beliefs about the present meritocracy in society are bounded up with judgments of its fairness. The assertion that poor people should not be getting welfare is predicated on the belief that people get what they deserve in life (high meritocracy). And the demand that wealthier individuals help out those who are worse off hinges on the assumption that the poor are less fortunate through no fault of their own (low meritocracy).

In other words, the way people think things *came to be* (causality) affects how they think they *ought to be* (morality).

A similar line of reasoning has been advanced by Starmans, Sheskin, & Bloom (2017), who point to recent studies showing that people aren't troubled by inequality per se but rather by unfairness. For example, Eriksson and Simpson (2012) asked participants to construct their *ideal* distribution of wealth, by prescribing the average household wealth in the top and bottom quintiles of the wealth distribution. Analyzing their responses, the authors found a startling result: the proportion of wealth allotted to the top and bottom quintiles reached a whopping 50:1 ratio. An earlier study yielded a smaller ratio of roughly 3:1, unequal nonetheless, but it probably underestimated the effect (Norton & Ariely, 2011; see commentary in Eriksson and Simpson, 2012).

In the next section, we go over studies showing how background assumptions regarding the meritocracy in society translate into specific policy preferences.

Folk theories of wealth and poverty

Why are some people richer than others, and others poorer? Lay causal attributions of wealth and poverty fall into three categories (Furnham, 1988, 2003), which we already encountered in Chapter 4 when discussing lay explanations of unemployment: individual, structural, and uncontrollable. Explanations for poverty, for example, include:

1. Individual factors: lack of effort, lack of motivation, money mismanagement
2. Structural factors: poor education, insufficient opportunities, an economic system that favors the rich
3. Uncontrollable factors: fate, bad luck

Causal explanations for wealth include:

1. Individual factors: effort, skills, intelligence, a business acumen
2. Structural factors: better education, more opportunities, high salaries in certain sectors, an economic system that favors the rich
3. Uncontrollable factors: good fortune, inheritance, being at the right place at the right time

In a cleverly designed experiment, Schneider and Castillo (2015) looked into how these causal theories feed into people's judgments of fairness. Participants in the study rated the importance of different causes for poverty, including individual, structural, and chance factors. In addition, they were asked to indicate how much they believed CEOs of large companies, and how much low-skilled workers, earned monthly. On the basis of these figures, the authors calculated a "perceived inequality" index, representing the degree of inequality people believe to exist. Participants then stated how much they thought the aforementioned CEOs and workers *ought* to earn monthly. On this basis, they calculated an index of "justified inequality" (what level of inequality people deem to be fair). Combining the two together, the researchers devised a measure of the perceived versus justified inequality ratio, indicating the *perceived fairness* of present inequality. In addition, participants indicated their beliefs regarding the causes of poverty (internal vs. external).

Consistent with the idea that causal attributions go hand in hand with moral judgments, it was found that attributions of poverty to individual factors ("high meritocracy") predicted the belief that present levels of inequality were fair, and attributions of poverty to external factors (structural and causal, i.e., "low meritocracy") that they were unfair.

Causal theories of wealth and poverty and policy preference

How people explain wealth and poverty also determines what policies they will be willing to support. For example, Zucker and Weiner (1993) found that attributions of poverty to personal responsibility predicted opposition to welfare policies. Bullock,

90 Lay understanding of capitalism

Williams, and Limbert (2003) found that individuals attributing wealth and poverty to external causes tended to support welfare policies such as extended healthcare, while those who explained wealth and poverty as internally driven were more likely to oppose them. Bradley and Cole (2002) examined the relationship between lay causal attributions of poverty and preferred solutions to poverty. Proposed solutions were either internally oriented (e.g., "every able-bodied individual should actively seek gainful employment") or externally oriented (e.g., "as a solution for poverty, the government should raise the minimum wage"). Participants rated the importance of several internal and external causes for poverty. The authors found that the more importance people placed on internal explanations, the more they were likely to endorse internally oriented solutions, and vice versa.

To sum up, in this section we asked: Why do pro- and anti-capitalists have vastly different intuitions about fairness? Pro-capitalists think that people deserve to be rewarded for their efforts and abilities. Anti-capitalists assert that we must strive to treat all people equally. What appears to be driving this divide is the degree to which each camp believes that, in the real world, rewards do depend on inputs.

These beliefs are captured in their causal theories of economic success. Those who believe that wealth and poverty derive from individual strivings celebrate economic success, and deem redistribution to be unfair. From these premises it follows that welfare is not for the less fortunate, but for the less deserving. But those who hold the opposite view, that wealth and poverty are largely the result of external factors such as the structure of the economic system, it is natural to support policies that extend help and protect those in need. To them, welfare is a welcome amendment to an unjust situation. And assuming inputs are only loosely connected to outcomes, they have no scruples in taxing the rich to fund these efforts.

Ideology and personality

One of the most powerful predictors for how a person explains wealth and poverty is their political ideology. Conservatives find the logic of internal explanations more appealing, while liberals think that external ones make more sense (Furnham, 1988, 2003). The same holds in other domains. In Chapter 4 we saw that when liberals explain unemployment, they consider political and social forces to be primary, with personal motivation and abilities as mere downstream consequences. For conservatives it is the other way around; they perceive government policy as a reaction to the features and behaviors of individuals.

It is as if liberals and conservatives live in different worlds. Or at least they have very different models for how they work, and this seeps into their economic worldviews (see Haidt, 2014 for a similar argument).

Another factor that affects how people see the world is their own personality. There is a personality-level analogue to causal explanations of wealth and poverty, that of internal versus external *locus of control*. Locus of control, which we have encountered several times in these pages, is a measure of the balance between a person's belief that their life is in their own hands versus the intuition that their life is controlled by outside forces. The original formulation is particularly telling: it refers to the expectancy that one's actions lead to consequent rewards, versus the expectancy that rewards arrive from the outside irrespective of personal inputs (Rotter, 1966). Those with a strongly internal locus of control tend to think that events in their lives emanate from their own behavior and enduring personal characteristics. Those with a stronger external locus of control are inclined to believe that what happens in their lives is the result of "luck, chance, fate, as under the control of powerful others, or as unpredictable because of the great complexity of the forces surrounding him" (Rotter, 1966, p. 1). It is measured using expressions such as "In the long run people get the respect they deserve in this world" (internal) versus "Unfortunately, an individual's worth often passes unrecognized no matter how hard he tries" (external) and "Trusting in fate has never turned out as well for me as making a decision to take a definite course of action" (internal) versus "I have often found that was is going to happen will happen" (external).

Recently in our lab, we tried to disentangle the different factors that go into shaping people's views of capitalism, pitting personality (locus of control) against ideology, while taking account of background demographic information. We devised a comprehensive questionnaire based on the views expressed by laypeople on social media (see *Contrasting views of capitalism*, above), including perceptions of the free market, attitudes to wealth inequality, and the role of the government in the economy.

In addition, we were interested in the factors that feed into people's causal theories of wealth and poverty. In addition to political ideology, we wanted to test the possibility that locus of control, as a habitual mode of understanding one's own life, would spill over into the domain of economics. The perception that one's life is internally driven could be projected onto the economic world as a belief that people, in general, are responsible for their economic fate. The perception that one's life events are externally driven could be applied to the economic world as the belief that people are not themselves responsible for their economic situation, good or bad.

What did we find? The most powerful and consistent predictor of people's views of capitalism was their self-described political ideology. In our sample, pro-capitalists almost exclusively identified as politically conservative, while anti-capitalists were almost completely liberal.

No surprise here. But what was striking was the potency of ideology. Political ideology consistently predicted the importance ascribed to each and every explanation for wealth and poverty: individual, structural, and uncontrollable. Conservatives emphasized individual factors and downplayed the importance of structural and uncontrollable ones across the board, and liberals the reverse.

Locus of control manifested in causal attributions as well, though to a lesser degree. Individuals with an internal locus of control thought that the most important factors in determining somebody's wealth is their effort and enduring personal characteristics, while downplaying the importance of uncontrollable factors, such as chance and fate. In fact, a person's locus of control was an even stronger predictor than their ideology regarding the power of chance and fate. Interestingly, locus of control had no effect whatsoever on what people thought regarding the role of structural and societal factors; these considerations, it appear, lie outside the scope of what locus of control can inform.

Thus we found, in line with many other studies featured in this chapter, that lay views of capitalism tightly align along a liberal-to-conservative continuum. In another recent study in our lab similar results were found when pitting ideology against people's self-declared values (using Schwartz's Value Inventory (Caprara, Vecchione, & Schwartz, 2009; Schwartz et al., 2014). Again, ideology was a potent and consistent predictor of views towards capitalism, above and beyond the values that people claim to espouse.

But why should people's views of capitalism go hand-in-hand with their opinions on immigration, gun control, and abortion? Part of the answer has to do with a form of "groupthink." In their book *The Knowledge Illusion: Why We Never Think Alone*, Steven Sloman and Philip Fernbach (2017, p. 16) write:

> Instead of appreciating complexity, people tend to affiliate with one or another social dogma. Because our knowledge is enmeshed with that of others, the community shapes our beliefs and attitudes. It is so hard to reject an opinion shared by our peers that too often we don't even try to evaluate claims based on their merits. We let our group do our thinking for us.

Nowadays, political affiliation does not simply entail membership in a group with shared beliefs. Rather, political affiliation functions as a kind of *social identity*, comparable to gender, religion, and ethnicity (Iyengar & Westwood, 2015). People of different ideological groups are averse to one another (Iyengar & Westwood, 2015); they are unlikely to associate with each other (McPherson, Smith-Lovin, & Cook, 2001); and they will go to great lengths to mold their opinions in ways that bolster their own group (Kahan, 2012). In today's online environment of "echo chambers" and "filter bubbles," people are all the more likely to entrench in their own group's beliefs.

Adopting the set of beliefs from one's ideological group has an additional benefit: it economizes the whole process of thinking about them. This caters to our general tendency for cognitive miserliness, discussed in Chapter 3. To answer an array of political and economic questions, difficult as they may be, one only need look to his or her ideological peers to "know" what he or she thinks. Beliefs about the meritocracy of society are part and parcel of these ideologies (Furnham, 1988, 2003; Rasinski, 1987). And as we have seen, from there the road is paved to broader views of the economy.

In Figure 7.7 we propose a model for how lay views of capitalism are formed. Personality and ideology jointly modulate the judgment as to whether the society is a meritocracy, and this assessment in turn moderates attitudes towards equality, the free market, and the need for regulation.

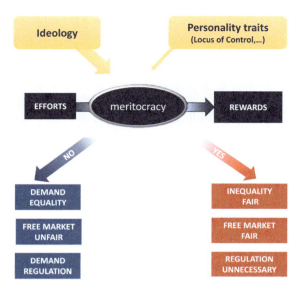

FIGURE 7.7 The joint contribution of personality and ideology to lay views of capitalism; wider line going from ideology to meritocracy perceptions indicates stronger influence.

Concluding remarks

In this chapter we tried to unearth the moral-psychological issues at the root of the capitalism debate. The first of these is how people relate to the profit motive. Many anti-capitalist beliefs are premised on a moral repugnance to self-interest (they call it "greed") and what it implies about humans and societies. Greed is thought by them to be a malign force that if only nurtured can unleash the worst of people. Greed can make people do anything to satisfy its appetite, including the exploitation of their fellow humans and the planet. That actions fueled by self-interest could bring about favorable outcomes – a core tenet of capitalism – is preposterous. Pro-capitalists are unmoved by these arguments. To them, self-interest is natural and inevitable. Capitalism offers an elegant, albeit counterintuitive mechanism, whereby the power of self-interest is harnessed in a way that brings benefits overall.

The second root of the debate is how different people judge the fairness of inequality (a duo that to some would seem inextricable). When people say inequality is unfair, they are actually attesting to much more. Namely, people harbor different theories about how wealth is *attained*. Those who believe that individuals' efforts and talents dictate how they will fare in life are not troubled by inequality. What *would* be unfair, however, was if someone were to subvert this just state of affairs by diverting wealth from the deserving to the undeserving. But for those who doubt that people always get what they deserve in life, an inequality in outcomes signals underlying unfairness, a state in need of a remedy. We pointed to two sources from which these opposing theories originate. The first and most dominant is political

94 Lay understanding of capitalism

ideology, which comes pre-packaged with these beliefs. The second is personality – in particular locus of control – the degree to which people believe they have control over their own lives.

Lay views of capitalism put on display some of the biases and cognitive constraints we discussed in Chapters 2 and 3. Chief among these is the tendency to moralize economic affairs. Economic policies and phenomena are not just efficient or inefficient but good or bad, right or wrong. Additionally, they demonstrate our propensity for cognitive miserliness, the attempt to economize cognitive resources to a minimum. In order to answer an array of economic questions, for example how to lift people out of poverty or how strictly to regulate markets, all one needs to do is look to the beliefs and theories espoused by his or her ideological peers. Since nowadays political ideology serves as a kind of social identity, policy proposals that go against one's ideological commitments cannot be expected to be considered impartially (if at all). Rather, they will be seen as threats to one's very sources of social belonging and meaning. In this way people get further and further entrenched in their own views, making the task of policy implementation all the more challenging.

Another important resource people draw upon is their own personality. The perceived link between efforts and rewards in one's own life, i.e., locus of control, quickly translates into grand theories of how stuff works "out in the world." Different control orientations (internal versus external) therefore can be expected to affect how people interpret what they observe in the economic domain and how they react to different policy proposals. For instance, some believe they have little control over what happens in their life, and they generalize this belief onto people in general. This may be a major source of resistance for them when they encounter economic phenomena that appear to take advantage of those that are vulnerable and powerless. And it may be a source of support for policies that protect them.

By means of understanding the deep moral-psychological factors that go into shaping economic views, we may hope to address people's concerns "where it matters." Our humble attempt here points to perceived meritocracy as the major determinant of people's views of the economic system. Whether liberal or conservative, people's top concern is whether the economic system is designed in a way that will ensure that people get what they deserve. Therefore, perceived meritocracy should be considered as a fundamental issue on which policy implementation will turn.

Alongside the hurdles to understanding laid down by people's ideological commitments, we would also like to point out some ways in which they might be of value. Some ideas packed into political ideologies are valid. In Chapter 2 we pointed to *aggregation* as a concept central to economic understanding. Aggregation refers to looking at the large-scale effects that emerge out of the interplay between many basic elements in a system. Conservatives are at a better position to grasp this concept. Their ability to transcend the intentions behind individual actions – be they greedy or benevolent – allows them to appreciate their outcomes at an aggregate level. Such is the requisite for comprehending the logic of the "invisible hand."

However, another idea prepacked into the conservative ideology is that people largely get what they deserve in life. And this belief blinds them to the fact that the structure of the economic system and the organization of society (and sometimes plain bad luck) can affect the link between personal inputs and economic outcomes. In this respect, liberals are better situated to understand the economy as a system complete with feedback loops and indirect effects. They factor into their reasoning precisely such considerations when they explain wealth and poverty as well as other macroeconomic concepts (Chapter 4). In other words, concepts essential to genuine economic understanding can take root in people's minds and become widespread.

8
MONEY AND WEALTH

Visitors to the Belgian coast in the summer may observe a charming activity amongst children there. Throughout the beach, groups of children, usually siblings and friends, sit in little "shops" dug out in the soft sand, and sell crepe paper flowers. Other children walk from stall to stall, a pail of seashells in their hand, and look to buy those flowers. The shells in the pail serve as the only medium of exchange. Not any shell will do, with the specific species differing from one municipal beach to the next. In Knokke-Heist, only elongated shells called *couteaux* ("knives") are accepted; elsewhere, other shapes are used exclusively. This is a spontaneous economic activity that has been going on for many dozens of years. This market is self-contained. You don't do anything with the flowers save sell them for those shells, while the *couteaux* themselves are used only for those transactions.

In these exchanges of flowers for shells, it is clear to all what are the goods and what the currency. Some of the flowers are simple, other more elaborate, there are smaller and larger ones, some more beautiful than others, and they are priced accordingly. *Couteaux* (the shells), by contrast, are all deemed equivalent regardless of their size or other physical characteristics, and flower prices are expressed by the number of shells demanded for each, in keeping with their appeal. It is much more convenient to use shells than trawling all over the beach with your own stock of flowers in the hope of finding someone willing to exchange the flowers you want against some of those you have. And if you (or Mum) are not so skilled at making pretty flowers, you can compose many of a simple design, sell them, and you will eventually be able to afford some really nice ones.

Supply and demand – money as tool

Centuries ago, Michel de Montaigne (1533–1592) commented on the difficulty of bringing together offer and demand:

Money and wealth   97

FIGURE 8.1 Paper flowers stall at the Belgian seaside.
Source: © 2012 – Regimsansel.blogspo

> My late father … long ago told me that he had once envisioned to introduce the following practice; that there might be in every town a certain place, so that those who stood in need of something might repair there, and have their business entered by an officer appointed for that purpose. As for example: I wish to sell my pearls; I am looking for pearls for sale; this man seeks company to travel to Paris; this man seeks a servant of such a quality; that one seeks a master; or a workman; some inquiring for one thing, some for another, each according to his needs. And it seems that this means of mutual advertisements would be of no mean advantage to the public intercourse: for there are always conditions that look for one another, and the want of knowing one another leaves men in very great necessity.
>
> *(Montaigne, 1595/1969, ch. XXXV, p. 275)*

The classic example of matching offer and demand was set up by the *Vereenigde Oost-Indische Compagnie* (VOC). That early corporation established an intricate trade route in the seventeenth and eighteenth centuries, and brought untold riches to the Dutch, who themselves had few resources. The main intra-Asian trade circuit was the so-called triangular trade connecting Japan, India, and Mainland South-East Asia. Japan sold metals to the VOC, that were then spent as means of payment for the purchase of cotton textiles in South Asia. Part of the Indian textiles were sent to Mainland South-East Asia, where they were bartered against commodities in demand on the Japanese market. Through this triangular trade the VOC obtained profits, which were transferred to Insular South-East Asia in the form of silver and cotton textiles in order to procure pepper and spices so highly sought after on the European market (Shimada, 2006).

The commercial activity of the VOC relied on a complicated system of barter. Money, as every introductory economics textbook tells us, affords flexibility. It

98 Money and wealth

makes it possible to do business indirectly, when there is no match between the needs of seller and buyer. One has pearls to sell, and no need for a ride. The other offers a ride, but needs no pearls. A third needs neither pearls nor a ride, but is willing to work. People get paid for their goods, services, or labor, and with the advent of cash, indirect trading is hugely facilitated.

Actually, this introductory presentation is more of an ideal reconstruction than the description of an actual historical development. It is not at all sure that pure barter ever existed as the fundamental way to exchange goods and services (Humphrey, 1985) within the confines of a stable social group. In reality, the fundamental element was trust in reciprocity, and exchanges took place flexibly in a context of fairness and mutual goodwill. Interestingly, studies of child development do not indicate that barter is easier to understand than transactions involving money (Leiser & Beth Halachmi, 2006). In trade between strangers, this model does occur but, as we will see, trust remains a fundamental aspect of money even after the advent of cash.

Let us return to the Belgian seaside commerce. Shells are not just useful as a mechanism of trade. They also store value in this insulated economy, as they are solid and durable. This makes it possible to accumulate wealth, and to transport it. For children, this means they can be brought home and conserved for next year's season, whereas existing stocks of paper flowers will no longer be saleable. In the world of grownups, these features lie behind the success of another kind of shell, the cowrie shell, which was extremely popular across much of Africa and other areas bordering the Indian Ocean, as a means of exchange and a store of value (Weatherford, 2009).

Money supply

Money supply (or money stock) is defined as the sum total of currency and other liquid instruments in a country's economy as of a particular time. A reduction in money supply can cause deflation (a decline in general price levels). Increase in money supply can cause inflation. In the sixteenth century, the vast quantities of precious metal that poured from the Americas caused tremendous inflation – the more silver people had, the more goods they wanted to buy, and the more people who wanted these goods, the higher the prices charged for them. The quantity of goods produced could not keep up with the increasing volume of silver.

Belgian children live in a stable world, where the going rates for flowers are known and unchanging, while money supply is stable too. Every child engaged in that trade knows the fair price range for a given flower. As we saw, this intuition of a stable, right, normative price, remains part of the adults' mental model, alongside a more mature conception. Yet if some climatic condition were to cause the shells to crumble within hours, this would bring this generations-old commerce to an end. So too, if the mollusks who secrete the shells were decimated in an ecological disaster, or on the contrary were to proliferate, this would surely affect prices. The

Money and wealth **99**

stock of the medium of exchange must be just right. Too little and the economy will grind to a stop, too much of it and prices will rise.

The distinction between wealth and money is hard to grasp for non-economists. Historically, the conflation of the two underlay the early attempt to devise a coherent economic policy by the Mercantilists. To them, a nation's wealth would be increased by regulating the nation's commercial activity. Restricting imports by imposing punishing tariffs and maximizing exports (against precious metal) was naïvely thought to increase the nation's wealth. It took a deeper understanding of trade to recognize that trade is not a zero-sum game, that trade profits both parties, and that the means of payment is merely the means to enable trade to take place for their mutual benefit.

Modern-day non-economists similarly don't differentiate clearly between the creation of wealth and an increase in money supply. The public "knows" that money is created exclusively by the central bank, by "the mint," while commercial banks collect deposits and then lend that money out, which is how they turn a profit. Andy Haldane, the chief economist of the Bank of England, recently gave a speech entitled "The Great Divide" in which he stressed the yawning perception gap between the financial sector and wider society (Haldane, 2016). Economic thinking on these matters is radically different from the views held by the public: "Far from banking other people's money, modern banks are primarily involved with making money by creating a most fundamental institution of capitalism: liquidity" (Sgambati, 2016, p. 274).

Do central banks want people to understand this, though? Not necessarily. According to Braun (2016) a central bank's legitimacy hinges on it being perceived as acting in line with the dominant folk theory of money, even though this theory accords poorly with how money actually works. Using the Bundesbank and the European Central Bank as examples, Braun suggests that under inflationary macroeconomic conditions, central bankers willingly nourished the folk-theoretical notion of money as a quantity under the direct control of the central bank. He then goes on to intimate that the Bank of England's recent refutation of the folk theory of money was motivated by an economic environment where the focus shifted from fighting inflation to staving off deflation.

It had its work cut out for it. Here are some examples of thoroughly unintuitive claims that were presented by the Bank of England in a document intended to enlighten non-economists about money creation. "Rather than banks receiving deposits when households save and then lending them out, bank lending creates deposits" (McLeay, Radia, & Thomas, 2014, p. 14). One would have thought that banks do the opposite. Another statement, from a BoE article entitled "Money creation in the modern economy," was quoted approvingly by MP Steve Baker in his opening remarks at the British House of Commons (2014), where MPs convened, for the first time in 147 years we are told, to discuss "Money Creation and Society." "Whenever a bank makes a loan, it simultaneously creates a matching deposit in the borrower's bank account, thereby creating new money." Baker commented: "I

100 Money and wealth

have been told many times that this is ridiculous," and indeed, that statement too does sound wildly paradoxical. *Qui paye ses dettes s'enrichit* (he who pays back his debts becomes richer) goes the prudential French proverb. Yet the Bank of England makes it sound as though taking a loan can enrich you.

Of course, a loan doesn't make you any richer, or poorer for that matter. Properly analyzed, what it does is supply you with liquidity. Consider a last statement, from the same document: "When a bank agrees to make a loan, say as a mortgage to buy a house, it credits the borrower's bank account with a deposit of the size of the mortgage. At that moment, new money is created." This makes sense, provided the two concepts, value (wealth, capital) and money, are properly differentiated. When a bank gives out a mortgage, money is put in circulation. The borrower then takes the money and spends it on a house, having promised to pay it back in successive installments, a promise backed by the possibility the bank has to foreclose on the house should they fail to do so. The total money supply has increased, while of course no wealth was created. Conversely, "repayment of bank loans destroys money" makes sense too: he who pays back his debt diminishes the money supply, whilst this has nothing to do with anyone becoming poorer or richer.

This fundamental failure to differentiate capital and money was illustrated later in that debate at the British House of Commons. In response to a question, MP Steve Baker pointed at the confusion with some irritation:

> If the Hon. Lady is saying that she would like rising real wage levels, of course I agree with her. Who wouldn't? I want rising real wage levels, but something about which I get incredibly frustrated is the use of that word "capital." I have heard economists talk about capital when what they really mean is money, and typically what they mean by money is new bank credit, because 97% of the money supply is bank credit. That is not capital; capital is the means of production. ... I fear that we have started to label as capital money that has been loaned into existence without any real backing.

In a recent study, 100 British MPs were asked, of several statements, whether they are true or false, including the following two: *Only the government – via the Bank of England or Royal Mint – has the authority to create money, including coins, notes and the electronic money in your bank account*; and *New money is created when banks make loans, and existing money is destroyed when members of the public repay loans* (Dods Group, 2014). The MPs' average understanding of the role played by banks in the financial system was low: 72% believe that the government alone is responsible for creating money, while only 12% said that it was true that bank loans create new money which is then destroyed on repayment.

We could not identify studies on lay conceptions about money, but one can safely assume that the average member of the public is no more knowledgeable about money than MPs who are regularly required to participate in debates about economic issues. Some preliminary studies we ran point to one of the causes of the confusion. A common misconception is that banks can only loan out money that was previously deposited by its customers. People are mostly unaware that the bank is allowed to lend out a multiple of their reserves, which themselves are often supposed to be backed by gold in the central bank's vaults. With such assumptions, no wonder the role and the functioning of the central bank remain wholly mysterious to most people, who rely on other clues to decide whether it deserves to be trusted (Kril, Leiser, & Spivak, 2016).

Fiat money

The simple distinction we made between goods and services that people want, and money that serves as the instrument to facilitate their exchange, is psychologically too restrictive. The standard account distinguishes two forms of money. First is *commodity money*, which derives its value from the commodity out of which the good/money is made, whether gold or a cigarette. The face value of the coin is merely a convenience, a way to express a standard quantity. Proponents of commodity money emphasize the material qualities of precious metals – their durability, malleability, resistance to rust, etc.

The other form is called *fiat money*, as in "*Fiat lux*" ("Let there be light"), the phrase uttered by the Divine Creator when He willed light into existence. Fiat money was first introduced as a more convenient form of money. Instead of having to carry around metal disks or loads of cigarettes, one could carry paper backed by the government. Over time governments have been less willing to back up their fiat currency with gold or other commodities and fiat money has become trust-based, firstly in the government who issues it, and secondly in the economic community that accepts it. With this arrangement, the status of money is what causes the piece of paper to have a value, which it does not have in virtue of its physical structure. Fiat money both requires trust and generates it: since everyone accepts this currency, I too will accept it. What makes the piece of paper in my hand count as money is the fact that we, collectively, accept and recognize that the piece of paper has the status of money. Our fates become linked, as I accept to belong to the social group of those who throw their fate with that currency (Aglietta & Orléan, 2002).

Fiat money is especially convenient for very large sums, where the bulk of the equivalent commodity would be unmanageable. The convenience is used extensively in criminal contexts as it facilitates crime, bribery, and tax evasion (Henry, 1976; Rogoff, 2016). Since the possibility to use paper money or coins to buy goods and services relies on a convention initiated by a government, a government can cancel the convention. Currency can be demonetized and removed from circulation, and this is not so uncommon as one might think. in late 2016, India's government cancelled all its high-denomination banknotes without warning, in an effort to curb corruption and force people to join the cashless digital economy. The point of doing so unannounced was to prevent criminals from shifting their money to other forms, such as buying real estate. In practice, it seems this surprise decree did little to "flush" illicit money as practically all the banknotes affected were deposited in the bank. At about the same time, Venezuela President Nicolás

102 Money and wealth

Maduro announced that the 100-bolívar note would cease to be legal tender within 72 hours, arguing (implausibly) that this would prevent putative speculators from harming the Venezuelan economy. Demonetization also happened a decade before in Europe, with the introduction of the euro that superseded national currencies.

Emotional value of money – money as drug

What preceded is a version of the standard presentation of money in an economic textbook. But that prosaic account of fiat money does not do justice to the passion money can evoke. Schumpeter summarized the two aspects of money a century ago: "There are only two theories of money which deserve the name ... the commodity theory and the claim [= fiat] theory. From their very nature, they are incompatible" (Gabor & Vestergaard, 2016, p. 3; Schumpeter, 1917). As Lawson (2016) points out, it seems unlikely that two traditional accounts could be endlessly maintained if they did not each capture something of the actual situation. While the fiat theory is endorsed by economists, the notion that all paper money is backed by gold stored in the central bank remains prevalent amongst non-economists, and is resistant in the face of even significant training (Vergès, 1989, p. 425). We suggest that this persistence expresses the intuition that money is truly valuable, and not just a convention. In a seminal paper, Lea and Webley (2006) describe all money-related phenomena as being subsumed under either of two broad theories. *Tool theory* captures all the ways money satisfies people's practical needs. While money has various functions (e.g., a store of value, a means of exchange, a unit of account), all these uses are instrumental. *Drug theory* proposes that money is akin to biological drugs, affecting behavior in ways that are not instrumental or adaptive (which parallels that of biological drugs) but still make use of evolved reward-related mechanisms in the human brain (just like biological drugs).

When money consists of precious metal, especially gold, it is experienced as inherently valuable. In actual fact, gold has relatively few practical uses, outside of decoration and some sophisticated modern technological applications; yet people throughout the world have been attracted to it. Even though it lacks utility, empirical evidence shows that humans everywhere have wanted to touch it, wear it, play with it, and possess it. Unlike copper, which turns green; iron, which rusts; and silver, which tarnishes, pure gold remains pure and unchanged (Weatherford, 2009), making it a natural peg for immaterial properties, such as purity, sanctity, perfection, or permanence. Gold features in pirates' hoards along with gems and pearls. One enamored by gold and gems, says Bachelard, "*aime une richesse qu'on ne vend pas*" ("loves riches that is not for sale"). Literature and movies are full of characters who hunger for gold (Virgil already spoke of *auri sacra fames*, the accursed hunger for gold [*Aeneid*, III, 57]), whether that of mountain dwarves, Tolkien's Smaug, or assorted pirates. Disney's character Scrooge McDuck had a telling favorite pastime: diving off a springboard into his money heap to swim in his "three cubic acres" pool of gold coins, in what Bachelard (1948, p. vi) would have called "a monstrosity of psychological valuation." Such gold is not for use or exchange. It is hoarded, and no

Money and wealth **103**

amount can satisfy the hoarder. "He who loves silver cannot be satiated by silver" (Ecclesiastes 5:10). One is indeed reminded of substance addiction.

Emotions are extended to fiat money

This phenomenon is not restricted to gold and silver. The emotions did not vanish with the introduction of the newer forms of fiat money. Instead, the emotional value of money became attached to the newer means of payment. Bills may be bits of paper that become valuable by convention, but once this has occurred, bills too become symbolically charged. Tim Harford (2015) tells of two financially successful artists, Bill Drummond and Jimmy Cauty, who filmed themselves burning £1 million worth of banknotes. As Harford points out, people wouldn't have minded if they had spent that money in any of the absurd lavish avenues open to the very rich. But they did mind this *destruction* of money, and jeered when Drummond explained to an assembled crowd that "burning that money doesn't mean there's any less loaves of bread in the world, any less apples, any less anything. The only thing that's less, is a pile of paper" (p. 57).

The situation contrasts cleanly with the practice of Potlatch amongst some Indian tribes. In the course of that ceremony, people would exchange gifts and sometimes destroy valuable belongings, possibly to reduce overly marked wealth inequalities within their communities. Potlatch truly destroys wealth, whereas Drummond and Cauty's burning of those notes didn't destroy any goods. Indeed, following their action, everyone who held pounds at the time became fractionally richer.

Drummond's action was of course neither candid not indifferent. The performer wasn't trying to make the economic point we are discussing here – although he understood it well – but to enact some sort of public provocation. He too presumably felt a frisson as he set fire to that pile of cash. As we saw, primitive conceptions are not eradicated by the acquisition of a mature conception. They subsist alongside it, remaining emotionally potent, and burning paper money is disturbing to people. This has been demonstrated experimentally. Becchio et al. (2011) prepared video clips of people cutting up or tearing banknotes, and other clips where valueless paper notes were being cut, and showed them to participants while measuring brain activity. Clips of banknote destruction were shown to provoke greater brain activation than the folding of the notes or the destruction of worthless papers.

Everyday cash has striking effects that cannot be accounted for by its instrumental role. Being around money, touching money, seeing pictures of money bills floating around on a screen saver in the background, all these have been shown to affect people's emotions and attitudes, and merely activating the concept of money in these peripheral ways affects both personal and interpersonal behavior. In a now classic series of experiments, Vohs, Mead, and Goode (2006) primed participants with money, by having money in one form or another around them, without any suggestion of the money belonging to the participants or accessible to them in any way. Those primed with money preferred to play and to work alone, were less helpful to others, and choose to put more physical distance between themselves

104 Money and wealth

and a new acquaintance. For instance, when requested to place a chair in view of a discussion with some other participant, they put the chair at some larger distance from them if money had been activated. They were also less willing to chip in when invited to contribute to some charity devoted to helping needy students (Vohs, Mead, & Goode, 2008), and reduced helpful behavior even towards a romantic partner (Savani, Mead, Stillman, & Vohs, 2016). Reminders of money also prompted participants to work harder on challenging tasks than did participants not reminded of money (Vohs et al., 2008). Mere exposure to money was also found to increase endorsement of free-market systems and social inequality (Caruso, Vohs, Baxter, & Waytz, 2013, p. 149).

At least some of these effects are precocious (Gasiorowska, Chaplin, Zaleskiewicz, Wygrab, & Vohs, 2016; Gasiorowska, Zaleskiewicz, & Wygrab, 2012). While young children (aged 3–6) do not yet understand the economic mechanisms of money and are incapable of using money properly (Leiser et al., 1990), they too behaved more selfishly following mental activation of the concept of money. For instance, when asked by the experimenter to help her out, they were less helpful than children from a control group who had not been exposed to money.

Money is a powerful psychological stimulus. It affects us in a variety of ways, and its impact is as evident in a wide range of behaviors, from hoarding and discomfort at its destruction to a range of social effects. Historically, money went from being commodity-based and possessed of intrinsic value to being conventional, and its value grounded in the trust of the community of users, as orchestrated by a central authority that set it up. This transition did not end the emotional effects, that remain visible in our relation to fiat money too.

Fungibility

A central theoretical postulate in economics is money fungibility, the notion that a unit of money is substitutable to another. Thaler (1990, 1999, 2015) has long contested the appropriateness of this convenient postulate when it comes to describe how people behave. We will look at a number of its violations.

Studies on attitudes towards transition from a national currency to the euro in European countries show that opposition to the common euro currency does not stem from the perceived economic personal drawbacks, but originates from emotional feelings towards the national currency (Burgoyne, Routh, & Ellis, 1999). People become attached to money, and reluctant to part with it, over and beyond the unwillingness to give away of their wealth. A common recommendation to help people stick to their budget is to pay in cash, handing over physical bills and coins, preferably one by one, as paying by credit card or checks is less painful than handing over currency. This recommendation is based on experiments such as that by Prelec and Simester (2001) who titled their paper "Always leave home without it." The use of credit cards makes people more willing to spend their money. Soman (1999) shows that there are several aspects to the transparency of payment in credit card payments: you are not made aware of the amount you pay in the same way as you do when writing a check, let alone when you need to count the bills and coins to reach the required amount, and there are temporal aspects to the transaction: are you out of money immediately or will this only occur in the future. Payment mechanisms that make the sum less salient (you just enter your PIN code) and deplete wealth with a temporal delay create an illusion of liquidity that causes people to spend more freely.

In the same spirit, Raghubir and Srivastava (2008) demonstrated that consumers spend more when spending "scrip" (a gift certificate introduced in the experiment) than when they must pay equivalent amounts of cash. They call this feature "payment transparency": the more transparent (in the sense of invisible) the payment form, the more likely people will be to buy goods and services. Cash is physical, embodied, money, and its use makes handing over wealth salient. These observations dovetail with the use of tokens and chips in gambling venues, where the house is interested in having the patrons gamble freely. Chips and tokens do not quite feel like real money. And they are therefore often re-gambled without hesitation as their emotional value is less than that of equivalent amounts in hard cash. Lapuz and Griffiths (2010) found that participants in their experiments gambled significantly more with chips than with cash, and conclude, rather disarmingly: "The finding suggests that it might be more socially responsible for gaming operators to provide the option for their clientele to gamble with real money rather than make them convert it to chips" (p. 38). When paying by cash, the feeling of parting with money is very vivid and is akin to "having one's meter running" (Thaler, 1999). As Ragubir and Srivastava put it,

> [payment] by credit card or gift card may not feel or appear as real as legal tender thereby reducing the salience of parting with real money. ... using a different payment form (other than legal tender) may seem like play money or "monopoly" money, making it easier to spend.
>
> *(2008, p. 215)*

It is worth reflecting upon the psychological difference between the novel "scrip" and regular cash, and asking why the former should be easier to spend. Indeed, what is so "real" about cash, considering that scrips and dollars are both plainly conventional "fiat" money? The answer is that cash *feels* like it has intrinsic value. You exchange it for real stuff, and the basis for this possibility is remote. Once a material support becomes imbued with symbolic meaning, its material properties and its value become psychologically intertwined. This is why burning money can provide a special kind of thrill. For the newly introduced scrips, the conventional aspect is still salient.

This interpretation is supported by neurological data. Money, a strong incentive and a strong reward, activates the same neural circuits as rewards associated with physiological needs. Brain imaging studies found exposure to money activated areas of the brain linked with immediate reward, and not delayed or long-term rewards (McClure, Laibson, Loewenstein, & Cohen, 2004), supporting the idea that

106 Money and wealth

money is perceived as more than a tool for the future purchasing of goods, and its possession is rewarding in itself. Tallon-Baudry, Meyniel, and Bourgeois-Gironde, 2011) took advantage of the changes in the euro area in 2002 to compare neural responses to valid coins with neural responses to demonetized coins, that were no longer legal tender. In this way, they were able to show that valid currency is identified as "special" extremely fast. Magneto-encephalographic recordings show that valid and invalid coins are distinguished within 150 ms of presentation, indicating that the mental process is automatic and unconscious.

Beyond the somewhat contrived contrast between cash and the newly introduced scrip, one can point to the way the same price expressed in different currency produces different affective responses. This was very striking in Eastern Europe, where the US dollars had an aura linked to the opulent lifestyle of the West. In Poland, the perceived status of the zloty (the local currency before Poland joined the euro zone) and that of the prestigious US dollar affected how prices were perceived. Depending on the currency used, the same price at a known exchange rate could be seen as more or less expensive (Przybyszewski & Tyszka, 2007; Tyszka & Przybyszewski, 2006). Parallel observations were made regarding the Russian ruble: "Not all cash is alike," notes Lemon (1998) in her anthropological study of the affective relationship Russians held toward US dollars after the Soviet period.

Not only are prices expressed in an admired currency magnified, so is the physical size of coins and bills. This phenomenon was called the "money size illusion," and it is a special case of a more general phenomenon, the influence of value on perception. Show someone a diamond, say, then remove it and ask them to draw a circle of the same size as the diamond. Chances are, they will draw it larger than the original. Do the same with a piece of cut glass, making sure to tell them it is worthless, and the effect disappears (Bruner & Goodman, 1947). Lea (1981) found that pre-decimal British coins were remembered as larger than the identical coins under their decimal names, devalued by a decade of rapid inflation. Leiser and Izak (1987) too showed that the perceived size of coin depends on their perceived value. They ran their experiments in Israel at a time of double-digit monthly inflation, and showed that for coins in use at the time, the money size illusion did not obtain, as coinage was felt to be of little value, whereas for coins that had been in use before the inflation period, the effect was again found. Related effects were also found by Furnham (1983).

Real money vs. money on paper

Another expression of the violation of fungibility is presented by the distribution of dividends. It is generally accepted that dividends and capital gains should be perfect substitutes for each other (if taxes and transaction costs are ignored). Roughly speaking, if you own stock, you should be indifferent between you (and all other stockholders) receiving the payment of a one-dollar cash dividend or the decision by the company not to distribute any, since the drop in the value of the stock equals the amount the company distributed.

Why then do firms distribute dividends? Because people prefer receiving them, and there are various interpretations for this preference. Shefrin and Statman (1984) propose an explanation based on "mental accounting" – the set of cognitive operations used by individuals and households to organize, evaluate, and keep track of financial activities. Shefrin and Statman argue that investors like dividends because the regular cash payment provides a simple self-control rule: spend the dividends and leave the principal alone. Spending the dividends but making sure not to touch the principal is akin to using only salaried income to indulge in luxuries, but staying away from the savings. This may be good advice, but economically speaking is not quite rational. The sum total of what you own includes both savings and monthly income. You should base your decision on whether the utility from that tempting luxury item is worth its price, taking into consideration your entire fortune. Yet this policy is reasonable because restricting the decision to just the state of your checking account serves as a commitment device that shields us from succumbing to temptation.

Laibson (1997) discusses dividends in terms of liquidity. Investments in bonds or in the stock markets generate benefits, but these are difficult to realize immediately: the check you receive is liquid, whereas stocks must be sold. A similar situation obtains regarding capital gains in the stock market. Using aggregate data, Hatsopoulos, Krugman, and Poterba (1989) show that capital gains do not boost consumption, whereas consumption does increase when takeovers generate cash for the stockholders. This is sometimes called the "mailbox effect": when the check arrives in the mailbox, it tends to get spent, whereas gains "on paper" are left alone.

What's the difference? We would suggest an additional, speculative interpretation, not incompatible with the previous one, that draws some support from existing phenomena. Psychologically, there exist two kinds of money. The one is real. It consists of cash, and by extension, includes also money deposited in a bank account. But financial money is another kind of money, it is virtual money, only a potential that has to be transformed into real money to become the kind you can spend. Economists will of course point to the transaction cost involved in selling virtual financial money, but we suspect that this aspect is secondary, though the question should be examined empirically. Some support might be found in data presented by Leiser et al. (2017) who asked non-economists the following question: In your opinion, what really happened to all the money that was said to have "disappeared" in the recent crisis? Participants selected, out of four explanations, the one that best matched their own view (or checked the "don't know" answer). The options were: (1) it never existed: its existence before the crisis was just an illusion; (2) shares fell, and as a result part of their value was lost during the crisis; (3) it was not lost for everyone, and is now in the hands of certain people; (4) its value existed only as a potential, and the crisis destroyed that potential. Despite its simplicity, this question is revealing.

The press reports stated the total value of the stock market dropped by several trillions during the crisis, just as the stock market valuation increases when times are good. Many people have trouble with the notion that value can decrease,

FIGURE 8.2 From concrete to insubstantial forms of money.

and only a quarter of those who agreed to answer at all (about 95% of the total) endorsed it. All the others rejected the possibility that value can truly vanish, and supported various other accounts instead. Half the respondents apparently believe in a Law of Conservation of Wealth (!) which states that "Wealth cannot be created or destroyed, it can only be transformed." To some, what happened during the crisis is that some clever operators managed to siphon money off discretely in some way, and it is now in their possession. To others, the money didn't disappear because it never existed in the first place: it was never more than an illusory bubble, a shiny, iridescent object that vanishes if you try to touch it. Lastly, a quarter of the respondents saw stock market valuation as potential money. It can be actualized if you sell your stock, and it then becomes real money, but if you don't, the potential may disappear, and this is what happened in the crisis. This latter conception fits the distinction between the financial industry and the real economy (de Rosa & Bulgarella, 2009), that distinguishes between the virtual world of finance that deals in insubstantial financial products produced by speculators, and the real economy anchored in the productivity of real people and their work that involves real money.

This chapter surveyed a variety of psychological phenomena related to money. Their range suggests that an integrative and clearly articulated account of lay understanding of money may be unattainable. Money is a polymorphous representation (Bourgeois-Gironde & Dimier, 2009), it implicates a nexus of attitudes, emotions, and confused knowledge. The ways money functions in a modern economy are not clearly differentiated by its users, and this confusion encourages an irrational attachment to the medium. The medium itself makes a difference, as some forms are felt to be intrinsically more valuable than others. We may tentatively summarize the studies and observations surveyed in this chapter by suggesting the following gradient (see Figure 8.2), starting from the material and emotion-laden to the most ethereal: gold, prestigious currencies, any cash, newly invented local moneys (such as the Brixton local urban pound and scrips in a lab experiment), lines in a bank account, and money in the form of financial instruments.

9
FINANCIAL AND ECONOMIC LITERACY

Throughout this book, we discuss the limited economic knowledge of members of the public, and focus on their understanding of broader economic issues, mostly to stress how challenging it is in the absence of formal training in the dismal science. In this chapter, we will take a somewhat different perspective, and discuss remediation. What can be done to fight the consequences of that challenge. Is education the solution, and if so, of what kind? And how effective is it?

We will take up these questions regarding two distinct domains: personal finance, and citizen participation in policy making. Accordingly, this chapter will be comprised of two parts, with little relation between them.

Financial literacy and education

We begin with everyday financial knowledge, the type of knowledge that people use to handle their financial affairs. Or rather, the knowledge the public should be using, but often doesn't. The intricacies of the workings of the economy are mystifying, of course, but navigating one's personal finances is challenging too. This difficulty has significant consequences for public policy (Congdon et al., 2011). The basic premise of rational choice theory is that aggregate social behavior results from the decisions and behavior of individual actors. Every individual has preferences among the available choice alternatives, and is assumed to take account of all available information concerning the probabilities of events and their potential costs and benefits. People are then supposed to act consistently in choosing the self-determined best choice of action. This is usually expressed by the dictum "economic agents are utility maximizing." When these and related assumptions obtain, it becomes possible to understand, model, and shape economic behavior.

This neat state of affairs falls apart if individuals cannot work out what is best for them. If they don't have access to the needed information or don't understand

110 Financial and economic literacy

its significance, comparing alternatives usefully is a serious challenge. Individuals therefore often fail to optimize their own welfare. It follows that the standard models used to capture consumer behavior and shape economic policy lose their usefulness, in some cases to the point of irrelevance. The finance ministry may well force banks and financial bodies to publish and disseminate the extensive information needed for informed decisions in the hope of shaping the market, yet this will come to naught if the public cannot understand the information provided. This is indeed by and large the case.

How much financial literacy does the public possess?

Over the past decade or so, the extent of the ignorance of economic and financial basics has become apparent. Surveys of financial and economic literacy have flourished since the financial crisis in 2008 (e.g., Aprea et al., 2016; Lusardi & Mitchell, 2011; Walstad, Rebeck, & Butters, 2013). Despite sizeable differences in different countries and target groups, the results consistently show that untrained people have difficulties understanding even basic economic and financial concepts such as the functioning of an interest rate or the principle of risk diversification (Di Girolamo, Harrison, Lau, & Swarthout, 2015; Lusardi & Mitchell, 2007, 2011).

Such questions typically relate to five key difficulties:

* *Basic understanding of interest on a deposit.* Suppose you had €100 in a savings account and the interest rate was 2% per year. After 5 years, how much do you think you would have in the account if you left the money to grow? (i) More than €102; (ii) Exactly €102; (iii) Less than €102; (iv) Do not know; (v) Refusal.
* *Interest compounding*: Suppose you had €100 in a savings account and the interest rate is 20% per year and you never withdraw money or interest payments. After 5 years, how much would you have on this account in total? (i) More than €200; (ii) Exactly €200; (iii) Less than €200; (iv) Do not know; (v) Refusal.
* *Inflation*: Imagine that the interest rate on your savings account was 1% per year and inflation was 2% per year. After 1 year, how much would you be able to buy with the money in this account? (i) More than today; (ii) Exactly the same; (iii) Less than today; (iv) Do not know; (v) Refusal.
* *Time value of money*: Assume a friend inherits €10,000 today and his sibling inherits €10,000 3 years from now. Who is richer because of the inheritance? (i) My friend; (ii) His sibling; (iii) They are equally rich; (iv) Do not know; (v) Refusal.
* *Money illusion*: Suppose that in the year 20xx, your income has doubled and prices of all goods have doubled too. In 20xx, how much will you be able to buy with your income? (i) More than today; (ii) The same; (iii) Less than today; (iv) Do not know; (v) Refusal.

The OECD recently completed a study of financial literacy in 30 countries with an extensive geographical spread, in Africa, Asia, Europe, Australasia, North America

Financial and economic literacy **111**

and South America. The study relied on the *OECD Toolkit* (OECD/INFE., 2015), a set of questionnaires developed over many years. The verdict is bleak. Many adults around the world are currently unable to reach even the minimum target score on financial knowledge.

Here are a few numbers, to get a sense of just how poorly people fare. The minimum target score is five out of seven on a range of simple questions. On average, only 56% of adults achieved this minimum score (OECD countries did only slightly better, with 63% across OECD countries, similar differences apply to each topic). Regarding the benefits of compound interest on savings, only 42% of adults across all participating countries gave the correct answer, while only 58% could compute a percentage to calculate a simple interest on savings). Only about two out of three adults were aware that it is possible to reduce investment risk by buying a range of different stocks, and half the respondents tend to financial short-termism (Aprea & Wuttke, 2016).

Consequences of deficient financial knowledge

Financial knowledge, then, is often very deficient, and people pay the price. Low levels of financial literacy are associated with the reluctance to plan for retirement (Lusardi & Mitchell, 2007), borrowing at higher interest rates (Stango & Zinman, 2009), a lower likelihood of participating in the stock market (Van Rooij et al., 2011), and countless more correlates of financial literacy have been documented, some of which are discussed in the comprehensive reviews by Fernandes, Lynch Jr., and Netemeyer (2014), Hastings, Madrian, and Skimmyhorn (2012), and Lusardi and Mitchell (2014).

The topic has become popular in research and in discussion of policy, due to several recent changes in the personal economic environment. The most obvious one is that, starting about a decade ago and with no end in sight, people have been compelled to be more involved in their finances. Recent changes in the labor market, growing availability of debt vehicles (credit cards, debit cards, mortgages, home equity loans, payday loans, etc.), and a vast range of savings alternatives require more decisions to be made by the individual (Hastings et al., 2012). Reforms of pension regimes, in particular the shift from Defined Benefits to Defined Contributions plans in many countries, have placed the onus of financial management on the individual consumer. The OECD warns that, although these arrangements have important advantages, they put more of the risks of saving for retirement and decision making in the hands of individuals (OECD, 2016). People are responsible to make sure that their contributions will be enough to live from after they retire, and this implies inter alia that they must understand how it is being invested until that time, whether the investment is a safe yet profitable one. They must also understand the ways financial institutions handle fees, compare across possibilities, negotiate better conditions and so forth, and expectedly, financial literacy was shown to be predictive of financial behavior (Allgood & Walstad, 2016). At the same time that the burden of responsibility was shifting

112 Financial and economic literacy

from government to the public, the financial industry has become much more sophisticated. Financial products and services have become more complicated, and advanced analysis is required to select between them. Those developments are not restricted to the developed world. With the growth of microfinance and the emergence of mobile money in many parts of the world, policy makers and NGOs are urging more widespread financial awareness and knowledge to enable the poor to better understand and utilize the new financial products at their disposal. Thus, the notion that financial education needs to be expanded has gained traction, in both the developed and developing world (Carpena, Cole, Shapiro, & Zia, 2015).

The promise of financial literacy training

In view of these developments, the natural response would be to impart financial literacy, at school, in the workplace, and wherever possible (Aprea & Wuttke, 2016; Fernandes et al., 2014). This is especially required, since people cannot be expected to learn from their experience, the way they acquire so many other skills. Experiential learning (learning through reflection on experience doing) will not be effective in this realm, because regarding some of the most important issues, faulty knowledge cannot be corrected by experience in a timely manner. Most consequential financial decisions, such as saving and investing for retirement, choosing a mortgage, or investing in an education, are undertaken infrequently and have delayed outcomes so that, if you didn't get it right the first time, you won't find out until too late (Hastings et al., 2012).

Economists entertain broader fears, beyond the concern for the financial well-being of the individuals directly involved. The analysis of the causes of the financial and economic crisis suggests that financial incompetence by household was a significant cause, besides other major causal factors. "Lack of financial literacy was one of the factors contributing to ill-informed financial decisions … these decisions could, in turn, have tremendous negative spill-over" (OECD, 2013, p. 140). The claim is that the financial crisis would not have occurred, had people declined the entreaties to buy houses on loans that required them to pay back amounts that they couldn't possibly earn. The crisis affected economically fragile families directly, and has also ominous consequences for long-term economic growth. As a result of all these considerations, financial education programs are currently at the forefront of the post-crisis reform agenda.

Financial training is mostly disappointing

However, while few would dispute that, all things equal, more knowledge is to be encouraged, extensive academic research questions the "financial literacy" approach to the improvement of financial abilities. Two links must hold for conventional financial education to be effective. Education must succeed in enhancing knowledge and understanding, and that improved knowledge must modify behavior.

The best empirical work finds that financial education is not likely to have significant and lasting effects on knowledge, and is even less likely to affect behavior (De Meza, Irlenbusch, & Reyniers, 2008). Hundreds of research papers have been written on the topic, most showing disappointing outcomes for financial literacy interventions, and only a few suggest that efforts are helpful. Participating in an economics course did not enhance minimal economic knowledge at all (Wobker, Kenning, Lehmann-Waffenschmidt, & Gigerenzer, 2014). Summarizing such studies is difficult. Fortunately, there exists a statistical technique to surmount these difficulties, called meta-analysis, which makes it possible to extract a conclusion from such a diverse corpus of published work. Three such meta-analytic surveys were completed in recent years. Fernandes et al. (2014) conducted their meta-analysis of the relationship of financial literacy and financial education to financial behaviors in 168 papers covering 201 prior studies. Their work led to two depressing conclusions: (1) attempts to increase financial literacy have a negligible effect on financial behavior – interventions to improve financial literacy explain only 0.1% of the variance in the financial behaviors studied; (2) such slight effect as there is decays over time, as is not uncommon for educational interventions. After 20 months, even substantial interventions amounting to 20 hours of instruction or more leave no discernible effects on behavior. It should also be noted that such meta-analyses suffer from an inherent bias: they summarize published studies only. It may well be that successful interventions are more likely to be reported and published than unsuccessful ones, and that the true effectiveness of those interventions is even lower.

Fernandes et al. do not dispute the strong correlation between financial literacy and sensible financial behavior. On the contrary, they insist on distinguishing correlation from causation, and demonstrate that the link between financial literacy and judicious financial behavior is not causal. Improving financial literacy does not improve financial behavior.

A second meta-analysis study, by Miller, Reichelstein, Salas, and Zia (2015), set out to demonstrate a more nuanced picture, but ultimately reached essentially the same conclusions. Their work was based on 188 papers and articles that report on the outcome of interventions designed to increase consumers' financial knowledge (financial literacy) or skills, attitudes, and behaviors (financial capability). Savings and retirement was the most common target for financial education intervention in their corpus. Meta-analysis to evaluate the impact of financial education interventions on retirement savings failed to produce evidence that those interventions boosted retirement savings, and Miller et al. (2015)'s findings regarding other, less popular topics were no different. Financial education and interventions do have a positive influence in some domains, especially when the participants have an immediate opportunity to use the newly acquired information, but it is no panacea. The literature review by Collins and O'Rourke (2010) suggests that counseling programs have a modest positive effect.

114 Financial and economic literacy

The most recent such study, by Kaiser and Menkhoff (2017) relies on the meta-analysis of 126 impact evaluation studies. They do find a very small effect of financial education on behavior, albeit restricted to certain cases only (saving, not borrowing; less effective for low-income participants and in less affluent countries). Importantly, the effect is reduced even further when financial education is made mandatory).

Summarizing, while it may pay to identify the specific circumstances where financial literacy training leads to some improvement, it is abundantly clear that training on its own will not solve the challenges of the new financial environment people have to contend with.

Correlation is not causation

This last conclusion may seem to contradict the findings we summarized earlier on, namely that financial literacy is predictive of economic success. An analogy will make clear what goes on here. People who manage to diet successfully are mostly nutritionally literate (Laz, Rahman, Pohlmeier, & Berenson, 2015). They know their main food categories, are aware of the ones that are more fattening, and can tell you that not all vegetables are made equal. Being determined to lose weight, they made it their business to do so efficiently.

It would be good to educate everyone about nutrition, but it would be unrealistic to expect nutrition education to solve the obesity crisis spreading in the Western world. "Dietary behaviour in members of commercial slimming clubs is not significantly influenced by nutrition knowledge. Although healthy eating recommendations can be valuable, other factors are more important for achieving weight loss" (Bray, 2014, p. 31). It is not out of ignorance that people eat more than is good for them. By the same token, financial literacy is surely to be encouraged, but cognitive intervention to teach financial literacy is ineffective as a means to promote appropriate financial behavior. If we consider the two main components of people's mental makeup, the cognitive and the emotional, it turns out that what people choose to know and what they do with their knowledge depend upon a range of specific and well-established personality traits (De Meza et al., 2008; Willis, 2008, 2011), in addition to environmental factors such as salience and accessibility, and these are crucial to financially responsible behavior.

Behavioral economics has identified a collection of deep-seated traits that influence decisions in both financial and non-financial contexts. Van Raaij (2016) lists some of the main relevant ones. *Numeracy* is the ability, motivation, and enjoyment to work with numbers and constitutes a significant predictor of both financial literacy and successful financial behavior. *Conscientiousness* is one of the "Big Five" personality variables, a set of five traits that was found time and time again in research as a valid means to describe psychological profiles. Conscientious people are those commonly described as having high willpower, high self-efficacy, or high self-control. These are people who keep records, plan ahead, and are less likely to give up or to postpone important tasks. This trait is of course invaluable in the personal financial context. Preparing a budget and keeping to it, preparing a shopping list before going shopping and then sticking to it, saving regularly, staying informed about the state of their checking accounts, and their retirement savings, all are more readily done by the conscientious. *Procrastination* is the tendency to postpone a task, start too late, or work too slowly to complete it on time (Steel, 2007). People may, for instance, be aware that they should check whether they are on course for saving sufficiently for their retirement, perhaps as the result of having attended a program of financial literacy, yet may postpone doing so because they find the task aversive. This reluctance may stem from any of various sources: it could stem from their low numeracy, or because thinking of retirement and old age may *stress* them, or because the pension is still many years off and they don't identify with their future and much older self, or again because they experience strong *present-time preference*, meaning that to them, postponing a cost, even one that generates high future benefits, is attractive. Conversely, so is advancing a benefit to the present, even if this implies high future costs. This leads to outcomes such as credit card borrowing at high interest rates and unwillingness to engage in painful activities such as financial planning. The last such trait we might mention is *locus of control*, one we already referred to in earlier chapters. To recall, this is the tendency to consider that your future is in your own hands (internal LOC) or to take the view that the future is determined by others, task difficulty, or luck (external LOC). As may be expected, those who experience an external locus of control are fatalistic, and less motivated to forge their financial fate by analyzing their options and following a carefully laid plan.

The reason for the correlation of financial literacy and a range of effective financial behaviors, and the direction of that causation is clear. People who possess the right combination of traits, who are intent on effectively handling their financial affairs, are more likely to do what it takes to acquire the necessary knowledge. Imparting that knowledge, by itself, doesn't give rise to sensible behavior.

Economic literacy to fight simplistic policies

A sound understanding of the economic world and of the economic systems which constitute this world is of vital concern for modern societies. It is crucial for citizens' political participation and their commitment to needed reforms. Economic considerations drive or at least influence political and social processes, making informed deliberation an essential prerequisite for the functioning of democracy (Caplan, 2011; Davies, 2015). Moreover, the views of the public also affect public policy indirectly through the political process. As Fornero (2015) shows with reference to the reform she led in the Italian pension system, policy makers hesitate to pursue what they consider the best policy if they know that the public will not understand its rationale and oppose it. Conversely, the public tends to judge unpopular policies as more necessary when they understand them better (Huston, 2010, 2012). The claim was raised in the context of many recent experiences in Europe (e.g., the handling of the migration issue, the Brexit referendum, or the

116 Financial and economic literacy

treatment of the Southern European countries in crisis) and elsewhere. Failure to understand economics breeds suspicion regarding ulterior motives of public policy (Berti et al., 2017; Leiser et al., 2017; Remmele, 2016). Distrust in turn affects economic behavior. For instance, we found (Slivanzky, Leiser, & Spivak, 2015) that the decision to take out retirement funds as annuity or as a lump sum is mostly driven by the degree of trust in the pension system. That mistrust may not be unjustified. Governments and financial institutions have sometimes misbehaved, and citizens should be in a position to understand whether they have been duped. Understanding the economy is indispensable for the effective functioning of economic and political institutions.

The need to support citizens in developing a sound economic understanding is not only recognized by professionals (e.g., Aprea, Wuttke, & Stock, 2015; for an early account see Beck, 1989; Davies, 2015; Lundholm & Davies, 2013; Retzmann & Seeber, 2016), it has entered public debate in many countries. For example, in Germany, the tweet of a high school student called Naina recently sparked a public discussion. In her tweet, Naina remarked: "I am almost 18 and am clueless about taxes, rent or insurances. But I can write a poem analysis. In 4 languages." The issue she raised was taken up intensively in the German media, she was invited to many talk shows, and even met the Secretary of Education. In Israel, the Social Protest movement of 2013 brought hundreds of thousands to the streets. Its main rhythmic slogan was rather vague: "*The people / want / social justice.*" As it became clear to all that they were unable to articulate a set of actionable demands, their slogan was spoofed by a very popular meme that ran: "*The people / want / all manner of things*" and was occasionally chanted in self-irony by the protesters themselves.

Existing programs focus mainly, often exclusively, on concrete actions and specific aspects of personal economic or financial behaviors such as budgeting, the adequate use of credit cards, or prevention of over-indebtedness (for an overview see, e.g., Frühauf & Retzmann, 2016 for Germany, and, e.g., Ben-Aharon, 2016; Bendavid-Hadar & Hadad, 2013; Lorenz, 2015; Niemand, 2016 for Israel). As such, they have little influence on the participants' conceptual understanding of the economic world or on the empowerment of citizenship and social responsibility.

A number of researchers have now emerged to criticize the narrow way economic education for the general public is conceived. We will present some of them.

Reforms and economic knowledge: Elsa Fornero

The first is Elsa Fornero, a respected economist with the University of Turin. We will describe her story in some detail, as it illustrates well how the lack of economic literacy affects policy decision making. In 2011 Fornero was invited by Prime Minister Mario Monti, himself an economist with no political affiliation, to join his government. This was to be a technocratic government, seeking broad consensus in Parliament to introduce urgently needed, clearly unpopular reforms – a result of many years of wanton promises, in particular under the leadership of premier Silvio Berlusconi, that no political party dared to put forward by itself. Fornero was tasked with reforming the unsustainable Italian pension system within weeks, and reforming labor law.

With a financial crisis looming, Parliament approved the new pension regime in a fortnight but the same parties who voted for it failed to support it outside Parliament and some, notably the populist Northern League, launched a personal hate-campaign against her. Fornero single-handedly defended the new law in heated public debates, never refusing an occasion to explain. She recalls as one of the most significant occasions the meeting with more than one thousand workers, who had signed up to meet and talk to the Minister. Fornero accepted the invitation and addressed the crowd, trying to explain why the austerity measures the government took were unavoidable and what benefits they could expect for themselves or for their children from those measures. Unsurprisingly, she failed to convince her audience, thought felt the audience's appreciation for having opened a dialogue. A dialogue that the political parties did not support, preferring to take advantage of an easy scapegoat. To this day, years after she ended her period in office, she is still under police protection.

This experience has had an interesting consequence: Fornero drew the conclusion that the reform's unpopularity was mainly the result of ignorance of the reform's economic bases, requiring present-day sacrifices in order to obtain long-term advantages at individual as well as general level. She became one of the most vigorous proponents of what she calls "economic-financial literacy" (Fornero, 2015) maintaining that it is a key requirement for sustainable economic reforms having a profound impact on people's lives, such as the pension reforms.

Her views are supported by a few studies. Boeri, Börsch-Supan, and Tabellini (2002) analyzed public opinion on pension reforms in Italy and Germany. The questionnaires included questions such as: Are citizens aware of the unsustainability of the pension systems and informed of its costs? Are reforms opposed by a majority or by a powerful minority? What reform options seem politically more feasible and why? What groups of citizens are more likely to favor reforms? The authors report that the majority of respondents were aware of the unsustainability of the system. However, many of those aware of the system's unsustainability were against further reform, which is maddening to a reformer, but in keeping with the lack of knowledge integration we have repeatedly observed. The important question is: Would more knowledgeable citizens think otherwise? Research about this hypothesis is sparse, but some studies do provide support. In a paper entitled "Does information increase political support for pension reform?" Boeri and Tabellini (2012) report on the results of an opinion poll on a representative sample of Italians, focused on reforms increasing retirement age or cutting pension benefits. They confirm that individuals who are more informed about the costs and functioning of the pension system are more willing to accept reforms.

Correlation does not imply causation. To determine whether the relation is indeed causal, the authors manipulated knowledge experimentally, and checked whether this increases participants' willingness to accept reforms. A randomly selected subset of their participants was therefore asked to read a descriptive note on

118 Financial and economic literacy

the Italian pension system before answering the questionnaire. Those who read the note were more willing to support pension reforms, supporting the causal interpretation of the link between the two (Boeri & Tabellini, 2012).

That situation is of course widespread (Bischoff & Siemers, 2013). Bonfiglioli and Gancia (2013) observe that governments of democratic countries often have a short-term bias because they intend to seek re-election. Reforms are often costly in the short run, even if they stand to deliver very substantive advantages in the long run. More understanding of such issues by the public would reduce the electoral risk, and encourage politicians to do the right thing, in the knowledge that they would receive credit for having done so. A simple example that we discuss elsewhere in this book is the issue of balanced governmental budgets (along with the household metaphor). When citizens fail to appreciate that governmental debt does not work like household debt does, this creates a poor democratic environment for government behavior. Fornero wants to educate the public because this will free politicians to implement the policies they consider best for their country.

Literacy and public policy

While Fornero (2015) wants to impart concrete contents (she details the specific mechanism of pension systems) there are more fundamental ideas that the public needs to acquire, before specific policies can be usefully discussed (Remmele, 2012, 2016). One such is the concept of a *Complex Designed System*, the notion that important aspects of the economy were designed deliberately. They neither evolved at random nor were they set up arbitrarily by the authorities. They were designed purposely to reach a goal or answer a need, while taking into account a set of constraints. The pension system does afford a good illustration of the variety of aspects that we would want the public to consider. The overall goal of a retirement system is to ensure that old people have sufficient resources to cover their needs. One important consideration is fairness, and this general requirement translates to several specific issues: some people have worked longer than others, some chose not to work while others were unable to, there are moral hazard issues, and inter-generational fairness must be observed. This in turn requires an appreciation of how the age distribution may affect the pension received, and this depends on how the pension system is set up. Further, mean longevity has been increasing for many years; some people enjoy a much longer life than others. As a last point, when pension funds are invested in a mix of instruments to balance risk and expected returns, the expected returns change over time (they are much lower today than they were a decade ago). This complexity contrasts sharply with the naïve understanding of pensions brought to light by Leiser (see Neuman, 2015) who used focus groups to study lay understanding of pensions in Israel. It was found that non-economists tend to use two models, and these models are both simplistic and wrong. One is the piggy-bank scheme (each month you put money in, and at retirement you take the money and that's your pension). The second is the contract model (you work for

40 years, then you get a percentage of something that remains a little vague, your last salary or average wage. Some version of this was true in the past and remains partly in place in some countries). Neither model recognizes the mutual insurance shared with the other people in the fund, nor do they incorporate the concept of return on investment and the fact that pension contributions are invested in order to increase the retirements payments.

These conceptions do not afford understanding of necessary steps by the authorities, which leads to suspicion towards them. The Israeli Finance Ministry recently concluded that the pension payments to newly retired people must henceforth be lower than in the past, because the expected ROI is lower than previously assumed, and the resulting shortfall must be shared fairly across generations. Many in the public felt that this move was tantamount to theft. Seen through their understanding of how the pension regime is set up, the government is taking money that was uniquely theirs, and must now do so because it has been "playing with their money on the stock market," while they don't see why the welfare of younger generations, important though it might be, should affect their own pension. Appreciation of the complexity of such issues might lead citizens to give more credit to the authorities for having thought the issues fairly and thoroughly, and may check the tendency to consider the administration as simply intent on appropriating their hard-earned money (Leiser et al., 2017; Remmele, 2012, 2016; Scharrer, Stadtler, & Bromme, 2014), assuming of course that the authorities did manage to gain the trust of the public.

This by no means implies that the public must accept the solutions offered by the authorities uncritically. Different countries have different designs. Any proposed or existing system may be modified if the citizens demand it, but they should think their criticisms through, because the present system does have its complex rationale that reflects one set of tradeoffs between competing values and benefits.

In praise of informed skepticism: Peter Davies

Fornero views governments as benevolent. She served in a technocratic government put in place specifically to enact necessary reforms. From her perspective, it is essential to educate the public, in order to facilitate the job of politicians who try to take the best decisions possible.

A contrasting perspective is taken by Peter Davies, a distinguished educationalist and editor of the *International Journal of Economic Education*. Davies (2015) contrasts the prevailing individualistic approach of financial literacy measurement and financial education with an educational framework that seeks to equip (young) people to play an active democratic role and to develop a broader understanding of the financial world. According to Davies, presenting uncritically a picture of the economy where the government and the financial institution all work for the common good would be misleading. Financial institutions and governments have sometimes misbehaved. Economically literate people should be made well aware of this, if the civil society is to defend itself, and make sure that no "dirty tricks" are played by those in a position to do so. At the present, the teaching resources that are available to help financial literacy are almost devoid of reference to financial wrongdoing. Present definitions of financial literacy are universally too limited. The responsibility for financial probity is placed on the individual, while responsibilities of banks and governments are ignored.

Davies remarks that this bias is unsurprising, given that so many teaching materials have been produced by the financial sector, but it does invite counter-measures. A situation where students' knowledge of the banking sector is largely dependent on the story that it chooses to tell about itself "does not look very healthy for democracy" (p. 314). The discourse about financial literacy is tendentious in other ways too. The very definition of financial literacy and the assessments designed to measure levels of financial literacy have uniformly placed all of the responsibilities on the individual. In view of the tarnished records of the financial sector and governments, it is very unfair to heap all the responsibility for financial problems upon individuals. It must be recognized that advocacy of financial education by bankers and politicians sometimes constitutes a deliberate attempt to distract populations from their own accountability.

The goal of financial and economic literacy education should be to empower laypeople to participate in an economy-driven society and to contribute to the development of a more sophisticated dialogue between policy makers and the general population. This can only take place if a larger portion of the public develops an appreciation for the breadth of considerations that need to be taken into account, the complexity and sometime unpredictability of the consequences of policies, the need to adjudicate between competing values, and the importance of long-term considerations.

An approach which merges financial, economic, and citizenship education is proposed by Carmela Aprea, a researcher in economics education and member of the OECD International Network of Financial Education Research Committee. In order to sustain a broader and educationally sound view of financial literacy, her comprehensive framework adopts an additional conceptualization, that of the "responsible economic citizen on financial issues" with a specific focus on systemic issues, which includes understanding of the economic system, participating within this system and changing it, if necessary (Aprea, 2016; Leumann, Heumann, Syed, & Aprea, 2016).

Financial competence is defined as the ability to adequately plan, implement, control, and evaluate personal financial decisions, embed these decisions within the broader systemic context, and critically reflect on this context. These different facets of financial competence (i.e., the cognitive and the non-cognitive, along with the individual and the systemic) need to be considered in financial education assessments, curricula, and interventions. Financial literacy education should foster the development of citizens able to think critically, respond compassionately, and act responsibly. It should embrace complexity, incorporate systemic thinking, and foster individual and collaborative reflection (Aprea et al., 2015).

Final words

"Educating the public" is a worthy goal, but it is a goal that demands careful scrutiny. Educating people to handle their personal finances better has proven disappointing, because the issue is rarely one of knowledge, and more one of commitment. There is every reason to make matters as intelligible as possible for members of the public, to fight unnecessary complications and deliberate obfuscation. But beyond this, responsible regulators must take stock of the limits that human nature imposes upon rationality, whether from the emotional or the cognitive direction. In practice, this means a careful mix of regulating the markets and encouraging, or requiring, the use of impartial advisers along with regulation that will directly protect citizens. Further, there is the important matter of educating citizens to enable their informed participation in debates on essential economic and social choices. That educational challenge is huge, and will require a sustained, indeed a permanent effort. But it must be faced. Only thus will it be possible to lessen the need for an overly paternalistic approach, and reduce the appeal of populist ideas.

10
PUBLIC POLICY CONSEQUENCES

> France is not a reformable country. The French detest reforms. We must explain to them where we are going.
>
> *French President Emmanuel Macron (August 24, 2017)*

Understanding economics is difficult. People navigate this field using intuitive theories and various cognitive devices such as naïve theories, metaphors, and heuristics that imbue them with a false confidence. People have an inflated confidence in the depth of their understanding in most domains (Keil, 2006; Rozenblit & Keil, 2002; Sloman & Fernbach, 2017).

> Intuitive theories are our untutored explanations for how the world works. They are our best guess as to why we observe the events we do and how we can intervene in those events to change them. ... The problem is, they are often wrong.
>
> *(Shtulman, 2017, p. 4)*

But this is especially true regarding economics. There is a huge gap between how economists and public policy experts think about economic matters and the way non-economists do. This book pointed out the main known causes that limit the general public's understanding and indicated some of their expressions. We will recap briefly some of the cognitive traits that shape lay perception of economics, causing it to diverge from professional views, before discussing the consequences and suggesting some recommendations for public policy.

The mismatch

Non-economists' thinking has a short range and a narrow scope. It focuses on direct links, and typically ignores indirect links, feedback loops, and aggregate effects.

Public policy consequences **123**

People without specialized training do not countenance complex causal networks. The narrow scope of their thinking is due to the organization of long-term memory and to the mechanisms responsible for retrieving relevant information from it. As a consequence, the default mode of thinking, the fast and intuitive Type 1, only brings to bear a very limited subset of the relevant knowledge, those that are salient and obvious. This type of thinking is further constrained by its short range (only direct effects are considered), due to the limitations of working memory, manifested whenever the slow and analytic Type 2 mode of thinking is used (Chapter 3). The result is that the public is largely unaware of emergent processes – the benevolent hidden hand is truly invisible. Here are some illustrative observations.

John Rentoul, chief political commentator for *The Independent on Sunday*, points out that public opinion favors non-market solutions, such as price controls, rent controls, and "affordable" housing (subsidies for first-time buyers). These policies have a feature in common: they tackle the matters in question *directly*. Therefore, there is one obvious solution for the public if the price of electricity or the rents are high: cap them. Alternative market solutions are not actively rejected: those possible solutions do not occur to them. In the same vein Chris Dillow, a British economist who writes the *Stumbling and Mumbling* blog, discusses the tendency of people to support renationalization, price controls, rent controls, and generally to think that the government should make things cheaper. He suggests that "because people underestimate the tendency of emergent processes to produce benign outcomes, demands for price and rent controls are stronger than most economists think they should be" (Dillow, 2015).

In a different domain, Srnicek and Williams (2016) in their discussion of the power of marches, protests, and other such manifestations to affect policies, observe that "folk politics" ignores the structural nature of problems in a modern world, and reduces complexity down to a human scale. "This impulse promotes authenticity-mongering, reasoning through individual stories, and a general inability to think systemically about change" (Heller, 2017).

We discussed various such tendencies, and in particular the disinclination of many people to admit tradeoffs, which constitutes one more obstacle to conveying public policy to the public and a topic that needs to be researched in order to find ways to overcome it. Many more doubtlessly remain to be identified.

Members of the public rely on a range of means to navigate abstruse economic topics, when the proper explanation eludes them. One is to rely on the deeply ingrained bias to attribute causation, if at all possible, to deliberate, intentional actions. Examples of this have been encountered throughout the book. If something goes wrong, the public will look for someone who was responsible for it. In analyzing the perception of the causes of the 2008 financial and economic crisis, many researchers found that people tend to attribute it primarily to foibles of individuals, rather than to systemic failings (Gangl, Kastlunger, Kirchler, & Voracek, 2012; Leiser et al., 2016; Leiser et al., 2010; Leiser & Rötheli, 2010). A particular expression of this tendency is to be found in the widespread incidence of various sorts of conspiracy theories. The tendency to imagine a conspiracy was checked

124 Public policy consequences

in the past by responsible media. With the development of online information channels of various sorts, their role has enormously decreased over just the past few years, and this has allowed that tendency to influence public opinion to an unprecedented degree (Bronner, 2013; Leiser et al., 2017).

A somewhat related factor is the *inherence* heuristic, an implicit bias that leads people to explain observed patterns chiefly by the inherent features of their constituents (Cimpian & Salomon, 2014a). In the case of prices, this bias expresses itself in the tendency to believe that goods and services have an intrinsic price. When prices deviate from that value, it means to them that something went awry, in a practical sense, but also morally. Rentoul (2015) comments about the familiar findings of opinion polls:

> House prices are the staple diet of the grumbler. Especially in London. Ridiculous, insane, wrong are some of the milder words. Which side of the supply and demand equation do people not understand? A significant proportion of the world's population wants to live in London.

Commonly used metaphors serve as one of several ways to understand. One notorious case in point is the household metaphor, that would equate the state with a family, the administration with the parents, and the state budget with the household budget. This metaphor, for all its huge faults, remains popular, because it is so natural. The mapping is easy to make, and it relies on a fundamental structure, that of the family, which is formative for the way we structure our relations of trust, authority, knowledge, etc. (Lakoff, 1987; Leiser & Zaltsman, 1990).

Another potent influence on economic views is the adoption of ideas prevalent in our environment. Many economic claims and conceptions circulate publicly. People don't need to frame accounts on their own and when the claims come embedded in a political ideology, as is often the case, they only need to endorse the one that suits their general outlook or that of their social environment. For instance, we discussed at length two ready-packaged accounts of capitalism in the US (Chapter 7). You only need to know which one your side endorses to know what you think – if such be the term – about various controverted economic claims. "As a rule, strong feelings about issues do not emerge from deep understanding" write Sloman and Fernbach (2017, p. 164). On unemployment, for instance, there are two opposing views. One considers the unemployed as responsible for their status, for being lazy, not preparing themselves for life with a proper training, etc. The alternative views them as victims of a system that didn't help them flourish as a person: a difficult environment, second-rate schools not conducive to learning, difficulty to enter more advanced training, the failure of the system to generate enough jobs for all (Chapters 4 and 7).

Yet another set of influences that shape economic views are related to broad personal traits. We encountered various personal traits in several chapters, and will here merely recall some of the main ones. One of them is locus of control (see Halpert & Hill, 2011). The locus of control construct is one of the most popular in cognitive social psychology, referring to the extent to which one believes that life events depend on one's own actions and/or qualities, as opposed to the actions of others. Another trait is "belief in a just world," the belief that the world is fair, and whatever happens probably is justified. Bastounis et al. (2004 and Christandl (2013) found that external locus of control and giving little credence that the world is just correlate with left-wing views: a belief constellation indicating low trust in the business world, protest against the unfair treatment of workers, and support for governmental intervention. In contrast, an internal locus of control and a strong belief in a just world were positively correlated with a conservative political orientation, a belief constellation characterized by satisfaction with the economy and disapproval of government intervention.

Many more personality traits, such as how anxious in general a person is, have been shown to affect economic views. To some extent, economic views flow from broad attitudes, that go way beyond economic issues. Consider the important questions of whether a national economy is stable or fragile? How likely is it that another economic crisis will erupt? Those are weighty questions, and rating agencies routinely analyze fundamentals to rate a country's prospect. The markets, for their part, express the collective insight of the masses, and price short- and long-term bonds according to the perceived risk they present. But what about individual ordinary people? How does each of them assess economic stability?

Leiser and Benita (in preparation) asked 300 people in the US for their view concerning economic fragility or stability, by checking the extent to which they agreed with the following sentences:

1. The economy is fundamentally sound, and will restore itself after occasional crises.
2. The economy is capable of absorbing limited shocks, but if the shocks are excessive, a major crisis and even collapse will ensue.
3. Deterioration in the economy, when it occurs, is a very gradual process.
4. The economy's functioning is delicate, and always at a risk of collapse.
5. The economy is an intricate system, and it is all but impossible to predict how it will evolve.
6. Economic experts can ensure that the economy will regain stability even after major crises.

These questions relate to the economy, and respondents answered them first. But we then asked corresponding questions, with minimal variations of wording, about three other widely disparate domains: personal relationships, climate change, and health. Participants rated to what extent they agree with each of the statements about each additional domain. The findings were clear: beliefs regarding economic stability are highly correlated with parallel beliefs in unrelated social and natural domains. People who believe that "The economy's functioning is delicate, and always at a risk of collapse" tend to agree that "Close interpersonal relationships are delicate, and always at a risk of collapse" (the sentiment expressed in the lyrics by

126 Public policy consequences

The Beatles: "yesterday came suddenly"). And people who hold that "The economy is capable of absorbing limited shocks, but if the shocks are excessive, a major crisis will occur" also tend to judge that "The human body is capable of absorbing limited shocks, but beyond a certain intensity of illness, body collapse will follow."

What we see in such cases is that people don't assess the economy as an intelligible system. Instead, they express their general feelings towards dangers. This interpretation was supported by the outcome of two attitude tests. The first was the locus of control scale, the second the "belief in a dangerous world" scale (Altemeyer, 1988a). BDW relates to the belief that the social environment of a person is dangerous and threatening. Sample questions are: "Every day as society become more lawless and bestial, a person's chance of being robbed, assaulted, and even murdered go up and up" and: "Any day now chaos and anarchy could erupt. All signs are pointing to it." As was expected, those who believe that the world is dangerous and who see an external locus of control see all four domains (economics, personal relations, health, and the environment) as unstable and unpredictable. Such judgments have little to do with an evaluation of the domain assessed, be it economic or something else. They attest personal traits, not comprehension.

Throughout the book, we mentioned many traits such as locus of control, social dominance orientation, and the like. It is worth explaining, especially to our economist readers, the status psychologists attribute to such constructs, and how they differ from how rational choice theory might view them. Rational choice theory would consider all such traits as specific prior beliefs. People who score high on belief in a dangerous world, for instance, deem danger to be ubiquitous. Asked about health, their estimation of the fragility of their health combines with the prior to produce an evaluation.

Psychologists don't consider such traits as beliefs at all, not even as implicit beliefs. They are seen as a proclivity to make certain evaluations and judgments. That proclivity may be more or less influential at a given time, and it can be modulated by priming certain feelings such as by evoking death, or by affecting mood by presenting essentially uninformative but emotionally potent material. Thus, conservatives become less conservative when they feel safe, whereas liberals endorse more conservative views when feeling threatened (Napier, Huang, Vonasch, & Bargh, 2017; Onraet, Van Hiel, Dhont, & Pattyn, 2013). The psychological approach involves a range of mental traits and states that jointly affect how a particular piece of information is perceived and used, ignored, or abused (Baekgaard, Christensen, Dahlmann, Mathiasen, & Petersen, 2017) under particular circumstances. Subsuming this rich dynamic interplay under the label "prior beliefs" constitutes a serious oversimplification of a complex matter intensively studied by psychologists (Allen et al., 2005; McNair & Crozier, 2017; Wood & Boyce, 2017).

Consequences

The views held by the public are consequential for two distinct reasons. The first is direct enough: economic beliefs affect economic behavior (Roos, 2007, 2008;

Shiller, 2017). People save or spend, negotiate salaries or accept an offer, buy or sell houses, all in accordance with how they perceive the economy and its prospects. Taken collectively, this influence on their behavior constitutes an important component of economic modelling (Darriet & Bourgeois-Gironde, 2015). As Nobel Laureate Robert Shiller stated in his Presidential address to the American Economic Association:

> We have to consider the possibility that sometimes the dominant reason why a recession is severe is related to the prevalence and vividness of certain stories, not the purely economic feedback or multipliers that economists love to model. The field of economics should be expanded to include serious quantitative study of changing popular narratives.
>
> *(Shiller, 2017, p. 4)*

If people believe that the current rate of inflation signals that the economy is going through a bad phase and predict that unemployment will rise in the future, this belief has economic consequences, and complicates the task of the central bank (Gaffeo & Canzian, 2011). The good-begets-good heuristic (Leiser & Aroch, 2009) explains how the public makes such predictions, by showing that the "sentiment" held by the public about the economy is deeply rooted in the globalizing way it perceives economic functioning (Chapter 5).

The second reason economic conceptions are important is that they affect policies. A first aspect of this is that decision makers are not necessarily conversant with economic ideas, and may promote policies consonant with lay thinking. We saw the example of British MPs and their understanding of money creation in Chapter 8. This is fairly typical. Lawmakers, even those involved in economic committees, usually have little background in economics. In the US, for instance, only about 20% of voting committee members had a business/accounting or economics background on the Senate and on the House budget committees, according to a 2011 report (Weinger, 2011), and in other committees, that proportion is probably even lower.

Public officials lacking economic knowledge are susceptible to metaphors such as "priming the pump," "a rising tide lifts all ships," or "starve the beast," the belief that tax cuts will be followed by spending cuts, thereby reducing government activity. While experience shows that tax cuts without immediate spending cuts tend to result in increased public debt rather than reduced public spending, the "starve the beast" metaphor still guides the decisions of many voters and politicians, though for the latter sometimes disingenuously (Baron & McCaffery, 2008; Schnellenbach & Schubert, 2015).

Here are two striking examples of economic ineptitude of officials in charge.

> The Central Bank of Nigeria is … puffing up its exchange rate. The naira has been hit hard by a fall in the price of oil, Nigeria's main export. … Instead of allowing the naira to devalue, the central bank is trying to defend it by

128 Public policy consequences

> blocking imports. … Economists find the policy baffling. Central banks usually prop up their currencies if they are worried about inflation, or allow them to devalue to depress imports and stimulate exports. Nigeria, by contrast, appears to be set on achieving both an uncompetitive exchange rate and higher inflation.
>
> *(The Economist, 2015b)*

That misguided policy was later reversed in view of its predictably disastrous consequences that had been anticipated by professional observers.

As a second illustration, *The Economist* wondered a few years ago about the policies of Turkey's President, Recep Erdogan:

> Mr Erdogan seems desperate to prop up growth … Lower rates, the president believes, are the answer. Mr Erdogan claims – against all the evidence and in complete contradiction to orthodox economics – that cutting rates will somehow lower inflation.
>
> *(The Economist, 2015a)*

Like many politicians and heads of states, Mr Erdogan has no training in economics, and reasons accordingly. Economists would point out that you can use monetary policy either to facilitate growth, by cutting rates, or to fight inflation, by raising them, but that you cannot do both: an wretched tradeoff. But to the untutored, far from being in competition, these two important goals are pursued jointly, and the right monetary policy will "get the economy back on track," in keeping with the underlying logic of the good-begets-good heuristic.

Striking as such examples may be, by far the more consequential avenue by which lay views affect public policy is through the political process (Christandl, 2008; Fornero, 2015; Haferkamp, Fetchenhauer, Belschak, & Enste, 2009). The public tends to judge unpopular policies as more necessary if they understand them better (Huston, 2010, 2012). Conversely, policy makers may hesitate to pursue what they consider the best policy if they know that the public won't understand its rationale, or its necessity, and will oppose it (Facchini, 2017). Voters vote "retrospectively" and punish the incumbent for poor economic performance. Political parties therefore face a tradeoff: offering popular yet economically harmful policies increases the chance of being elected today, but decreases the chance of re-election. Bischoff and Siemers (2013, p. 163) conclude that this combination makes for mediocre policies: parties offer strategic mixtures of policies rather than purely populist or purely good policy platforms, resulting in "mediocre policy choices and half-hearted reforms." We mentioned above the importance of consumer sentiment. It is worth noting here that the relation between sentiment and retrospective voting is itself complex and based in psychology (Soroka & McAdams, 2015). In both congressional and presidential elections, only negative developments (rising unemployment and inflation) affect the re-election chances whereas improved economic outcomes has no effect at all (Soroka, 2014).

Discussing policy implications to be drawn from behavioral failings or quirks, Dan Ariely presents a programmatic conception:

> I do hope that the debate between standard and behavioral economics will not take the shape of an ideological battle. We would make little progress if the behavioral economists took the position that we have to throw standard economics – invisible hands, trickle-downs, and the rest of it – out with the bathwater. Likewise, it would be a shame if rational economists continue to ignore the accumulating data from research into human behavior and decision making.
>
> *(Ariely, 2011)*

But as Bill Congdon (2012, p. 485) observes, the challenge of translating such information into policy is huge:

> Taxes can be used to discourage, subsidies to encourage, and so on. Behavioral tendencies make these relationships less straightforward. By attending to the detailed psychology of how individuals choose and act, behavioral economics helps us to understand why and how some policies work the way they do, or fail to work as predicted.

It behooves the authorities to learn what the public cares about, and this requires extensive and diligent research. The insights gained would serve not only to facilitate communication with the public, but lead to improved and psychologically informed regulation, by focusing the debate on whether a given policy is defendable in terms of its fairness or other principled grounds, as judged by the public.

Recommendations

What should be clear from reading the previous chapters is that misunderstanding economics is a natural state of affairs, in view of the mismatch between cognitive tendencies and the particular type of analyses and concepts that economic science has developed. Much of these insights are not accessible to people untrained in economics, and vulgarization articles will not be enough to bridge the fundamental gaps described in Chapters 2 and 3.

This is the fundamental starting point, though its implications for policy are far from clear. We would like to suggest one way to approach the subject, and introduce the somewhat whimsically named Druze Model. The Druze are an ethnic and religious group in the Levant with a distinct and secretive theology. Remarkably, most Druze know only a few of the tenets of their religion, whose esoteric teachings are reserved for people of high moral character who also studied and progressed over

FIGURE 10.1 Policy-making template.
Source: Template by John Kleckner, hejibits.com. Contents by authors, inspired by twitter.com/UnlearningEcon/status/863014072316547072.

the years in their understanding of its secrets. Everyone in the community can, in principle, gain access to those higher realms. In practice, few do, and the knowledgeable ones provide guidance to the others (Russell, 2014).

We suggest a similar two-tier model for economic understanding. Some knowledge cannot be shared with the public, not because it is secret but because it is inaccessible, and therefore perforce kept to the initiated. Other parts are exoteric: they are potentially accessible, and every effort should be made to convey them. The present work did its best to characterize where the boundary between the two is likely to be found, though much more research is needed to settle the matter empirically in each case.

The distinction between what can and what cannot be explained may be crossed with another dichotomy, between personal finances and political economics, leading to four combinations. We will examine them in turn.

Personal finances

What you can explain

Behavioral economics has identified three classes of tendencies that have consequences for public policy: imperfect optimization, bounded self-control, and non-standard preferences. Imperfect optimization captures mistakes that people make in choosing among alternatives. Bounded self-control means that people, even when they are accurate in what they want, may be unable to implement their wants, while non-standard preferences mean that what individuals want is not what one would presume on the basis of standard economic models of decision making (Congdon et al., 2011).

To these tendencies, *and in interaction with them*, we added the dimension of knowledge and understanding. Here is a simple example. In Israel, it is allowed, and easy, to have an overdraft in your checking account. Banks will honor checks or allow withdrawals up to a significant sum related to the customer's income. The interest on this kind of loan is almost twice as high as that on a regular loan, and similar to what people pay on credit card balance. Many people avail themselves of this possibility. Such loans total about €4 billion, an average of €1750 per household. We ran a survey to try to understand this behavior, and heard some remarkable explanations. In essence, people don't consider the overdraft as a loan at all. Indeed, they use the overdraft *because* they wouldn't want to be in debt and pay interest, and consider the overdraft as a service rendered by the bank which allows them to avoid taking out a loan. While they are aware that the bank charges for this convenience, and even that the fees are proportional to the size of the overdraft, they nevertheless don't consider this as an interest-bearing loan, hence their seemingly irrational financial decisions. Explaining that an overdraft is tantamount to a loan may not be difficult. Conveying this fact does not mean a public campaign. The regulator in Israel could require bank statements and apps to include the overdraft in the section on loans, for instance, and also to condition the permission to use it on signing clearly formulated loan papers. This may be sufficient to change the distorted perception. Then again, the misperception may be too entrenched and other means might be needed, though it doesn't seem that this case involves a fundamental difficulty.

Some aspects of public policy relating to personal finances can be taught too. Consider the following anecdote. A woman was furious when she learned about a regulation regarding inheritance of pension funds. She had raised her children entirely alone and, by dint of great effort, managed to save enough for a passable

132 Public policy consequences

pension. When she learned that her now adult children would not inherit all her retirement savings when she dies, even if this should come to pass soon after she retires, she was incensed. This seemed to her outrageous, until the symmetrical benefit was pointed out to her: if she happens to live out a very long life, she will continue to receive a monthly pension for as long as she lives. At no point will anyone tell her that her retirement savings are all used up. Moreover, it was also explained to her, the two aspects are intimately linked: longevity varies, and the pension of the longer-lived is paid with the money left unused by those who departed early. This explanation totally floored the lady in question, who until that time had never considered such regulations as part of a coherent system with intelligible fairness, but rather as a set of arbitrary, sometimes wanton rules.

What the public can understand should be explained, by all means available: by introducing the material in school curriculum, by information campaigns, and by regulating communication between financial service providers and the public. Every opportunity to make clear to the public what is what, but also what intelligible policies are meant to achieve and why they are fair, should be exploited.

Besides the cognitive dimension, this approach may in time produce a measure of trust in the authorities. Citizen buy-in may be secured. Fornero and Lo Prete (2017) show that the electoral cost of a pension reform is significantly lower in countries where the level of economic-financial literacy is higher. Even in the absence of reform, the trust people have in the pension system is a strong predictor of their tendency to save for retirement.

Trust, we submit, can be earned, if its importance is realized and proper means are deployed. Some commercial firms are committed to build consumer trust and the administration has much to learn. Doing so is a continuous, relentless effort, more difficult in some countries than in others for cultural and historic reasons. But it should be engaged in, to enlist support for painful yet necessary reforms, as the sorry example of several European countries remind us. When policies are opaque to ordinary people and trust is absent, the public will try to oppose them, and often succeed.

What you cannot explain

Then again, some matters cannot be successfully explained to the public. Following a detailed review of countless ways ordinary people are challenged by financial demands in the modern world, Lauren Willis (2008, p. 208) infers that financial education cannot be the solution.

> The knowledge, comprehension, and skills necessary to make independent, welfare enhancing decisions in today's personal financial marketplace are prodigious ... The gulf between the knowledge, comprehension, and skills of most ... adults and those needed in today's market cannot be bridged by financial literacy education.

Taking a broader perspective, Bernd Remmele points out that whereas the phrase "financial literacy" imply that the "financial" is readable, this is far from being the case.

> Financial literacy is not to be reduced to seemingly restricted decisions on household consumption, saving, borrowing, etc. These household decisions happen within the wider context of financial capitalism. Without understanding the mechanisms behind inflation, stock market cycles, the development of interest rates, etc., household decisions remain systemically blind ... these mechanisms can appear to be of sublime incomprehensibility.
>
> *(Remmele, 2016, p. 44)*

Moreover, "If the cognitive is not available, the alternative reactions are conative, i.e. getting practical, or emotional, remaining in wonder or panicking" (Remmele, 2016, p. 43). This leaves us with various ways to experience what cannot be understood: the market as absurd and evil; the market as sham; the market as nature; the market as muddle.

The fact must be faced. Certain matters are only intelligible to professionals who appreciate the complex and indirect effects of policies, and are able to map which tradeoffs are feasible and to formulate balanced policies.

There are several possible routes to face this, and their effectiveness should be compared. Some policies that don't depend on sophisticated understanding of economic concepts can work very well (e.g., defaults, automatic adjustments). This may be unsavory to those who believe in giving the individuals all the choices and letting them select according to their lights. But the lights in question, on many topics, are dim indeed.

At times, it is necessary to protect from misunderstanding by regulation, including by enacting legal requirements. The public sometimes welcomes such heavy-handed intervention. In a new unpublished national sample, we found that 73% of the public strongly supports the legal obligation imposed on all Israeli workers, whether employees and self-employed, to save for retirement.

In important cases, it may be appropriate to encourage, perhaps even mandate, reliance on independent financial advice, which might be *pro bono* (Willis, 2011) or paid. Candidate circumstances would be taking out a mortgage, or managing retirement savings. In many countries, public policy forces individuals to manage their individual retirement accounts. But investment possibilities are hard to compare, regulations are intricate and calculations complex. The government could set up a licensing scheme and the legal framework for the operation of a large-scale activity of trained independent advisers. We are not referring here to financial investment advisers, whose contribution to the profitability of investment remains to be demonstrated, but rather to prudential advice, in particular to middle-class households. Research does indicate that those who receive comprehensive advice on financial planning are much better prepared for retirement and more likely to enjoy a

134 Public policy consequences

generally sound economic situation (Marsden, Zick, & Mayer, 2011; Winchester & Huston, 2015).

The public may even be grateful for such a requirement. The survey we just mentioned also showed that (1) people do not know how the pension system works; (2) they are aware they don't understand much about the saving instruments available to them; and (3) they realize that as a consequence they may be losing big. Fully 70% of the sample reported that they would be *interested* or *probably interested* in paid independent advice regarding their retirement savings (vs. 10% who are *probably uninterested* or *uninterested*).

Governance

Governance was of course implied in most of what precedes, but indirectly, as the focus was on personal finances. In this short section, we would like to focus specifically on the relation between the public and the administration. We noted that misunderstanding sometimes leads people to oppose policies that professional economists would call for, and many examples of this were mentioned in previous chapters. There is a great deal that the public does not know or understand (Somin, 2016) or understands differently, and this raises questions about how democracy can produce effective policies. There are divergences on issues such as rent control, budget deficits, countercyclical spending, inflation goals, welfare policy, and tradeoffs. Brennan (2011, p. 700) goes as far as to maintain that: "The practice of unrestricted universal suffrage is unjust. Citizens have a right that any political power held over them should be exercised by competent people in a competent way."

While we certainly won't enter this debate, we do have some recommendations to lessen the tension. We advocate teaching principles of public policy in high schools and colleges. The emphasis should be on the nature of the enterprise: for the chosen topic, learning to appreciate that many aspects are involved, consequences are non-obvious, tradeoffs often need to be recognized, alternatives formulated, each representing an adjudication between the importance of the aspects involved in the tradeoff, and some way has to be found to decide in a principled way (see Chapter 9). Such a training will prepare the students to consider public policy as something more than an arbitrary collection of senseless rules.

The same goal would be also promoted by adopting a simple principle: policies whose rationale is understandable should be publicized and explained to the public. This should become a matter of standard communication policy, even if no particular opposition is expected. By the same token, of two comparable policies, preference should be given to the more intelligible one, or the one that is perceived as more fair or moral. This will garner more support for the policies in question of course, but beyond that, help build up trust in the institutions. Here is an example. Retirement age is increasing in most countries, as a consequence of the increase in life expectancy. However, a later retirement age is disliked by people. Framing the law in terms of an automatic linkage between the two would bring an important benefit, besides its purely economic merits (Alexander & Etienne, 2013). It would make the rationale of that linkage very clear, which might be expected to diminish opposition to the policy, while promoting understanding that the policy makers are taking sensible, if sometimes unpleasant, measures.

The lay conceptions we documented involve more than knowledge and understanding. We saw how, for members of the public, the economic dimension is not dissociated from morality. All too often, economists are happy to set policy by relying on their own intuitions, shaped as they were by their specific training, which exposes them to the criticism of forming an "*econocracy*" (Earle, Moran, & Ward-Perkins, 2016). But laymen have "non-standard" preferences which are at variance with neoclassical economics (Enste, Haferkamp, & Fetchenhauer, 2009). Economists promote reforms by considering their efficiency (Lazear, 2000), whereas laypersons care also about their perceived fairness (Haferkamp et al., 2009) and while it sometimes appears that they object to inequality, it may be *unfair* inequality that they resent (Starmans et al., 2017) (see Chapter 7).

Consider two approaches to cut greenhouse gas emissions: cap-and-trade and a carbon tax. A carbon tax directly establishes a price on emissions: companies are charged a set amount for every ton of emissions they produce. A cap-and-trade program issues a set number of emissions "allowances" each year. These allowances can be auctioned to the highest bidder, creating a carbon price. According to researchers at the World Resources Institute, either policy will do, if well designed (Kaufman, Obeiter, & Krause, 2016). In terms of public acceptance, however, the two policies are profoundly different. Pollution is harmful, so that slapping a tax on those who go on polluting seems right and proper. The approach is wholly in keeping with the intuitive mode of thinking, as it counteracts directly the offending factor, the impunity of irresponsible greed. Is a company trying to profit by spewing out pollutants? Let us hit it where it hurts, this will dissuade it alright! A cap-and-trade program, by contrast, is convoluted, and more importantly, appears profoundly immoral. It mandates the administration to license companies to pollute, and in so doing legitimizes pollution (Sandel, 2012). Would anyone support a policy to reduce crime whereby each precinct gets a number of licenses to kill per year, licenses that could be traded and so forth? *Ceteris paribus*, the carbon tax policy is superior, because it fits the way people feel about the issue, and contributes to establish the administration as moral and responsible. A similar situation is created by the "debt illusion." While the form of finance of a public program (tax or debt) has no effects on substantive outcomes, voters prefer debt over tax finance (Banzhaf & Oates, 2012). This is so because they systematically underestimate the true, indirect, costs of public goods when financed through public debt, rather than through taxes (Dell'Anno & Dollery, 2014). This being the case, debt financing is to be preferred (again, assuming all other things are equal).

Awareness of how people misunderstand macroeconomics has another benefit. It helps plan how to elude avoidable conflicts with the public. For instance, deficit spending is thoroughly counterintuitive, yet held by many to be necessary to prevent downturns from turning into a recession. However, the public and its representatives may oppose discretionary stabilization (as in the US with the

Balanced Budget Amendment), in part based on the notorious household analogy. It may therefore be judicious to introduce *automatic* stabilizers as part of fiscal policy.

The range and variety of psychological elements we surveyed means that the insights of economic psychology cannot readily be incorporated into economic theories. There isn't a simple theory of non-economist economic thinking. Misunderstandings add up, but there are many different kinds of mistakes.

To what extent is it possible to remedy this ignorance and those biases? Where does the boundary lie, between what can and what cannot be explained to the public (Caplan, 2011; Facchini, 2017; Killick, 2017)? We believe that many difficulties are insuperable. The disparities are just too large and the foundations are lacking for this to be remedied. Short of a universal proper course in economics – which most would fail in any event – essential parts of economic reasoning will have to remain entrusted to people who acquired the necessary knowledge.

And yet, we don't really know the boundaries. We made much in this work of the tendency to focus on individuals and their motivations rather than on systemic aspects, on the person rather than on the emerging effects of many people interacting. Our intensive study of contrasting views about capitalism (Chapter 7) showed that this tendency can be overcome. Conservatives who believe in the hidden hand evince an understanding that the aggregate outcome is unlike that of the individual actions. Liberals who fault the system for difficulties experienced by individuals transcend the focus on the individual.

The preceding pages are the fruit of a limited effort. This is the time to call for more research into people's conceptions of every aspect of the economic world, into pedagogical methods that may succeed in shifting the boundary, and in insights about what has to remain the preserve of professionally trained specialists. Policy makers must make sure they learn what people think and want, not in order to hector, nudge, or lecture them, but to engage in a true if challenging dialogue.

REFERENCES

Abric, J.-C. (2005a). *Méthodes d'étude des représentations sociales.* Toulouse: Erès.

Abric, J.-C. (2005b). La recherche du noyau central et de la zone muette des représentations sociales. In J.-C. Abric (Ed.), *Méthodes d'étude des représentations sociales* (pp. 59–80). Toulouse: ERES.

Ackermann, F., Cropper, S., Eden, C., & Cook, J. (1991). *Cognitive mapping for policy analysis in the public sector.* Paper presented at the Academy of Management Meeting, Miami.

Adams, D. (2010). *The restaurant at the end of the universe.* London: Pan Macmillan.

Aglietta, M., & Orléan, A. (2002). *Monnaie (la): Entre violence et confiance.* Paris: Odile Jacob.

Akerlof, G. A., & Shiller, R. J. (2010). *Animal spirits: How human psychology drives the economy, and why it matters for global capitalism.* Princeton, NJ: Princeton University Press.

Alejo, R. (2010). Where does the money go? An analysis of the container metaphor in economics: The market and the economy. *Journal of Pragmatics, 42*(4), 1137–1150.

Alexander, S., & Etienne, S. (2013). *Assessing the economic and budgetary impact of linking retirement ages and pension benefits to increases in longevity.* IDEAS. Retrieved January 9, 2018, from https://ideas.repec.org/p/euf/ecopap/0512.html.

Allen, M. W., Ng, S. H., & Leiser, D. (2005). Adult economic model and values study: Cross-national differences in economic and related general beliefs. *Journal of Economic Psychology, 26*, 159–185.

Allgood, S., & Walstad, W. B. (2016). The effects of perceived and actual financial literacy on financial behaviors. *Economic Inquiry, 54*(1), 675–697.

Altemeyer, B. (1988a). *Enemies of freedom: Understanding right-wing authoritarianism.* San Francisco, CA: Jossey-Bass.

Altemeyer, B. (1998b). The other "authoritarian personality." *Advances in Experimental Social Psychology, 30*(C), 47–92. doi:10.1016/S0065-2601(08)60382-2

Ames, D. L., & Fiske, S. T. (2013). Intentional harms are worse, even when they're not. *Psychological Science, 24*(9), 1755–1762.

Angelini, P., & Lippi, F. (2008). Did prices really soar after the euro cash changeover? Evidence from ATM withdrawals. In P. Giovane & R. Sabbatini (Eds.), *The euro, inflation and consumer's perceptions* (pp. 109–124). Berlin: Springer.

138 References

Aprea, C. (2016). Conceptions of financial literacy. In C. Aprea, E. Wuttke, K. Breuer, N. K. Koh, P. Davies, B. Greimel-Fuhrmann, & J. S. Lopus (Eds.), *International handbook of financial literacy*. Singapore: Springer.

Aprea, C., & Wuttke, E. (2016). Financial literacy of adolescent and young adults: Setting the course for a competence-oriented assessment approach. In C. Aprea, E. Wuttke, K. Breuer, N. K. Keng, P. Davies, B. Greimel-Fuhrmann, & J. Lopus (Eds.), *International handbook of financial literacy* (pp. 397–414). Singapore: Springer.

Aprea, C., Wuttke, E., Breuer, K., Koh, N. K., Davies, P., Greimel-Fuhrmann, B., & Lopus, J. S. (Eds.). (2016). *International handbook of financial literacy*. Singapore: Springer.

Aprea, C., Wuttke, E., & Stock, M. (2015). Exploring the possibilities for a bildungs-oriented conceptualisation of financial literacy education. In S. Hillen & C. Aprea (Eds.), *Instrumentalism in education – where is bildung left?* (pp. 89–104). Münster: Waxmann.

Ariely, D. (2011, January 10). A gentler and more logical economics. Retrieved January 9, 2018, from http://danariely.com/2011/01/10/a-gentler-and-more-logical-economics/.

Ariely, D., & Jones, S. (2008). *Predictably irrational*. New York: HarperCollins.

Armantier, O., Bruine de Bruin, W., Topa, G., Klaauw, W., & Zafar, B. (2015). Inflation expectations and behavior: Do survey respondents act on their beliefs? *International Economic Review, 56*(2), 505–536.

Arrese, Á., & Vara-Miguel, A. (2016). A comparative study of metaphors in press reporting of the euro crisis. *Discourse & Society, 27*(2), 133–155.

Awab, S. A., & Norazit, L. (2013). "Challenging" times or "turbulent" times: A study of the choice of metaphors used to refer to the 2008 economic crisis in Malaysia and Singapore. *Intercultural Pragmatics, 10*(2), 209–233.

Axelrod, R. (1976). The analysis of cognitive maps. In R. Axelrod (Ed.), *Structure of decision: The cognitive maps of political elites* (pp. 55–72). Princeton, NJ: Princeton University Press.

Bachelard, G. (1948). *La terre et les rêveries de la volonté*. Paris: Librairie José Corti.

Baekgaard, M., Christensen, J., Dahlmann, C. M., Mathiasen, A., & Petersen, N. B. G. (2017). The role of evidence in politics: Motivated reasoning and persuasion among politicians. *British Journal of Political Science*, 1–24. doi:10.1017/S0007123417000084

Banzhaf, H. S., & Oates, W. E. (2012). *On fiscal illusion and Ricardian equivalence in local public finance*. NBER Working Papers, No. 18040. Retrieved January 9, 2018, from https://econpapers.repec.org/paper/nbrnberwo/18040.htm.

Barbas, A., & Psillos, D. (1997). Causal reasoning as a base for advancing a systemic approach to simple electrical circuits. *Research in Science Education, 27*(3), 445–459.

Barman, C. R., Griffiths, A. K., & Okebukola, P. A. O. (1995). High school students' concepts regarding food chains and food webs: A multinational study. *International Journal of Science Educational and Psychological Measurement, 17*(6), 775–782.

Barnett White, T. (2005). Consumer trust and advice acceptance: The moderating roles of benevolence, expertise, and negative emotions. *Journal of Consumer Psychology, 15*(2), 141–148. doi:http://dx.doi.org/10.1207/s15327663jcp1502_6

Baron, J., & McCaffery, E. J. (2008). Starving the beast: The political psychology of budget deficits. In E. Garrett, E. A. Graddy, & H. E. Jackson (Eds.), *Fiscal challenges: An inter-disciplinary approach to budget policy* (pp. 221–239). Cambridge, UK: Cambridge University Press.

Baron, J., Scott, S., Fincher, K., & Metz, S. E. (2015). Why does the cognitive reflection test (sometimes) predict utilitarian moral judgment (and other things)? *Journal of Applied Research in Memory and Cognition, 4*(3), 265–284.

Bastiat, F. (1848). What is seen and what is not seen. *Library of Economics and Liberty*. Retrieved January 9, 2018, from www.econlib.org/library/Bastiat/basEss1.html.

Bastounis, M., Leiser, D., & Roland-Levy, C. (2004). Psychosocial variables involved in the construction of lay thinking about the economy: Results of a cross-national survey. *Journal of Economic Psychology, 25*(2), 263–278.

Batchelor, R. A. (1986). The psychophysics of inflation. *Journal of Economic Psychology, 7*, 269–290.

Becchio, C., Skewes, J., Lund, T. E., Frith, U., Frith, C., & Roepstorff, A. (2011). How the brain responds to the destruction of money. *Journal of Neuroscience, Psychology, and Economics, 4*(1), 1–10.

Beck, K. (1989). "Ökonomische Bildung": Zur Anatomie eines wirtschaftspädagogischen Begriffs. *Zeitschrift für Berufs-und Wirtschaftspädagogik, 85*(7), 579–596.

Beilharz, H.-J., & Gersbach, H. (2016). Voting oneself into a crisis. *Macroeconomic Dynamics, 20*(04), 954–984.

Ben-Aharon, O. (2016). *Content analysis of teaching material in economic literacy in Israel.* Student Report. Ben-Gurion University of the Negev, Beer Sheva, Israel.

Bendavid-Hadar, I., & Hadad, Y. (2013). Financial education for children: The Israeli case. *Citizenship, Social and Economics Education, 12*(1), 48–57.

Berlin, I. (1978). Herzen and Bakunin on liberty. In I. Berlin, *Russian thinkers.* New York: Viking Penguin.

Bernanke, B. (2006). A message from Chairman Bernanke. *Federal Reserve Bank of Dallas*, July. Cited by Frederic S. Mishkin: "The importance of economic education and financial literacy." Speech by Frederic S. Mishkin, Member of the Board of Governors of the US Federal Reserve System, at the Third National Summit on Economic and Financial Literacy, Washington DC, February 27, 2008. Retrieved January 30, 2018, from www.federalreserve.gov/newsevents/speech/mishkin20080227a.htm.

Berti, A. E., Ajello, A. M., Aprea, C., Castelli, I., Lombardi, E., Marchetti, A., ... Valle, A. (2017). Adolescents' and young adults' naïve understandings of the economic crisis. *Europe's Journal of Psychology, 13*(1), 143–161.

Bice, D., Curtis, E. S., Geerling, W., Goffe, W., Hoffer, A., Lindahl, S., ... Stock, W. (2014). *Preconceptions of principles students.* Paper presented at the Allied Social Sciences Association Annual Meetings, Boston, MA, January.

Bischoff, I., & Siemers, L.-H. (2013). Biased beliefs and retrospective voting: Why democracies choose mediocre policies. *Public Choice, 156*(1), 163–180. doi:10.1007/s11127-011-9889-5

Blanchard, O. (2016). The United States economy: Where to from here? The Phillips Curve: Back to the '60s? *The American Economic Review, 106*(5), 31–34.

Blanchflower, D. G., Bell, D. N., Montagnoli, A., & Moro, M. (2014). The happiness trade-off between unemployment and inflation. *Journal of Money, Credit and Banking, 46*(S2), 117–141.

Bobbio, A., Canova, L., & Manganelli, A. M. (2010). Conservative ideology, economic conservatism, and causal attributions for poverty and wealth. *Current Psychology, 29*(3), 222–234. doi:10.1007/s12144-010-9086-6

Boeri, T., Börsch-Supan, A., & Tabellini, G. (2002). Pension reforms and the opinions of European citizens. *The American Economic Review, 92*(2), 396–401.

Boeri, T., & Tabellini, G. (2012). Does information increase political support for pension reform? *Public Choice, 150*(1), 327–362.

Boers, F., & Demecheleer, M. (1997). A few metaphorical models in (western) economic discourse. *Amsterdam Studies in the Theory and History of Linguistic Science Series, 4*, 115–130.

Boeynaems, A., Burgers, C., Konijn, E. A., & Steen, G. J. (2017). The effects of metaphorical framing on political persuasion: A systematic literature review. *Metaphor and Symbol, 32*(2), 118–134.

140 References

Bonfiglioli, A., & Gancia, G. (2013). Uncertainty, electoral incentives and political myopia. *The Economic Journal, 123*(568), 373–400.

Booth, W. C. (1974). *A rhetoric of irony* (Vol. 641). Chicago: University of Chicago Press.

Bourgeois-Gironde, S., & Dimier, D. (2009). *Comment l'argent vient à l'esprit: étude d'une représentation polymorphe.* Paris: Vrin.

Bovi, M. (2009). Economic versus psychological forecasting. Evidence from consumer confidence surveys. *Journal of Economic Psychology, 30*(4), 563–574. doi:http://dx.doi.org/10.1016/j.joep.2009.04.001

Bowdle, B. F., & Gentner, D. (2005). The career of metaphor. *Psychological Review, 112*(1), 193–216.

Boyer, P., & Petersen, M. B. (in press). Folk-economic beliefs: An evolutionary cognitive model. *Behavioral and Brain Sciences.*

Brachinger, H. W. (2008). A new index of perceived inflation: Assumptions, method, and application to Germany. *Journal of Economic Psychology, 29*(4), 433–457. doi:10.1016/j.joep.2008.04.004

Bradley, C., & Cole, D. J. (2002). Causal attributions and the significance of self- efficacy in predicting solutions to poverty. *Sociological Focus, 35*(June), 381–396. doi:10.1080/00380237.2002.10570710

Braun, B. (2016). Speaking to the people? Money, trust, and central bank legitimacy in the age of quantitative easing. *Review of International Political Economy, 23*(6), 1064–1092.

Bray, B. (2014). *Nutrition knowledge and dietary behaviour of members of commercial slimming clubs in Greater Manchester* (Master Thesis), University of Chester, UK. Retrieved January 9, 2018, from http://hdl.handle.net/10034/615917.

Brennan, J. (2011). The right to a competent electorate. *The Philosophical Quarterly, 61*(245), 700–724.

Brennan, J. (2016). *Against democracy.* Princeton, NJ: Princeton University Press.

Briskman-Mazliach, R. (1998). *On the relation between attitudes and perceptions about the economy and personality and occupational variables* (MA), Ben-Gurion University of the Negev, Beer Sheva, Israel.

Brkic, J. (2013, July 31). Milton Friedman on capitalism and greed. Freedom&Prosperity.TV. Retrieved January 22, 2018, from www.slobodaiprosperitet.tv/en/node/847.

Bronner, G. (2013). *La démocratie des crédules.* Paris: Presses Universitaires de France.

Brotherton, R., & French, C. C. (2015). Intention seekers: Conspiracist ideation and biased attributions of intentionality. *PLoS ONE, 10*(5), e0124125.

Brown, D. E. (1991). *Human universals.* New York: McGraw-Hill.

Brown, T. C. (2005). Loss aversion without the endowment effect, and other explanations for the WTA–WTP disparity. *Journal of Economic Behavior & Organization, 57*(3), 367–379.

Bruine de Bruin, W., Vanderklaauw, W., Downs, J. S., Fischhoff, B., Topa, G., & Armantier, O. (2010). Expectations of inflation: The role of demographic variables, expectation formation, and financial literacy. *Journal of Consumer Affairs, 44*(2), 381–402.

Bruner, J. S., & Goodman, C. C. (1947). Value and need as organizing factors in perception. *The Journal of Abnormal and Social Psychology, 42*(1), 33–44. doi:10.1037/h0058484

Bullock, H. E., Williams, W. R., & Limbert, W. M. (2003). Predicting support for welfare policies: The impact of attributions and beliefs about inequality. *Journal of Poverty, 7*(3), 35–56. doi:10.1300/J134v07n03_03

Burgoyne, C. B., Routh, D. A., & Ellis, A.-M. (1999). The transition to the euro: Some perspectives from economic psychology. *Journal of Consumer Policy, 22*(1–2), 91–116.

Busom, I., & Lopez-Mayan, C. (2015). *Student preconceptions and learning economic reasoning.* Available at SSRN 2704371 (Working Paper No. 862). GSE, Barcelona, Spain.

References 141

Camerer, C. F., Loewenstein, G., & Rabin, M. (2011). *Advances in behavioral economics*. Princeton, NJ: Princeton University Press.

Caplan, B. (2011). *The myth of the rational voter: Why democracies choose bad policies (2nd ed.)*. Princeton, NJ: Princeton University Press.

Caprara, G., Vecchione, M., & Schwartz, S. H. (2009). Mediational role of values in linking personality traits to political orientation. *Asian Journal of Social Psychology, 12*(2), 82–94.

Carey, S. (1985). *Conceptual change in children*. Cambridge, MA: MIT Press.

Carey, S. (2009). *The origin of concepts*. Oxford: Oxford University Press.

Carey, S., Zaitchik, D., & Bascandziev, I. (2015). Theories of development: In dialog with Jean Piaget. *Developmental Review, 38*, 36–54.

Carpena, F., Cole, S. A., Shapiro, J., & Zia, B. (2015). The ABCs of financial education: Experimental evidence on attitudes, behavior, and cognitive biases. *World Bank Policy Research Working Paper* No. 7413.

Caruso, E. M., Vohs, K. D., Baxter, B., & Waytz, A. (2013). Mere exposure to money increases endorsement of free-market systems and social inequality. *Journal of Experimental Psychology: General, 142*(2), 301–306.

Caruso, E. M., Waytz, A., & Epley, N. (2010). The intentional mind and the hot hand: Perceiving intentions makes streaks seem likely to continue. *Cognition, 116*(1), 149–153.

Charteris-Black, J., & Ennis, T. (2001). A comparative study of metaphor in Spanish and English financial reporting. *English for Specific Purposes, 20*(3), 249–266.

Charteris-Black, J., & Musolff, A. (2003). "Battered hero" or "innocent victim"? A comparative study of metaphors for euro trading in British and German financial reporting. *English for Specific Purposes, 22*(2), 153–176.

Cheng, W., & Ho, J. (2015). A corpus study of bank financial analyst reports: Semantic fields and metaphors. *International Journal of Business Communication*, 1–25. doi:10.1177/2329488415572790

Chi, M. (1992). Conceptual change within and across ontological categories: Examples from learning and discovery in science. In R. N. Giere (Ed.), *Cognitive models of science* (Vol. 15, pp. 129–186). Minneapolis: University of Minnesota Press.

Chi, M., Roscoe, R. D., Slotta, J. D., Roy, M., & Chase, C. C. (2012). Misconceived causal explanations for emergent processes. *Cognitive Science, 36*(1), 1–61.

Chiou, C. C. (2008). The effect of concept mapping on students' learning achievements and interests. *Innovations in Education and Teaching International, 45*(4), 375–387.

Chow, M. Y. V. (2014). The movements of the economy: Conceptualizing the economy via bodily movement metaphors. *Metaphor and the Social World, 4*(1), 3–26.

Christandl, F. (2008). *How economic laypeople perceive economic growth and inflation* (PhD dissertation). Cologne University.

Christandl, F. (2013). The belief in a just world as a personal resource in the context of inflation and financial crises. *Applied Psychology, 62*(3), 486–518.

Cimpian, A. (2015). The inherence heuristic: Generating everyday explanations. In R. A. Scott, S. M. Kosslyn, & M. C. Buchmann (Eds.), *Emerging trends in the social and behavioral sciences*. New York: John Wiley & Sons, Inc.

Cimpian, A., & Salomon, E. (2014a). The inherence heuristic: An intuitive means of making sense of the world, and a potential precursor to psychological essentialism. *Behavioral and Brain Sciences, 37*(05), 461–480.

Cimpian, A., & Salomon, E. (2014b). Refining and expanding the proposal of an inherence heuristic in human understanding. *Behavioral and Brain Sciences, 37*(05), 506–527.

Cimpian, A., & Steinberg, O. D. (2014). The inherence heuristic across development: Systematic differences between children's and adults' explanations for everyday facts. *Cognitive Psychology, 75*, 130–154. doi:http://dx.doi.org/10.1016/j.cogpsych.2014.09.001

142 References

Clark, T. G. (2015). National economies are not the same as family budgets. *Another Angry Voice*. Retrieved January 9, 2018, from http://anotherangryvoice.blogspot.co.uk/2015/08/national-economies-not-like-family.html.

Clémence, A. (2005). Sens et analyse des différences dans les représentations sociales. In J.-C. Abric (Ed.), *Méthodes d'étude des représentations sociales* (pp. 165–178). Toulouse: ERES.

Colbert, S. (Writer). (2005). Comedy Central (Producer), *The Colbert Report*.

Collett-Schmitt, K., Guest, R., & Davies, P. (2015). Assessing student understanding of price and opportunity cost through a hybrid test instrument: An exploratory study. *Journal of Economics and Economic Education Research, 16*(1), 115–134.

Collins, J. M., & O'Rourke, C. M. (2010). Financial education and counseling: Still holding promise. *Journal of Consumer Affairs, 44*(3), 483–498.

Coluche. (1989). *Coluche: l'intégrale* (Vol. 4). Paris: Carrère.

Congdon, W. J. (2012). Psychology and public policy. In E. Shafir (Ed.), *The behavioral foundations of public policy*. Princeton, NJ: Princeton University Press.

Congdon, W. J., Kling, J. R., & Mullainathan, S. (2011). *Policy and choice: Public finance through the lens of behavioral economics*. Washington, DC: Brookings Institution Press.

Corcos, A., & Moati, P. (2008) La perception du prix juste par les Français. *Cahier de Recherche No. 254*. Centre de recherche pour l'étude et l'observation des conditions de vie.

Cowan, N. (2001). The magical number 4 in short-term memory: A reconsideration of mental storage capacity. *Behavioral and Brain Sciences, 24*(3), 87–114.

Craighead, B. (2011, August 24). The wrong budget analogy. *LA Times*. Retrieved January 9, 2017, from http://articles.latimes.com/2011/aug/24/opinion/la-oe-craighead-spending-20110824.

Cushman, F. (2008). Crime and punishment: Distinguishing the roles of causal and intentional analyses in moral judgment. *Cognition, 108*, 353–380. doi:10.1016/j.cognition.2008.03.006

Dal Bó, E., Dal Bó, P., & Eyster, E. (2017). The demand for bad policy when voters underappreciate equilibrium effects. *The Review of Economic Studies*, rdx031–rdx031. doi:10.1093/restud/rdx031.

Dahlgreen, W. (2015). *British people keener on socialism than capitalism*. Retrieved March 11, 2018, from https://yougov.co.uk/news/2016/02/23/british-people-view-socialism-more-favourably-capi/.

Darriet, E., & Bourgeois-Gironde, S. (2015). Why lay social representations of the economy should count in economics. *Mind & Society*, 1–14. doi:10.1007/s11299-015-0177-9

Davies, P. (2011). Multiple-choice questions to assess first-year undergraduates' understanding of opportunity cost used by Shanahan et al. (2006). *Citizenship, Social and Economics Education, 10*(2–3), 101–110.

Davies, P. (2015). Towards a framework for financial literacy in the context of democracy. *Journal of Curriculum Studies, 47*(2), 300–316.

de los Ríos, M. E. C. (2010). Cognitive devices to communicate the economic crisis: An analysis through covers in *The Economist*. *Ibérica* (20), 81–106.

De Meza, D., Irlenbusch, B., & Reyniers, D. (2008). *Financial capability: A behavioural economics perspective*. London: Financial Services Authority.

de Rosa, A. S., & Bulgarella, C. (2009). *Good "real" economics vs bad "virtual" finance: A rhetorical device in the media and expert discourse*. Paper presented at the Behavioural Economics, Economic Psychology: Theory and Policy conference, Halifax, Canada.

de Rosa, A. S., Jesuino, J., & Gioiosa, C. (2003). *Euro currency system: Familiarisation processes the introduction of the euro*. Paper presented at the workshop on The Euro: Currency and Symbol, Vienna, Austria.

References   143

Del Giovane, P., & Sabbatini, R. (2008). *The euro, inflation, and consumers' perceptions.* Berlin: Springer.

Dell'Anno, R., & Dollery, B. E. (2014). Comparative fiscal illusion: A fiscal illusion index for the European Union. *Empirical Economics, 46*(3), 937–960.

Di Girolamo, A., Harrison, G. W., Lau, M. I., & Swarthout, J. T. (2015). Subjective belief distributions and the characterization of economic literacy. *Journal of Behavioral and Experimental Economics, 59*, 1–12.

Diamond, A. (2013). Executive functions. *Annual Review of Psychology, 64*, 135–168. doi:10.1146/annurev-psych-113011-143750

Dillow, C. (2015, October 30). On misunderstanding economics. Retrieved January 16, 2018, from http://stumblingandmumbling.typepad.com/stumbling_and_mumbling/2015/10/index.html.

Dillow, C. (2016, November 16). On the doctrine of signatures. Retrieved January 9, 2018, from http://stumblingandmumbling.typepad.com/stumbling_and_mumbling/2016/11/on-the-doctrine-of-signatures.html.

DiSessa, A. A. (2006). *A history of conceptual change research: Threads and fault lines.* Cambridge, UK: Cambridge University Press.

DiSessa, A. A. (2009). A bird's-eye view of the "pieces" vs "coherence" controversy (from the "pieces" side of the fence"). In S. Vosniadou (Ed.), *International handbook of research on conceptual change* (pp. 35–60). New York: Routledge.

Dixon, R., Griffiths, W., & Lim, G. (2014). Lay people's models of the economy: A study based on surveys of consumer sentiments. *Journal of Economic Psychology, 44*, 13–20.

Dods Group. (2014). Parliamentary perceptions of the banking system. Retrieved January 9, 2018, from http://positivemoney.org/wp-content/uploads/2014/08/Positive-Money-Dods-Monitoring-Poll-of-MPs.pdf.

Domaradzki, M. (2016). Conceptualizing the economy as a living organism: Vivification in Arab economic discourse. *Text & Talk, 36*(4), 417–443.

Donovan, E., & Kelemen, D. (2011). Just rewards: Children and adults equate accidental inequity with intentional unfairness. *Journal of Cognition and Culture, 11*(2), 137–150.

Doyle, A. C. (1903). *A study in scarlet.* London: Smith, Elder.

Dräger, L., Menz, J.-O., & Fritsche, U. (2014). Perceived inflation under loss aversion. *Applied Economics, 46*(3), 282–293.

Dräger, L., Lamla, M. J., & Pfajfar, D. (2016). Are consumer expectations theory-consistent? The role of central bank communication and news. *European Economic Review, 85*, 84–111.

Drews, S., & van den Bergh, J. C. J. M. (2016). Public views on economic growth, the environment and prosperity: Results of a questionnaire survey. *Global Environmental Change, 39*(Supplement C), 1–14. doi:https://doi.org/10.1016/j.gloenvcha.2016.04.001

Duckitt, J. (2001). A dual-process cognitive-motivational theory of ideology and prejudice. In M. P. Zanna (Ed.), *Advances in experimental social psychology* (Vol. 33, pp. 41–113). San Diego, CA: Academic Press. doi:10.1016/S0065-2601(01)80004-6

Duckitt, J., & Sibley, C. G. (2010). Personality, ideology, prejudice, and politics: A dual-process motivational model. *Journal of Personality, 78*(6), 1861–1894. doi:10.1111/j.1467-6494.2010.00672.x

Duckitt, J., Wagner, C., Du Plessis, I., & Birum, I. (2002). The psychological bases of ideology and prejudice: Testing a dual process model. *Journal of Personality and Social Psychology, 83*(1), 75–93.

Dunning, D., Heath, C., & Suls, J. M. (2004). Flawed self-assessment. *Psychological Science in the Public Interest, 5*(3), 69–106.

144 References

Duriez. B., Van Hiel, A., & Kossowska, M. (2005). Authoritarianism and social dominance in Western and Eastern Europe: The importance of the sociopolitical context and of political interest and involvement. *Political Psychology*, *26*(2), 299–320. doi:10.1111/j.1467-9221.2005.00419.x

Earle, J., Moran, C., & Ward-Perkins, Z. (2016). *The econocracy: The perils of leaving economics to the experts*. Oxford: Oxford University Press.

Eden, C., & Spender, J.-C. (Eds.). (1998). *Managerial and organizational cognition: Theory, methods and research*. London: Sage.

Ehrlinger, J., Johnson, K., Banner, M., Dunning, D., & Kruger, J. (2008). Why the unskilled are unaware: Further explorations of (absent) self-insight among the incompetent. *Organizational Behavior and Human Decision Processes*, *105*(1), 98–121.

Enste, D. H., Haferkamp, A., & Fetchenhauer, D. (2009). Unterschiede im Denken zwischen Ökonomen und Laien–Erklärungsansätze zur Verbesserung der wirtschaftspolitischen Beratung. *Perspektiven der Wirtschaftspolitik*, *10*(1), 60–78.

Erickson, K. (1994, December). Interview with Alan S. Blinder. *The Region*. Retrieved January 9, 2018, from www.minneapolisfed.org/publications/the-region/interview-with-alan-s-blinder.

Eriksson, K., & Simpson, B. (2012). What do Americans know about inequality? It depends on how you ask them. *Judgment & Decision Making*, *7*(6), 741–745.

Ernst-Vintila, A., Delouvee, S., & Rouquette, M.-L. (2010). La crise financière de 2008: menace collective ou défi individuel? Une analyse de la pensée sociale mobilisée en situation de crise. *Les cahiers internationaux de psychologie sociale*, *87*, 515–542.

Evans, J. S. B. T. (2010). *Thinking twice: Two minds in one brain*. Oxford: Oxford University Press.

Everett, J. A. C. (2013). The 12 item Social and Economic Conservatism Scale (SECS). *PLoS ONE*, *8*(12), e82131–e82131. doi:10.1371/journal.pone.0082131

Facchini, F. (2017). Public choice failure and voter incompetence in France. *The Political Quarterly*, *88*(2), 258–264.

Faricy, C., & Ellis, C. (2014). Public attitudes toward social spending in the United States: The differences between direct spending and tax expenditures. *Political Behavior*, *36*(1), 53–76.

Fernandes, D., Lynch Jr., J. G., & Netemeyer, R. G. (2014). Financial literacy, financial education, and downstream financial behaviors. *Management Science*, *60*(8), 1861–1883.

Ferrari, M., & Chi, M. T. H. (1998). The nature of naive explanations of natural selection. *International Journal of Science Education*, *20*(10), 1231–1256.

Financial Crisis Inquiry Commission. (2011). *The financial crisis inquiry report, authorized edition: Final report of the National Commission on the Causes of the Financial and Economic Crisis in the United States*. Washington, DC: US Government Printing Office. Retrieved January 30, 2018, from www.gpo.gov/fdsys/pkg/GPO-FCIC/pdf/GPO-FCIC.pdf.

Flament, C., & Rouquette, M.-L. (2003). *Anatomie des idees ordinaires: Comment etudier les representations sociales*. Paris: Armand Colin/VUF.

Fornero, E. (2015). Economic-financial literacy and (sustainable) pension reforms: Why the former is a key ingredient for the latter. *Bankers, Markets & Investors*, *134*, 6–16.

Fornero, E., & Lo Prete, A. (2017). *Voting in the aftermath of a pension reform: The role of economic-financial literacy*. Torino, Italy: Center for Research on Pensions and Welfare Policies.

Frederick, S., Novemsky, N., Wang, J., Dhar, R., & Nowlis, S. (2009). Opportunity cost neglect. *Journal of Consumer Research*, *36*(4), 553–561. doi:10.1086/599764

Friedkin, N. E., Proskurnikov, A. V., Tempo, R., & Parsegov, S. E. (2016). Network science on belief system dynamics under logic constraints. *Science*, *354*(6310), 321–326. doi:10.1126/science.aag2624

References **145**

Frühauf, F., & Retzmann, T. (2016). Financial literacy in Germany. In C. Aprea, E. Wuttke, K. Breuer, N. K. Keng, P. Davies, B. Greimel-Fuhrmann, & J. Lopus (Eds.), *International handbook of financial literacy* (pp. 263–276). Singapore: Springer.

Furnham, A. (1982). Explanations for unemployment in Britain. *European Journal of Social Psychology*, *12*(4), 335–352.

Furnham, A. (1983). Inflation and the estimated sizes of notes. *Journal of Economic Psychology*, *4*(4), 349–352.

Furnham, A. (1988). *Lay theories: Everyday understanding of problems in the social sciences*. Oxford: Pergamon Press.

Furnham, A. (2003). Poverty and wealth. In S. C. Carr & T. S. Sloan (Eds.), *Poverty and psychology*. International and Cultural Psychology Series (pp. 163–183). Boston, MA: Springer US.

Furnham, A., & Lewis, A. (1986). *The economic mind: The social psychology of economic behaviour*. Brighton, UK: Wheatsheaf.

Gabor, D., & Vestergaard, J. (2016). Towards a theory of shadow money. Institute for New Economic Thinking Working Paper. Retrieved January 29, 2018, from https://ineteconomics.org/uploads/papers/Towards_Theory_Shadow_Money_GV_INET.pdf.

Gaffeo, E., & Canzian, G. (2011). The psychology of inflation, monetary policy and macroeconomic instability. *Journal of Socio-Economics*, 40, 660–670. doi:10.1016/j.socec.2011.05.005

Gangl, K., Kastlunger, B., Kirchler, E., & Voracek, M. (2012). Confidence in the economy in times of crisis: Social representations of experts and laypeople. *The Journal of Socio-Economics*, *41*(5), 603–614.

Ganzach, Y. (2000). Judging risk and return of financial assets. *Organizational Behavior and Human Decision Processes*, *83*(2), 353–370. doi:http://dx.doi.org/10.1006/obhd.2000.2914

Gasiorowska, A., Chaplin, L. N., Zaleskiewicz, T., Wygrab, S., & Vohs, K. D. (2016). Money cues increase agency and decrease prosociality among children: Early signs of market-mode behaviors. *Psychological Science*, *27*(3), 331–344.

Gasiorowska, A., Zaleskiewicz, T., & Wygrab, S. (2012). Would you do something for me? The effects of money activation on social preferences and social behavior in young children. *Journal of Economic Psychology*, *33*(3), 603–608.

Gelman, S. A., & Legare, C. H. (2011). Concepts and folk theories. *Annual Review of Anthropology*, *40*, 379–398.

Gentner, D., Bowdle, B., Wolf, P., & Boronat, C. (2001). Metaphor is like analogy. In D. Centner, K. J. Holyoak, & B. N. Kokinov (Eds.), *The analogical mind: Perspectives from cognitive science* (pp. 199–253). Cambridge, MA: MIT Press.

Gibbs Jr., R. W. (2015). The allegorical character of political metaphors in discourse. *Metaphor and the Social World*, 5(2), 264–282.

Gick, M. L., & Holyoak, K. J. (1980). Analogical problem solving. *Cognitive Psychology*, *12*(3), 306–355.

Gick, M. L., & Holyoak, K. J. (1983). Schema induction and analogical transfer. *Cognitive Psychology*, *15*(1), 1–38.

Gielissen, R., Dutilh, C. E., & Graafland, J. J. (2008). Perceptions of price fairness: An empirical research. *Business & Society*, 3(47), 370–389.

Gigerenzer, G. (2007). *Gut feelings: The intelligence of the unconscious*. New York: Penguin.

Gigerenzer, G., & Gaissmaier, W. (2011). Heuristic decision making. *Annual Review of Psychology*, *62*, 451–482.

Gilg, O., Hanski, I., & Sittler, B. (2003). Cyclic dynamics in a simple vertebrate predator-prey community. *Science*, *302*(5646), 866–868.

Gilovich, T., Vallone, R., & Tversky, A. (1985). The hot hand in basketball: On the misperception of random sequences. *Cognitive Psychology*, *17*(3), 295–314.

146 References

Goffe, W. L. (2013). Initial misconceptions in macro principles classes. *Unpublished manuscript.* University Park, PA: Penn State University, Department of Economics.

Green, D., McManus, I., & Derrick, B. (1998). Cognitive structural models of unemployment and employment. *British Journal of Social Psychology, 37*(4), 415–438.

Green, D. W. (1997). Explaining and envisaging an ecological phenomenon. *British Journal of Psychology A, 88,* 199–217.

Grotzer, T. A. (2012). *Learning causality in a complex world: Understandings of consequence.* Lanham, MD: Rowman & Littlefield Education.

Grotzer, T. A., & Basca, B. B. (2003). How does grasping the underlying causal structures of ecosystems impact students' understanding? *Journal of Biological Education, 38*(1), 16–29.

Grotzer, T. A., Kamarainen, A. M., Tutwiler, M. S., Metcalf, S., & Dede, C. (2013). Learning to reason about ecosystems dynamics over time: The challenges of an event-based causal focus. *BioScience, 63*(4), 288–296.

Haferkamp, A., Fetchenhauer, D., Belschak, F., & Enste, D. (2009). Efficiency versus fairness: The evaluation of labor market policies by economists and laypeople. *Journal of Economic Psychology, 30*(4), 527–539. doi:10.1016/j.joep.2009.03.010

Haidt, J. (2013). Of freedom and fairness. *Democracy Journal, Spring* (28).

Haidt, J. (2014, January 9). Your personality makes your politics. *TIME.*

Haldane, A. (2016). *The great divide: Speech at the New City Agenda annual dinner.* London: Bank of England. Retrieved January 9, 2018, from www.bankofengland.co.uk/publications/Documents/speeches/2016/speech908.pdf.

Halford, G. S., Wilson, W. H., & Phillips, S. (1998). Processing capacity defined by relational complexity: Implications for comparative, developmental and cognitive psychology. *Behavioral and Brain Science, 21*(6), 803–864.

Halford, G. S., Wilson, W. H., & Phillips, S. (2010). Relational knowledge: The foundation of higher cognition. *Trends in Cognitive Sciences, 14*(11), 497–505.

Halpert, R., & Hill, R. (2011). *The locus of control construct's various means of measurement: A researcher's guide to some of the more commonly used locus of control scales.* Beach Haven, NJ: Will to Power Press.

Harford, T. (2015, December 22). In praise of Scrooge. Retrieved January 9, 2018, from timharford.com/2015/12/in-praise-of-scrooge/.

Hastings, J. S., Madrian, B. C., & Skimmyhorn, W. L. (2012). *Financial literacy, financial education and economic outcomes.* NBER Working Papers No. 18412.

Hatsopoulos, G. N., Krugman, P. R., & Poterba, J. M. (1989). *Overconsumption: the challenge to US economic policy.* Paper presented at American Business Conference.

Heaven, P. C. (1990). Suggestions for reducing unemployment: A study of Protestant work ethic and economic locus of control beliefs. *British Journal of Social Psychology, 29*(1), 55–65.

Heider, F., & Simmel, M. (1944). An experimental study of apparent behavior. *The American Journal of Psychology, 57*(2), 243–259.

Heller, N. (2017, August 21). Is there any point to protesting. *The New Yorker.* Retrieved January 29, 2018, from www.newyorker.com/magazine/2017/08/21/is-there-any-point-to-protesting.

Henry, J. (1976). Calling in the big bills. *Washington Monthly, 5*(6), 27–33.

Hiel, A. V., & Kossowska, M. (2007). Contemporary attitudes and their ideological representation in Flanders (Belgium), Poland, and the Ukraine. *International Journal of Psychology, 42*(1), 16–26. doi:10.1080/00207590500411443

Higgins, E. T. (1996). Knowledge activation: Accessibility, applicability, and salience. In E. T. Higgins & A. Kruglanski (Eds.), *Social psychology: Handbook of basic principles* (pp. 133–168). New York: Guilford Press.

Ho, A. K., Sidanius, J., Pratto, F., Levin, S., Thomsen, L., Kteily, N., & Sheehy-Skeffington, J. (2012). Social dominance orientation: Revisiting the structure and function of a variable predicting social and political attitudes. *Personality and Social Psychology Bulletin*, *38*(5), 583–606. doi:10.1177/0146167211432765

Holyoak, K. J., & Thagard, P. (1989). Analogical mapping by constraint satisfaction. *Cognitive Science*, *13*, 295–355.

Horton, P. B., McConney, A. A., Gallo, M., Woods, A. L., Senn, G. J., & Hamelin, D. (1993). An investigation of the effectiveness of concept mapping as an instructional tool. *Science Education*, *77*(1), 95–111.

House of Commons. (2014). *Money creation and society*. Retrieved January 9, 2018, from www.publications.parliament.uk/pa/cm201415/cmhansrd/cm141120/debtext/141120-0001.htm#14112048000001.

Hu, C., & Chen, Z. (2015). Inflation metaphor in contemporary American English. *Higher Education Studies*, *5*(6), 21–35.

Hu, C., & Liu, H. (2016). Inflation metaphor in the TIME Magazine corpus. *English Language Teaching*, *9*(2), 124–135.

Humphrey, C. (1985). Barter and economic disintegration. *Man*, *20*(1), 48–72. doi:10.2307/2802221

Huston, S. J. (2010). Measuring financial literacy. *Journal of Consumer Affairs*, *44*(2), 296–316.

Huston, S. J. (2012). Assessing financial literacy. In D. Durband & S. Britt (Eds.), *Student financial literacy* (pp. 109–124). Boston, MA: Springer.

IGM Forum. (2017). Behavioral economics. Retrieved January 29, 2018, from www.igmchicago.org/surveys/behavioral-economics.

Iyengar, S., & Westwood, S. J. (2015). Fear and loathing across party lines: New evidence on group polarization. *American Journal of Political Science*, *59*(3), 690–707. doi:10.1111/ajps.12152

James, S., Lahti, T., & Thaler, R. H. (2006). Individual preferences, monetary gambles, and stock market participation: A case for narrow framing. *The American Economic Review*, *96*(4), 1069–1090.

Jost, J. T., Gaucher, D., & Stern, C. (2015). "The world isn't fair": A system justification perspective on social stratification and inequality. In J. Dovidio & J. Simpson (Eds.), *APA handbook of personality and social psychology* (Vol. 2, pp. 317–340). Washington, DC: American Psychological Association.

Kahan, D. M. (2012). Ideology, motivated reasoning, and cognitive reflection: An experimental study. *SSRN Electronic Journal*, *8*(4), 407–424. doi:10.2139/ssrn.2182588

Kahneman, D. (2011). *Thinking, fast and slow*. New York: Farrar, Straus and Giroux.

Kahneman, D., Knetsch, J. L., & Thaler, R. (1986). Fairness as a constraint on profit seeking: Entitlements in the market. *American Economic Review*, *76*(4), 728–741.

Kaiser, T., & Menkhoff, L. (2017). Does financial education impact financial literacy and financial behavior, and if so, when? *The World Bank Economic Review*, *31*(3), 611–630.

Kallaugher, K. (2007, June 14). Vote for me, dimwit. *The Economist*, 1–2. Retrieved January 9, 2018, from www.economist.com/node/9340166.

Kashima, Y., McKintyre, A., & Clifford, P. (1998). The category of the mind: Folk psychology of belief, desire, and intention. *Asian Journal of Social Psychology*, *1*(3), 289–313.

Katona, G. (1960). *The powerful consumer: Psychological studies of the American economy*. New York: McGraw-Hill.

Katona, G. (1975). *Psychological economics*. New York: Elsevier.

Kaufman, N., Obeiter, M., & Krause, E. (2016). *Putting a price on carbon: Reducing emissions*. Washington, DC: World Resources Institute.

148 References

Keefer, L. A., & Landau, M. J. (2016). Metaphor and analogy in everyday problem solving. *Wiley Interdisciplinary Reviews: Cognitive Science, 7*(6), 394–405.

Keen, S. (2015). Beware of politicians bearing household analogies. *Forbes*. Retrieved January 9, 2018, from www.forbes.com/sites/stevekeen/2015/01/14/beware-of-politicians-bearing-household-analogies-3/#1db9482eb12a.

Keil, F. C. (1989). *Concepts, kinds, and cognitive development*. Cambridge, MA: MIT Press.

Keil, F. C. (1992). The origins of an autonomous biology. In M. R. Gunnar & M. Maratsos (Eds.), *Modularity and constraints in language and cognition: The Minnesota Symposia on Child Development*. Hillsdale: NJ: Erlbaum.

Keil, F. C. (2003). Folkscience: Coarse interpretations of a complex reality. *Trends in Cognitive Sciences, 7*(8), 368–373. doi:10.1016/s1364-6613(03)00158-x

Keil, F. C. (2006). Explanation and understanding. *Annual Review of Psychology, 57*, 227–254.

Keil, F. C. (2010). The feasibility of folk science. *Cognitive Science, 34*(5), 826–862. doi:10.1111/j.1551-6709.2010.01108.x

Keil, F. C., & Newman, G. E. (2015). Order, order everywhere, and only an agent to think: The cognitive compulsion to infer intentional agents. *Mind & Language, 30*(2), 117–139.

Kelemen, D., & Rosset, E. (2009). The human function compunction: Teleological explanation in adults. *Cognition, 111*(1), 138–143.

Kelemen, D., Rottman, J., & Seston, R. (2013). Professional physical scientists display tenacious teleological tendencies: Purpose-based reasoning as a cognitive default. *Journal of Experimental Psychology: General, 142*(4), 1074–1083.

Keynes, J. M. (1922). Introduction to the series. In D. H. Robertson (Ed.), *Cambridge economic handbooks, vol. 2*. Cambridge, UK: Harcourt, Brace.

Killick, A. (2017). Do people really lack knowledge about the economy? A reply to Facchini. *The Political Quarterly, 88*(2), 265–272. doi:10.1111/1467-923X.12365

Klamer, A., & Leonard, T. C. (1994). So what's an economic metaphor. In P. Mirowski (Ed.), *Natural images in economic thought: Markets read in tooth and claw* (pp. 20–51). New York: Cambridge University Press.

Klein, N. (2009). Naomi Klein interviews Michael Moore on the perils of capitalism. Retrieved January 22, 2018, from www.alternet.org/story/142871/naomi_klein_interviews_michael_moore_on_the_perils_of_capitalism.

Klein, N. (2014). *This changes everything: Capitalism vs. the climate*. London: Penguin.

Kohut, A., Wike, R., Menasce Horowitz, J., Simmons, K., Poushter, J., Barker, C., … Mueller Gross, E. (2012). *Pervasive gloom about the world economy*. Retrieved January 9, 2018, from www.pewglobal.org/2012/07/12/pervasive-gloom-about-the-world-economy/#.

Korinek, A. (2015). *Thoughts on DSGE macroeconomics: Matching the moment, but missing the point*. Paper presented at A Just Society: Honoring Joseph Stiglitz, Columbia Business School, New York.

Krennmayr, T. (2015). What corpus linguistics can tell us about metaphor use in newspaper texts. *Journalism Studies, 16*(4), 530–546.

Kril, Z., Leiser, D., & Spivak, A. (2016). What determines the credibility of the Central Bank of Israel in the public eye? *International Journal of Central Banking, 12*(1), 67–94.

Kruger, J., & Dunning, D. (2009). Unskilled and unaware of it: How difficulties in recognizing one's own incompetence lead to inflated self-assessments. *Psychology, 1*, 30–46.

Krugman, P. (2010, December 12). Block those metaphors. *New York Times*. Retrieved January 29, 2018, from www.nytimes.com/2010/12/13/opinion/13krugman.html.

Kuhn, T. S. (1977). A function for thought experiments. In T. S. Kuhn, *The essential tension: Selected studies in scientific tradition and change* (pp. 240–265). Chicago: University of Chicago Press.

Laibson, D. (1997). Golden eggs and hyperbolic discounting. *The Quarterly Journal of Economics, 112*(2), 443–477.

Lakoff, G. (1987). *Women, fire and dangerous things: What categories reveal about the mind.* Chicago: University of Chicago Press.

Lakoff, G. (2010). *Moral politics: How liberals and conservatives think.* Chicago: University of Chicago Press.

Lakoff, G., & Johnson, M. (1980). *Metaphors we live by.* Chicago: University of Chicago Press.

Landale, J. (2017, July 28). Brexit means what? Time for the metaphors to stop. *BBC.* Retrieved January 9, 2018, from www.bbc.co.uk/news/uk-politics-40726215.

Landau, M. J., Keefer, L. A., & Rothschild, Z. K. (2014). Epistemic motives moderate the effect of metaphoric framing on attitudes. *Journal of Experimental Social Psychology, 53,* 125–138.

Lapuz, J., & Griffiths, M. D. (2010). The role of chips in poker gambling: An empirical pilot study. *Gambling Research: Journal of the National Association for Gambling Studies (Australia), 22*(1), 34–39.

Laukkanen, M. (1996). Conducting cause mapping research: Opportunities and challenges. In B. Wintersheid & C. Eden (Eds.), *Managerial and organizational cognition: New directions in theory, methods and research.* London: Sage.

Lawson, T. (2016). Social positioning and the nature of money. *Cambridge Journal of Economics, 40*(4), 961–996.

Laz, T. H., Rahman, M., Pohlmeier, A. M., & Berenson, A. B. (2015). Level of nutrition knowledge and its association with weight loss behaviors among low-income reproductive-age women. *Journal of Community Health, 40*(3), 542–548. doi:10.1007/s10900-014-9969-9

Lazear, E. P. (2000). Economic imperialism. *The Quarterly Journal of Economics, 115*(1), 99–146.

Lea, S. E. G. (1981). Inflation, decimalization and the estimated sizes of coins. *Journal of Economic Psychology, 1*(1), 79–81.

Lea, S. E. G., & Webley, P. (2006). Money as tool, money as drug: The biological psychology of a strong incentive. *Behavioral and Brain Science, 29*(2), 161–209.

Leiser, D. (2001). Scattered naive theories: Why the human mind is isomorphic to the internet web. *New Ideas in Psychology, 19*(3), 175–202.

Leiser, D., & Ackerman, R. (2010). Heuristic and operational bases of the sense of understanding (Les fondements heuristique et opérationnel du sentiment de compréhension). In P. Y. Brandt, J. Czellar, D. Desbiez-Piat, H. Kilcher, & J. Vonèche (Eds.), *Festschrift in honor of Christiane Gillièron.* Geneva: Labor et Fides.

Leiser, D., & Aroch, R. (2009). Lay understanding of macroeconomic causation: The good-begets-good heuristic. *Applied Psychology, 58*(3), 370–384.

Leiser, D., Benita, R., & Bourgeois-Gironde, S. (2016). Differing conceptions of the causes of the economic crisis: Effects of culture, economic training, and personal impact. *Journal of Economic Psychology, 53,* 154–163. doi:http://dx.doi.org/10.1016/j.joep.2016.02.002

Leiser, D., & Beth Halachmi, R. (2006). Children's understanding of market forces. *Journal of Economic Psychology, 27*(1), 6–19.

Leiser, D., Bourgeois-Gironde, S., & Benita, R. (2010). Human foibles or systemic failure: Lay perceptions of the 2008–2009 financial crisis. *Journal of Socio-Economics, 39*(2), 132–141. doi:10.1016/j.socec.2010.02.013

Leiser, D., & Drori, S. (2005). Naïve understanding of inflation. *Journal of Socio-Economics, 34*(2), 179–198. doi:10.1016/j.socec.2004.09.006

Leiser, D., Duani, N., & Wagner-Egger, P. (2017). The conspiratorial style in lay economic thinking. *PLoS ONE, 12*(3), e0171238.

150 References

Leiser, D., & Izak, G. (1987). The money size illusion as a barometer of confidence? The case of high inflation in Israel. *Journal of Economic Psychology*, *8*(3), 347–356.

Leiser, D., & Rötheli, T. F. (2010). The financial crisis: Economic and psychological perspectives. Introduction to the special issue of the *Journal of Socio-Economics* on "The Financial Crisis." *Journal of Socio-Economics*, *39*(2), 117–118. doi:10.1016/j.socec.2010.02.017

Leiser, D., Sevon, G., & Levy, D. (1990). Children's economic socialization: Summarizing the cross-cultural comparison of ten countries. Special Issue: Economic socialization. *Journal of Economic Psychology*, *11*(4), 591–631.

Leiser, D., & Zaltsman, J. (1990). Economic socialization in the kibbutz and the town in Israel. *Journal of Economic Psychology*, *11*(4), 557–565.

Lemon, A. (1998). "Your eyes are green like dollars": Counterfeit cash, national substance, and currency apartheid in 1990s Russia. *Cultural Anthropology*, *13*(1), 22–55.

Leumann, S., Heumann, M., Syed, F., & Aprea, C. (2016). Economic competence and financial literacy of young adults: Status and challenges. In E. Wuttke, J. Seifried, & S. Schumann (Eds.), *Towards a comprehensive financial literacy framework: Voices from stakeholders in European vocational education and training* (pp. 19–39). Opladen: Barbara Budrich.

Levitt, S. D., & Dubner, S. J. (2005). *Freakonomics: A rogue economist explains the hidden side of everything*. New York: William Morrow.

Liu, D., Wellman, H. M., Tardif, T., & Sabbagh, M. A. (2008). Theory of mind development in Chinese children: A meta-analysis of false-belief understanding across cultures and languages. *Developmental Psychology*, *44*(2), 523–531.

Lombrozo, T., Kelemen, D., & Zaitchik, D. (2007). Inferring design. *Psychological Science*, *18*(11), 999–1006.

Lorenz, M. (2015). *Lehrmaterial zum Themengebiet "finanzielle Vorsorge": Überblick und kritische fachdidaktische Analyse* (Master thesis), Friedrich-Schiller-Universität Jena.

Lotz, S., & Fix, A. R. (2013). Not all financial speculation is treated equally: Laypeople's moral judgments about speculative short selling. *Journal of Economic Psychology*, *37*, 34–41.

Lucas Jr., G. M. (2015). Out of sight, out of mind: How opportunity cost neglect undermines democracy. *New York University Journal of Law & Liberty*, *9*, 249.

Lundholm, C., & Davies, P. (2013). Conceptual change in the social sciences. In S. Vosniadou (Ed.), *International handbook of research on conceptual change* (pp. 288–304). New York: Routledge.

Lunt, P. K. (1989). The perceived causal structure of unemployment. In K. G. Grunert & F. Ölander (Eds.), *Understanding economic behaviour* (pp. 107–120). Dordrecht: Springer Netherlands.

Lusardi, A., & Mitchell, O. S. (2007). Financial literacy and retirement preparedness: Evidence and implications for financial education. *Business Economics*, *42*(1), 35–44.

Lusardi, A., & Mitchell, O. S. (2011). Financial literacy around the world: An overview. *Journal of Pension Economics and Finance*, *10*(04), 497–508.

Lusardi, A., & Mitchell, O. S. (2014). The economic importance of financial literacy: Theory and evidence. *Journal of Economic Literature*, *52*(1), 5–44.

Malle, B. F., Guglielmo, S., & Monroe, A. E. (2014). A theory of blame. *Psychological Inquiry*, *25*(2), 147–186. doi:10.1080/1047840X.2014.877340

Malmendier, U., & Nagel, S. (2016). Learning from inflation experiences. *The Quarterly Journal of Economics*, *131*(1), 53–87.

Mankiw, N. G. (1997). Comment on "Why do people dislike inflation?" In C. D. Romer & D. H. Romer (Eds.), *Reducing inflation: Motivation and strategy*. Chicago: University of Chicago Press.

Mankiw, N. G. (2014). *Principles of macroeconomics* (7th ed.). Stamford, CT: Cengage Learning.

Manning, A. (2016). *The elusive employment effect of the minimum wage.* CEP Discussion Paper No. 1428. London School of Economics: Centre for Economic Performance.

Marsden, M., Zick, C. D., & Mayer, R. N. (2011). The value of seeking financial advice. *Journal of Family and Economic Issues, 32*(4), 625–643. doi:10.1007/s10834-011-9258-z

May, T. (2016). Britain, the great meritocracy: Prime Minister's speech. Retrieved January 22, 2018, from www.gov.uk/government/speeches/britain-the-great-meritocracy-prime-ministers-speech.

McCaffery, E. J., & Baron, J. (2006). Thinking about tax. *Psychology, Public Policy, and Law, 12*(1), 106–135.

McCloskey, D. N. (1983). The rhetoric of economics. *Journal of Economic Literature, 21*(2), 481–517.

McClure, S. M., Laibson, D. I., Loewenstein, G., & Cohen, J. D. (2004). Separate neural systems value immediate and delayed monetary rewards. *Science, 306*(5695), 503–507.

McGraw, A. P., & Tetlock, P. E. (2005). Taboo trade-offs, relational framing, and the acceptability of exchanges. *Journal of Consumer Psychology, 15*(1), 2–15.

McLeay, M., Radia, A., & Thomas, R. (2014). Money creation in the modern economy. *Bank of England Quarterly Bulletin,* 54(1), 14–27.

McNair, S., & Crozier, W. (2017). Assessing psychological dispositions and states that can influence economic behaviour. In R. Ranyard (Ed.), *Economic psychology* (pp. 69–87). Hoboken, NJ: Wiley-Blackwell.

McPherson, M., Smith-Lovin, L., & Cook, J. M. (2001). Birds of a feather: Homophily in social networks. *Annual Review of Sociology, 27,* 415–444. doi:10.1146/annurev.soc.27.1.415

Miller, M., Reichelstein, J., Salas, C., & Zia, B. (2015). Can you help someone become financially capable? A meta-analysis of the literature. *The World Bank Research Observer, 30*(2), 220–246.

Mitchell, G., & Tetlock, P. E. (2009). Disentangling reasons and rationalizations: Exploring perceived fairness in hypothetical societies. In J. Jost, A. C. Kay, & H. Thorisdottir (Eds.), *Social and psychological bases of ideology and system justification* (pp. 126–158). New York: Oxford University Press.

Mitchell, G., Tetlock, P. E., Mellers, B. A., & Ordonez, L. D. (1993). Judgments of social justice: Compromises between equality and efficiency. *Journal of Personality and Social Psychology, 65*(4), 629–639.

Moati, P. (2009). Les consommateurs trouvent les prix "injustes." *Consommation & Modes de Vie, 220.*

Moliner, P. (1996). *Images et représentations sociales.* Grenoble: Presses Universitaires de Grenoble.

Montaigne, M., de (1595/1969). *Essais* (Livre 1). Paris: Garnier-Flammarion.

Moore, J., & Newell, A. (1973). How can MERLIN understand? In L. W. Gregg (Ed.), *Knowledge and cognition* (pp. 201–252). Hillsdale, NJ: Erlbaum.

Moore, M. (Writer). (2009). *Capitalism: A love story.* Overture Films.

Moore, P. (2015). *One third of millennials view socialism favorably.* Retrieved March 11, 2018, from https://today.yougov.com/news/2015/05/11/one-third-millennials-like-socialism/.

Morris, M. W., Sheldon, O. J., Ames, D. R., & Young, M. J. (2007). Metaphors and the market: Consequences and preconditions of agent and object metaphors in stock market commentary. *Organizational Behavior and Human Decision Processes, 102*(2), 174–192.

Moscovici, S. (1981). On social representations. In J. Forgas (Ed.), *Social cognition: Perspectives on everyday understanding* (pp. 181–210). London: Academic Press.

Moscovici, S. (1984). The phenomenon of social representations. In R. M. Farr & S. Moscovici (Eds.), *Social representations* (pp. 3–69). Cambridge, UK: Cambridge University Press.

Mueller, E. (1963). Public attitudes toward fiscal programs. *The Quarterly Journal of Economics,* 77, 210–235.

152 References

Mullainathan, S., & Shafir, E. (2013). *Scarcity: Why having too little means so much*. London: Allen Lane.

Murray, M., & Millar, R. (1992). Lay explanations of and solutions to unemployment in Northern Ireland. *Work & Stress, 6*(4), 367–378.

Mylonas, K., Furnham, A., Alvaro, J. L., Papazoglou, S., Divale, W., Cretu, R. Z., ... Filus, A. (2016). Explanations of unemployment: An eight-country comparison. *International Journal of Academic Research in Business and Social Sciences, 6*(9), 344–361.

Napier, J. L., Huang, J., Vonasch, A. J., & Bargh, J. A. (2017). Superheroes for change: Physical safety promotes socially (but not economically) progressive attitudes among conservatives. *European Journal of Social Psychology, 68*, 83–92.

Nesbit, J. C., & Adesope, O. O. (2006). Learning with concept and knowledge maps: A meta-analysis. *Review of Educational Research, 76*(3), 413–448.

Neuman, E. (2015, December 29). When it comes to Israel's economy, most of us are just plain stupid. *Haaretz*. Retrieved January 9, 2018, from www.haaretz.com/israel-news/business/.premium-1.694105.

Neumark, D. (2015). The effects of minimum wages on employment. *FRBSF Economic Letter, 37*.

Ng, T., & Wright, M. (2007). Introducing the MONIAC: An early and innovative economic model. *Reserve Bank of New Zealand Bulletin, 70*.

Niemand, R. (2016). *Finanzielle Allgemeinbildung an Gymnasien – eine Curriculumanalyse* (Staatsexamensarbeit). Friedrich Schiller Universität Jena.

Norton, M. I., & Ariely, D. (2011). Building a better America: One wealth quintile at a time. *Perspectives on Psychological Science, 6*(1), 9–12. doi:10.1177/1745691610393524

Norton, R. (2008). Unintended consequences. *The Concise Encyclopedia of Economics*. Retrieved January 9, 2018, from www.econlib.org/library/Enc/UnintendedConsequences.html.

O'Mara-Shimek, M., Guillén-Parra, M., & Ortega-Larrea, A. (2015). Stop the bleeding or weather the storm? Crisis solution marketing and the ideological use of metaphor in online financial reporting of the stock market crash of 2008 at the New York Stock Exchange. *Discourse & Communication, 9*(1), 103–123.

Oberauer, K. (2009). Design for a working memory. In B. H. Ross (Ed.), *The psychology of learning and motivation* (Vol. 51, pp. 45–100). San Diego, CA: Elsevier.

Oberauer, K., Süß, H.-M., Wilhelm, O., & Sander, N. (2007). Individual differences in working memory capacity and reasoning ability. In A. R. A. Conway, C. Jarrold, M. J. Kane, A. Miyake, & J. N. Towse (Eds.), *Variation in working memory* (pp. 49–75). Oxford: Oxford University Press.

OECD. (2013). Financial literacy framework. In *PISA 2012 assessment and analytical framework*. Paris: OECD Publishing.

OECD. (2016). *OECD pensions outlook 2016*. Paris: OECD Publishing. Retrieved from http://dx.doi.org/10.1787/pens_outlook-2016-en.

OECD. (2017). *Use of behavioural insights in consumer policy* (Vol. 36). Paris: OECD Publishing.

OECD/INFE. (2015). *2015 OECD/INFE toolkit for measuring financial literacy and financial inclusion*. Retrieved January 9, 2018, from www.oecd.org/daf/fin/financial-education/2015_OECD_INFE_Toolkit_Measuring_Financial_Literacy.pdf.

Olen, H. (2013, March 26). Why the federal budget can't be managed like a household budget. *The Guardian*. Retrieved January 9, 2018, from www.theguardian.com/money/us-money-blog/2013/mar/26/federal-budget-household-finances-fed.

Onraet, E., Van Hiel, A., Dhont, K., & Pattyn, S. (2013). Internal and external threat in relationship with right-wing attitudes. *Journal of Personality, 81*(3), 233–248.

Orland, A. (2013). Personality traits and the perception of macroeconomic indicators – survey evidence. *Bulletin of Economic Research, 69*(4), E150–E172.

References **153**

Pang, M.-F., & Marton, F. (2005). Learning theory as teaching resource: Enhancing students' understanding of economic concepts. *Instructional Science*, *33*(2), 159–191.

Pennycook, G., Fugelsang, J. A., & Koehler, D. J. (2015). What makes us think? A three-stage dual-process model of analytic engagement. *Cognitive Psychology*, *80*, 34–72. doi:http://dx.doi.org/10.1016/j.cogpsych.2015.05.001

Pennycook, G., Ross, R. M., Koehler, D. J., & Fugelsang, J. A. (2017). Dunning–Kruger effects in reasoning: Theoretical implications of the failure to recognize incompetence. *Psychonomic Bulletin & Review*, *25*(6), 1774–1784. doi:10.3758/s13423-017-1242-7

Perkins, D. N., & Grotzer, T. A. (2005). Dimensions of causal understanding: The role of complex causal models in students' understanding of science. *Studies in Science Education*, *41*, 117–166.

Perry, R., & Sibley, C. G. (2013). A dual-process motivational model of social and economic policy attitudes. *Analyses of Social Issues and Public Policy*, *13*(1), 262–285. doi:10.1111/asap.12019

Perry, R., Sibley, C. G., & Duckitt, J. (2013). Dangerous and competitive worldviews: A meta-analysis of their associations with Social Dominance Orientation and Right-Wing Authoritarianism. *Journal of Research in Personality*, *47*(1), 116–127. doi:10.1016/j.jrp.2012.10.004

Pinker, S. (1997). The brain's versatile toolbox. *Natural History*, *106*(8), 42–45.

Pinker, S. (1999). How the mind works. *Annals of the New York Academy of Sciences*, *882*(1), 119–127.

Pinker, S. (2003). *The blank slate: The modern denial of human nature*. London: Penguin.

Pinker, S. (2005). So how does the mind work? *Mind and Language*, *20*(1), 1–24.

Pinker, S. (2006). The blank slate. *General Psychologist*, *41*(1), 1–8.

Pinker, S. (2010). Colloquium paper: The cognitive niche: coevolution of intelligence, sociality, and language. *Proceedings of the National Academy of Sciences of the United States of America*, *107 Suppl 2*, 8993–8999. doi:10.1073/pnas.0914630107 [doi]

Pinker, S. (2012). *The better angels of our nature: Why violence has declined*. New York: Viking.

Plender, J. (2015). *Capitalism: Money, morals and markets*. London: Biteback Publishing.

Polanyi, M. (1951). *The logic of liberty*. London: Routledge & Kegan Paul.

Pratto, F., Sidanius, J., Stallworth, L. M., & Malle, B. F. (1994). Social dominance orientation: A personality variable predicting social and political attitudes. *Journal of Personality and Social Psychology*, *67*(4), 741–763. doi:10.1037/0022-3514.67.4.741

Prelec, D., & Simester, D. (2001). Always leave home without it: A further investigation of the credit-card effect on willingness to pay. *Marketing Letters*, *12*(1), 5–12.

Przybyszewski, K., & Tyszka, T. (2007). Emotional factors in currency perception. *Journal of Consumer Policy*, *30*(4), 355–365.

Pühringer, S., & Hirte, K. (2013). *The financial crisis as a tsunami: Discourse profiles of economists in the financial crisis*. ICAE Working Paper Series No. 14.

Raghubir, P., & Srivastava, J. (2008). Monopoly money: The effect of payment coupling and form on spending behavior. *Journal of Experimental Psychology: Applied*, *14*(3), 213–255.

Ranyard, R., Missier, F. D., Bonini, N., Duxbury, D., & Summers, B. (2008). Perceptions and expectations of price changes and inflation: A review and conceptual framework. *Journal of Economic Psychology*, *29*(4), 378–400. doi:10.1016/j.joep.2008.07.002

Ranyard, R., Missier, F. D., Bonini, N., & Pietroni, D. (2017). The citizen's judgments of prices and inflation. In R. Ranyard (Ed.), *Economic psychology: The science of economic mental life and behaviour*. Chichester, UK: Wiley-Blackwell.

154 References

Rasinski, K. A. (1987). What's fair is fair – or is it? Value differences underlying public views about social justice. *Journal of Personality and Social Psychology, 53*(1), 201–211. doi:10.1037/0022-3514.53.1.201

Remmele, B. (2012). Macht ökonomische Bildung die Marktwirtschaft sozialer? *Österreichische Zeitschrift für Soziologie, 37*(1), 171–187.

Remmele, B. (2016). Financial literacy and financial incomprehensibility. In C. Aprea, E. Wuttke, K. Breuer, N. K. Koh, P. Davies, B. Greimel-Fuhrmann, & J. S. Lopus (Eds.), *International handbook of financial literacy* (pp. 39–55). Singapore: Springer.

Rentoul, J. (2015, September 24). Why do the British dislike the free market? *CapX*. Retrieved January 29, 2018, from https://capx.co/why-do-the-british-dislike-the-free-market/.

Resende, M., & Zeidan, R. (2015). Psychological biases and economic expectations: Evidence on industry experts. *Journal of Neuroscience, Psychology, and Economics, 8*(3), 160–172. doi:10.1037/npe0000043

Resnick, M. (1997). *Turtles, termites, and traffic jams: Explorations in massively parallel microworlds.* Cambridge, MA: MIT Press.

Retzmann, T., & Seeber, G. (2016). Financial education in general education schools: A competence model. In C. Aprea, E. Wuttke, K. Breuer, N. K. Koh, P. Davies, B. Greimel-Fuhrmann, & J. S. Lopus (Eds.), *International handbook of financial literacy* (pp. 9–23). Singapore: Springer.

Robins, S., & Mayer, R. E. (2000). The metaphor framing effect: Metaphorical reasoning about text-based dilemmas. *Discourse Processes, 30*(1), 57–86.

Rodrik, D. (2011). *The globalization paradox: Why global markets, states and democracy can't coexist.* Oxford: Oxford University Press.

Rogoff, K. S. (2016). *The curse of cash.* Princeton, NJ: Princeton University Press.

Roos, M. W. M. (2007). Nonexpert beliefs about the macroeconomic consequences of economic and noneconomic events. *Public Choice, 132*(3–4), 291–304.

Roos, M. W. M. (2008). Predicting the macroeconomic effects of abstract and concrete events. *European Journal of Political Economy, 24*, 192–201.

Rosset, E. (2008). It's no accident: Our bias for intentional explanations. *Cognition, 108*(3), 771–780.

Roth, A. E. (2007). Repugnance as a constraint on markets. *Journal of Economic Perspectives, 21*(3), 37–58.

Roth, A. E. (2015). *Who gets what – and why: The new economics of matchmaking and market design.* New York: Eamon Dolan/Houghton Mifflin Harcourt.

Rotter, J. B. (1966). Generalized expectancies for internal versus external control of reinforcement. *Psychological Monographs: General and Applied, 80*(1), 1–28. doi:10.1037/h0092976

Rozenblit, L., & Keil, F. (2002). The misunderstood limits of folk science: An illusion of explanatory depth. *Cognitive Science: A Multidisciplinary Journal, 26*(5), 521–562.

Rubin, D. (2001). *The psychological structuring of causal links in macro-economics.* (MA Thesis), Ben-Gurion University, Beer Sheva, Israel.

Rubin, P. H. (2003). Folk economics. *Southern Economic Journal, 70*(1), 157–172.

Rubin, P. H. (2014). Emporiophobia (fear of markets): Cooperation or competition? *Southern Economic Journal, 80*(4), 875–889.

Russell, G. (2014). *Heirs to forgotten kingdoms: Journeys into the disappearing religions of the Middle East.* New York: Basic Books.

Salter, W. J. (1986). *Tacit theories of economics* (PhD dissertation), Department of Psychology, Yale University, New Haven, CT.

Samuelson, P. A. (1971). Generalized predator-prey oscillations in ecological and economic equilibrium. *Proceedings of the National Academy of Sciences, 68*(5), 980–983.

References   155

Sandel, M. J. (2012). *What money can't buy: The moral limits of markets*. New York: Farrar, Straus & Giroux.

Sarnikar, S. (2015). What prevents thinking like an economist. In S. Sarnikar, *What can behavioral economics teach us about teaching economics?* (pp. 46–75). New York: Palgrave MacMillan.

Savadori, L., Nicotra, E., Rumiati, R., & Tamborini, R. (2001). Mental representation of economic crisis in Italian and Swiss samples. *Swiss Journal of Psychology, 60*(1), 11–14. doi:10.1024//1421-0185.60.1.11

Savani, K., Mead, N. L., Stillman, T., & Vohs, K. D. (2016). No match for money: Even in intimate relationships and collectivistic cultures, reminders of money weaken sociomoral responses. *Self and Identity, 15*(3), 342–355.

Scharrer, L., Stadtler, M., & Bromme, R. (2014). You'd better ask an expert: Mitigating the comprehensibility effect on laypeople's decisions about science-based knowledge claims. *Applied Cognitive Psychology, 28*(4), 465–471. doi:10.1002/acp.3018

Scheve, K. (2003). *Public demand for low inflation*. Bank of England Working Paper No. 172, International economic analysis division. Available at SSRN: http://ssrn.com/abstract=392361 or http://dx.doi.org/10.2139/ssrn.392361.

Schneider, S. M., & Castillo, J. C. (2015). Poverty attributions and the perceived justice of income inequality. *Social Psychology Quarterly, 78*(3), 263–282. doi:10.1177/0190272515589298

Schnellenbach, J., & Schubert, C. (2015). Behavioral political economy: A survey. *European Journal of Political Economy, 40*, 395–417. doi:http://dx.doi.org/10.1016/j.ejpoleco.2015.05.002

Schumpeter, J. (1917). Das Sozialprodukt und die Rechenpfennige. *Archiv für Sozialwissenschaft und Sozialpolitik, 44*, 627–715.

Schwartz, S. H., Caprara, G. V., Vecchione, M., Bain, P., Bianchi, G., Caprara, M. G., … Lönnqvist, J.-E. (2014). Basic personal values underlie and give coherence to political values: A cross national study in 15 countries. *Political Behavior, 36*(4), 899–930.

Semino, E. (2002). A sturdy baby or a derailing train? Metaphorical representations of the euro in British and Italian newspapers. *Text, 22*(1), 107–140.

Sevon, G. (1984). Cognitive maps of past and future economic events. *Acta Psychologica, 56*, 71–79.

Sgambati, S. (2016). Rethinking banking: Debt discounting and the making of modern money as liquidity. *New Political Economy, 21*(3), 274–290. doi:10.1080/13563467.2016.1113946

Shahaeian, A., Peterson, C. C., Slaughter, V., & Wellman, H. M. (2011). Culture and the sequence of steps in theory of mind development. *Developmental Psychology, 47*(5), 1239–1247.

Shefrin, H. (2002). *Beyond greed and fear: Understanding behavioral finance and the psychology of investing*. Oxford: Oxford University Press.

Shefrin, H. M., & Statman, M. (1984). Explaining investor preference for cash dividends. *Journal of Financial Economics, 13*(2), 253–282.

Shiller, R. J. (1997). Why do people dislike inflation? In C. D. Romer & D. H. Romer (Eds.), *Reducing inflation: Motivation and strategy* (pp. 13–70). Chicago: University of Chicago Press.

Shiller, R. J. (2017). *Narrative economics*. Cowles Foundation Discussion Paper No. 2069. Yale University, New Haven, CT.

Shimada, R. (2006). *The intra-Asian trade in Japanese copper by the Dutch East India Company during the eighteenth century* (Vol. 4). Leiden: Brill.

Shtulman, A. (2015). How lay cognition constrains scientific cognition. *Philosophy Compass, 10*(11), 785–798.

156 References

Shtulman, A. (2017). *Scienceblind: Why our intuitive theories about the world are so often wrong.* New York: Basic Books.

Shtulman, A., & Harrington, K. (2016). Tensions between science and intuition across the lifespan. *Topics in Cognitive Science, 8*(1), 118–137. doi:10.1111/tops.12174

Shtulman, A., & Lombrozo, T. (2016). Bundles of contradiction: A coexistence view of conceptual change. In D. Barner & A. S. Baron (Eds.), *Core knowledge and conceptual change* (pp. 53–72). Oxford: Oxford University Press.

Shtulman, A., & Valcarcel, J. (2012). Scientific knowledge suppresses but does not supplant earlier intuitions. *Cognition, 124*(2), 209–215.

Sibley, C. G., & Duckitt, J. (2013). The dual process model of ideology and prejudice: A longitudinal test during a global recession. *The Journal of Social Psychology, 153*(4), 448–466. doi:10.1080/00224545.2012.757544

Silaški, N., & Đurović, T. (2010). The conceptualization of the global financial crisis via the economy is a person metaphor: A contrastive study of English and Serbian. *Facta universitatis-series: Linguistics and Literature, 8*(2), 129–139.

Slivanzky, O., Leiser, D., & Spivak, A. (2015). *There is no annuity puzzle in the DB system: Annuity – preferences and psychological factors in Israel* (M.Sc.), Ben-Gurion University of the Negev, Beer Sheva, Israel.

Sloman, S. A. (1996). The empirical case for two systems of reasoning. *Psychological Bulletin, 119*(1), 3–22.

Sloman, S. A., & Fernbach, P. M. (2017). *The knowledge illusion: Why we never think alone.* New York: Riverhead Books.

Smith, A. (1776/2000). *The wealth of nations.* New York: Random House.

Smith, G. P. (1995). How high can a dead cat bounce?: Metaphor and the Hong Kong stock market. *Hong Kong Papers in Linguistics and Language Teaching, 18*, 43–57.

Smith, N. (2017, March 23). Capitalism will shrink inequality. In fact, it's happening. *Bloomberg.* Retrieved January 9, 2018, from www.bloomberg.com/view/articles/2017-03-23/capitalism-will-shrink-inequality-in-fact-it-s-happening.

Smith, W. (2014). Why the federal budget is not like a household budget. *The Conversation.* Retrieved January 9, 2018, from https://theconversation.com/why-the-federal-budget-is-not-like-a-household-budget-35498.

Soman, D. (1999). Effects of payment mechanism on spending behavior: The illusion of liquidity. *Journal of Consumer Research, 27*(4), 460–474.

Somin, I. (2016). *Democracy and political ignorance: Why smaller government is smarter* (2nd ed.). Stanford, CA: Stanford University Press.

Soroka, S. N. (2014). *Negativity in democratic politics: Causes and consequences.* Cambridge, UK: Cambridge University Press.

Soroka, S. N., & McAdams, S. (2015). News, politics, and negativity. *Political Communication, 32*(1), 1–22. doi:10.1080/10584609.2014.881942

Srnicek, N., & Williams, A. (2016). *Inventing the future: Postcapitalism and a world without work* (revised and updated ed.). London: Verso Books.

Stango, V., & Zinman, J. (2009). Exponential growth bias and household finance. *The Journal of Finance, 64*(6), 2807–2849.

Stanovich, K. E., & Toplak, M. E. (2012). Defining features versus incidental correlates of Type 1 and Type 2 processing. *Mind and Society, 11*, 3–13.

Stanovich, K. E., West, R. F., & Toplak, M. E. (2011). Individual differences as essential components of heuristics and biases research. In K. Manktelow, D. Over, & S. Elqayam (Eds.), *The science of reason: A festschrift for Jonathan St B. T. Evans.* Hove, UK: Psychology Press.

Starmans, C., Sheskin, M., & Bloom, P. (2017). Why people prefer unequal societies. *Nature Human Behaviour, 1*(0082). doi:10.1038/s41562-017-0082

References 157

Steel, P. (2007). The nature of procrastination: A meta-analytic and theoretical review of quintessential self-regulatory failure. *Psychological Bulletin, 133*(1), 65–94.

Stigler, G. J. (1970). The case, if any, for economic literacy. *The Journal of Economic Education, 1*(2), 60–66.

Sunstein, C., & Thaler, R. (2008). *Nudge: Improving decisions about health, wealth and happiness.* New York: Penguin Books.

Takahashi, H. (2010). Central banking as "fluid dynamics": A comparative study of English and Japanese metaphors of money. *ICU Language Research Bulletin* (25).

Tallon-Baudry, C., Meyniel, F., & Bourgeois-Gironde, S. (2011). Fast and automatic activation of an abstract representation of money in the human ventral visual pathway. *PLoS ONE, 6*(11), e28229.

Tardiff, N., Bascandziev, I., Sandor, K., Carey, S., & Zaitchik, D. (2017). Some consequences of normal aging for generating conceptual explanations: A case study of vitalist biology. *Cognitive Psychology, 95*, 145–163. doi:https://doi.org/10.1016/j.cogpsych.2017.04.004

Thaler, R. H. (1980). Toward a positive theory of consumer choice. *Journal of Economic Behavior & Organization, 1*(1), 39–60. doi:http://dx.doi.org/10.1016/0167-2681(80)90051–7

Thaler, R. H. (1990). Anomalies: Saving, fungibility, and mental accounts. *The Journal of Economic Perspectives, 4*(1), 193–205.

Thaler, R. H. (1999). Mental accounting matters. *Journal of Behavioral Decision Making, 12*(3), 183–206.

Thaler, R. H. (2015). *Misbehaving: The making of behavioral economics.* New York: W.W. Norton.

The Economist. (2006, January 12). Les misérables: The misery index celebrates its 30th birthday. Time for a revamp?. Retrieved January 8, 2018, from www.economist.com/node/5389316.

The Economist. (2015a, March 12). A frenzy about interest. Retrieved January 8, 2018, from www.economist.com/news/finance-and-economics/21646264-president-and-governor-central-bank-are-loggerheads-frenzy.

The Economist. (2015b, July 4). Toothpick alert: Desperate measures from the bank. Retrieved January 8, 2018, from www.economist.com/news/middle-east-and-africa/21656700-desperate-measures-bank-toothpick-alert

The Economist. (2017, May 13). The contradiction at the heart of Trumponomics. Retrieved January 8, 2018, from www.economist.com/news/briefing/21721936-you-cant-have-tax-cuts-investment-boom-and-smaller-trade-deficit-contradiction.

The Rachel Maddow Show. (2013). Why government, family budgets aren't the same. Retrieved January 8, 2018, from www.msnbc.com/rachel-maddow-show/why-government-family-budgets-arent-th.

Thibodeau, P. H., Hendricks, R. K., & Boroditsky, L. (2017). How linguistic metaphor scaffolds reasoning. *Trends in Cognitive Sciences, 21*(11), 852–863.

Thompson, V. A., Turner, J. A. P., Pennycook, G., Ball, L. J., Brack, H., Ophir, Y., & Ackerman, R. (2013). The role of answer fluency and perceptual fluency as metacognitive cues for initiating analytic thinking. *Cognition, 128*(2), 237–251.

Thorndike, E. L. (1920). A constant error in psychological ratings. *Journal of Applied Psychology, 4*(1), 25–29.

The transcript of Bernie Sanders's victory speech. (2016). *Washington Post.* Retrieved January 9, 2018, from www.washingtonpost.com/news/post-politics/wp/2016/02/10/the-transcript-of-bernie-sanderss-victory-speech/?utm_term=.ba4bc440934a.

Tyszka, T., & Przybyszewski, K. (2006). Cognitive and emotional factors affecting currency perception. *Journal of Economic Psychology, 27*(4), 518–530.

van Bavel, R., & Gaskell, G. (2004). Narrative and systemic modes of economic thinking. *Culture & Psychology, 10*(4), 417–439.

158 References

Van Gelder, S. (2011). *This changes everything: Occupy Wall Street and the 99% movement.* San Francisco, CA: Berrett-Koehler Publishers.

van Raaij, W. F. (2016). *Understanding consumer financial behaviour: Money management in an age of financial illiteracy.* New York: Palgrave Macmillan.

Van Rooij, M., Lusardi, A., & Alessie, R. (2011). Financial literacy and stock market participation. *Journal of Financial Economics, 101*(2), 449–472.

Vergès, P. (1989). Representations sociales de l'economie: une forme de connaissance. In D. Jodelet (Ed.), *Les representations sociales* (pp. 407–428). Paris: PUF.

Vergès, P. (1992). L'evocation de l'argent: une methode pour la definition du noyau central d'une representation. *Bulletin de Psychologie, 45*(405), 203–209.

Vergès, P. (1994). Approche du noyau central: proprietes quantitatives et structurales. In C. Guimelli (Ed.), *Structures et transformations des representations sociales* (pp. 233–253). Neuchatel: Delachaux et Niestle.

Vergès, P., & Bastounis, M. (2001). Toward the investigation of social representations and economy: Questionnaire methods and techniques. In C. Roland-Levy, E. Kirchler, E. Penz, & C. Gray (Eds.), *Everyday representations of the economy* (pp. 19–48). Vienna: WUV Universitatverlag.

Vergès, P., & Ryba, R. (2012). Social representations of the economy. In A. S. de Rosa (Ed.), *Social representations in the "social arena"* (pp. 233–244). London: Routledge.

Vohs, K. D., Mead, N. L., & Goode, M. R. (2006). The psychological consequences of money. *Science, 314*(5802), 1154–1156.

Vohs, K. D., Mead, N. L., & Goode, M. R. (2008). Merely activating the concept of money changes personal and interpersonal behavior. *Current Directions in Psychological Science, 17*(3), 208–212.

Vosniadou, S., & Skopeliti, I. (2014). Conceptual change from the framework theory side of the fence. *Science & Education, 23*(7), 1427–1445.

Vukićević-Đorđević, L. (2014). On biological metaphors in economic discourse. *Journal of Teaching English for Specific and Academic Purposes, 2*(3), 429–443.

Wallon, H. (1945). *Les origines de la pensée chez l'enfant.* Paris: Presses Universitaires de France.

Walstad, W. B., Rebeck, K., & Butters, R. B. (2013). The test of economic literacy: Development and results. *The Journal of Economic Education, 44*(3), 298–309.

Warneryd, K.-E. (1986). The psychology of inflation: Introduction. *Journal of Economic Psychology, 7*(3), 259–268.

Warneryd, K.-E. (1999). *The psychology of saving: A study on economic psychology.* Cheltenham, UK: Edward Elgar.

Warneryd, K.-E., & Wahlund, R. (1985). Inflationary expectations. In H. Brandstaetter & E. Kirchler (Eds.), *Economic psychology* (pp. 327–336). Linz, Austria: Lund.

Watson, T. J. (1996). How do managers think? Identity, morality and pragmatism in managerial theory and practice. *Management Learning, 27*(3), 323–341.

Weatherford, J. (2009). *The history of money.* New York: Crown Business.

Weick, K. E., & Bougon, M. G. (1986). Organisations as cognitive maps: Charting ways to success and failure. In H. P. Sims & D. A. Gioia (Eds.), *The thinking organisation* (pp. 102–135). San Francisco, CA: Jossey-Bass.

Weinger, M. (2011, August 23). Study: 8 in 10 pols lack econ studies. *Politico.* Retrieved January 9, 2018, from www.politico.com/story/2011/08/study-8-in-10-pols-lack- econ-studies-061929.

Wellman, H. M. (1990). *The child's theory of mind.* Cambridge, MA: Bradford Books / MIT Press.

Wellman, H. M., Fang, F., & Peterson, C. C. (2011). Sequential progressions in a theory-of-mind scale: Longitudinal perspectives. *Child Development, 82*(3), 780–792.

Wellman, H. M., & Gelman, S. A. (1992). Cognitive development: Foundational theories of core domains. *Annual Review of Psychology, 43*(1), 337–375.

Wellman, H. M., & Gelman, S. A. (1998). Knowledge acquisition in foundational domains. In W. Damon (Ed.), *Handbook of child psychology: Vol. 2. Cognition, perception, and language* (pp. 523–573). Hoboken, NJ: John Wiley.

White, M. (2003). Metaphor and economics: The case of growth. *English for Specific Purposes, 22*(2), 131–151.

White, P. A. (1995). Common-sense construction of causal processes in nature: A causal network analysis. *British Journal of Psychology, 86*(3), 377–395.

Williams, A. E. (2013). News of corporate failure: Evaluating the relationship between individual assessments and market investments. *Communication Quarterly, 61*(1), 59–71.

Williamson, M. R., & Wearing, A. J. (1996). Lay people's cognitive models of the economy. *Journal of Economic Psychology, 17*(1), 3–38.

Willis, L. E. (2008). Against financial-literacy education. *Iowa Law Review, 94*(1), 197–285.

Willis, L. E. (2011). The financial education fallacy. *The American Economic Review, 101*(3), 429–434.

Winchester, D. D., & Huston, S. J. (2015). All financial advice for the middle class is not equal. *Journal of Consumer Policy, 38*(3), 247–264. doi:10.1007/s10603-015-9290-8

Winter, H. (2013). *Trade-offs: An introduction to economic reasoning and social issues.* Chicago: University of Chicago Press.

Wobker, I., Kenning, P., Lehmann-Waffenschmidt, M., & Gigerenzer, G. (2014). What do consumers know about the economy? *Journal für Verbraucherschutz und Lebensmittelsicherheit, 9*(3), 231–242.

Wood, A. M., & Boyce, C. J. (2017). Developing, evaluating, and using subjective scales of personality, preferences, and well-being: A guide to psychometrics for psychologists and economists. In R. Ranyard (Ed.), *Economic psychology* (pp. 88–104). Hoboken, NJ: Wiley-Blackwell.

Woodford, R. (2003, September). Lemming suicide myth. *Alaska Fish & Wildlife News.* Retrieved January 9, 2018, from www.adfg.alaska.gov/index.cfm?adfg=wildlifenews.view_article&articles_id=56.

World Economic Forum. (2016). *The global risks report 2016* (11th ed.). *Insight Report,* 103. doi:10.1017/CBO9781107415324.004

Worstall, T. (2016, June 13). Pope Francis is right about poverty – just wrong about the cause and the solution. *Forbes.* Retrieved January 9, 2018, from www.forbes.com/sites/timworstall/2016/06/13/pope-francis-is-right-about-poverty-just-wrong-about-the-cause-and-the-solution/#2f1839d8441a.

Young, L., & Waytz, A. (2013). Mind attribution is for morality. In S. Baron-Cohen, M. Lombardo, & H. Tager-Flusberg (Eds.), *Understanding other minds: Perspectives from developmental social neuroscience* (pp. 93–103). Oxford: Oxford University Press.

Ziv, I., & Leiser, D. (2013). The need for central resources in answering questions in different domains: Folk psychology, biology and economics. *Journal of Cognitive Psychology, 25*(7), 816–832. doi:10.1080/20445911.2013.826663

Zucker, G. S., & Weiner, B. (1993). Conservatism and perceptions of poverty: An attributional analysis1. *Journal of Applied Social Psychology, 23*(12), 925–943. doi:10.1111/j.1559-1816.1993.tb01014.x

Zumbrunnen, J., & Gangl, A. (2008). Conflict, fusion, or coexistence? The complexity of contemporary American conservatism. *Political Behavior, 30*(2), 199–221. doi:10.1007/s11109-007-9047-4

INDEX

Note: Page numbers in *italics* refer to a figure.

Adams, Douglas 23
AEVEMS (Adult Economic Values and Economic Models Study) 41–42, **43**
affordable housing 23–24, 31–32, 123
agency theory 30
aggregate demand 13, 22n2, 34, 58
aggregate variables 18, 31
aggregation 10, 11–15, 19–20, 34, 46, 94
Akerlof, G.A. and Shiller, R.J. 50, 51
Ames, D.L. and Fiske, S.T. 74
anti-capitalism 78, 79, 86
Aprea, Carmela 120
Ariely, Dan 129
Arrese, Á and Vara-Miguel, A. 70
Artificial Intelligence 27
Associated Press 69
"augmented misery index" 56
"*l'avoir fiscal*" concept 4

Bachelard, G. 102
Baker, S. 99–100
Bakunin, M. 37
Bank of England 99–100
banknotes 101, 103
Barman, C.R., Griffiths, A.K. and Okebukola, P.A.O. 17
barter 97–98
Bastiat, F. 15, 24
Bastounis, M., Leiser, D. and Roland-Levy, C. 29, 125
BBC News 62

BDW ("belief in a dangerous world") scale 126
Becchio, C. et al. (2011) 103
behavioral economics 2–3, 114, 131
"behavioral public finance" 3
Beilharz, H.-J. and Gersbach, H. 38
Berlin, Sir I. 37
Bernanke, B. 2
bias: anti-capitalist 78, 79; and causality 123; *continuance* bias 67; halo effect 35–37; inherence bias 43, 44, 124; intentionality bias 30–31, 72–74; publication bias 113
binary relations 53, 58
Bischoff, I. and Siemers, L.-H. 128
Blinder, A. 2, 4
Boeri, T., Börsch-Supan, A. and Tabellini, G. 117
Boeri, T. and Tabellini, G. 117
Bogart, J. 5
Bonfiglioli, A. and Gancia, G. 118
bounded self-control 131
Boyer, P. and Petersen, M.B. 3
Bradley, C. and Cole, D.J. 90
Braun, B. 99
Bray, B. 114
Brennan, J. 134
Brexit 32, 62, 79
Brkic, J. 84
Brotherton, R. and French, C.C. 73
Brown, D.E. 58
Brown, T.C. 33

Index **161**

Bullock, H.E., Williams, W.R. and Limbert, W.M. 90
Bundesbank 99

capital gains 106, 107
capitalism 77–95; fairness and 86–89; folk theory 90; ideology and 84–86; in media 78; pro-and anti-capitalism 79–82, *83*, 90; and profit-motive 83–86
Carey, S. 3, 13
Carey, S. et al. (2015) 13, 14
Caruso, E.N., Waytz, A. and Epley, N. 74
cash 69, 98, 103, 104–108
causality: direct and indirect effects 15–17, 42; economic variables 54–55; household finance 112; of inflation 50; intuitive theories 71–72; lack of understanding of 10, 13, 14, 15–17, 31, 34, 123; MONIAC system 19, 20; and morality 88; and personality 89–93; training 117, 118; of unemployment 43, 44–46
Cauty, J. 103
Central Bank of Nigeria 127–128
central banks 2, 57, 62, 99, 128
Chaban-Delmas, J. 9n2
children and concept of money 104
Christandl, F. 125
Cimpian, A. and Salomon, E. 44
circular flow of economic activity 20
Clinton, H. 77
Cobra effect *see* Law of Unintended Consequences
cognitive functioning; Type 1 (intuitive) 21, 30–34, 58–59, 123, 135; Type 2 (deliberate) 30, 32, 33, 58, 123
Colbert, S. 8
Collins, J.M. and O'Rourke, C.M. 113
Coluche 23
commodity money 101
competitive worldview 85
Complex Designed System 118
Congdon, B. 129
conscientiousness 114–115
consequences 31–33; and agency 74; good-begets-good heuristic 57–59; lack of economic knowledge 111–112; public policy 122–136; unintended 24–25
Conservative supporters, on unemployment 43, 44, *45*, 48
conservatives 85, 87–88, 90–91, 94–95, 125–126, 136
conspiracy theories 7, *8*, 31, 73, 123, 124
continuance bias 67
cooperative worldview 85

Corcos, A. and Moati, P. 21
Craighead, B. 62
credit cards 104–105, 115
crime and fiat money 101, 102
currency and emotions 106

Dal Bó, E., Dal Bó, P. and Eyster, E. 35
Davies, P. 119–120
"debt illusion" 135
deflation 51, 61, 98, 99
deliberate (Type 2) reasoning 30, 32, 33, 58, 123
demand-siders 29
Democrats 62, 77
demonetization 101, 102, 106
Dillow, C. 32, 123
directness 31, 32
discretionary stabilization 135, 136
distortion 72, 131
dividends 106–108
Dixon, R., Griffiths, W. and Lim, G. 53
domino effects 15
Donahue, P. 84
Doyle, A.C. 27
Dräger, L., Lamla, M.J. and Pfajfar, D. 53
Dräger, L., Menz, J.-O. and Fritsche, U. 57
Drews, S. and van den Bergh, J.C.J.M. 58
drug theory 102
Drummond, B. 103
Druze Model 129–130
DSGE (*Dynamic Stochastic General Equilibrium* modeling) 17
Dual-Process Model 85
Duckitt, J. 85
Dunning–Kruger effect 6, 32

Eastern Europe, effect of US dollar pricing 106
economic cognition: behavioral economics 114; heuristics 9, 60–61; ideology 92, 94; mapping 53–57; metaphorical language 63–75; preparedness 3; system 10–22, 23–39
economic conservatism 85
economic ideology 84–86
economic liberalism 85
economics textbook approach 7, *8*
Economist, The 38, 127–128
ecosystems 16–17
egalitarianism 87–88
Elphicke, C. 62
emergent processes 7, 13, 34, 123
equilibria 11, 12, 17–20, 34–35; general 24, 38; partial 24

162 Index

Erdogan, R. 128
Erickson, K. 2, 4
Eriksson, K. and Simpson, B. 88
euro 47, 70, 102, 104, 106
European Central Bank 99
evolutionary psychology 3
expenses 33
exports *18*, *19*, 99, 127, 128
extended metaphors 68

fairness: barter 98; and capitalism 79, *83*;
    and morality 21, 86–90, 93; in pension
    system 118; and public policy 135
fallacy of composition 34
fatalistic factors and unemployment 43,
    46, 115
feedback effects 11, 15–17, 22, 31, 95
Fernandes, D. et al. (2014) 113
fiat money 101–104
financial crisis 2008: and capitalism 77, 82;
    'disappearance' of money 107–108; as
    failure of individuals 123; and financial
    literacy 112; intentionality bias 74; in
    media 68; metaphorical language in 60, 63
financial literacy: and economic success
    114–115; education 109–115, 132–134;
    OECD study 110–111; public policy
    115–116, 118–119; reforms and 116–118,
    132; scepticism 119–120
Financial Times, The 68, 69
fishing industry 24
"folk psychology" 14
food trade, profit margin 21
Fornero, E. 115, 116–117, 118, 119
Fornero, E. and Lo Prete, A. 132
framework theories 14, 71, 72
Freakonomics (Levitt and Dubner) 15, 16
Frederick, S. et al. (2009) 33
Friedman, M. 50, 84
Furnham, A. 21, 43, 46
Furnham, A. and Lewis, A. 28

Gabor, D. and Vestergaard, J. 102
Gaffeo, E. and Canzian, G. 57–58
"gambler's fallacy" 74
gambling and cash 105
Ganzach, Y. 36
GBG (good-begets-good) heuristic 53–59,
    61, 127
Gelman, S.A. and Legare, C.H. 71
general equilibrium 24, 38
Germany 28, 40, 47, 99, 116, 117
Gick, M.L. and Holyoak, K.J. 27–28
Giscard d'Estaing, V. 4
globalization 80, 127

globalization paradox 38–39
Godfather, The (film) 20
gold 101–102, 108
good/bad dichotomy 59
good-begets-good heuristic *see* GBG
governance 134–136
government bonds 5, 36, 62, 107
government malfunction 7, *8*
government services and taxation 28,
    29, 33–34
Green, D.W. 17
Green, D.W., McManus, I. and
    Derrick, B. 46
greenhouse gas emission reduction 135
"groupthink" 92

Haldane, A. 99
halo effect 35–37
Harford, T. 103
Hatsopoulos, G.N., Krugman, P.R. and
    Poterba, J.M. 107
Heaven, P.C. 46
Heider, E. and Simmel, M. 72–73
Heller, N. 123
Hibbler, W. 17
hidden hand *see* invisible hand
Hitchhiker's Guide to the Galaxy, The (radio
    program) 23
Holmes, Sherlock 27
"hot hand fallacy" 74
housing 5, 23–24, 31–32, 56, 63, 64, 123
Hu, C. and Chen, Z. 70
"human universals" 58
hyperinflation 47

ideological entrenchment 92, 94
ideology 9, 124; and capitalism 77–95
IGM Forum poll 2017 1–2
imperfect optimization 131
imports *18*, *19*, 32, 50, 99
Income Fisher equation 57
Index of Consumer Sentiment survey
    (University of Michigan) 47, 53, 57
India 101
indirect effects 11, 15–17, 31, 42, 95, 133
individualistic factors and
    unemployment 43
inequality 77, 79–81, 85, 86–89, 93, 104, 135
inflation 47–51; central psychological
    core 49–51; metaphorical language 70;
    and money supply 98; official statistics
    40; perceptions and expectations 47;
    predictions 52–53; prices 48–49; public
    view of 40–41, 52–53, 56–57; social
    representations 48–49

inherence heuristic 43, 44, 124
intentionality bias 30–31, 72–74
interest rates 5, 57, 58, 62, 110, 111, 115;
  negative 34, 42
intrinsic price 124
intuitive psychology 73–74
intuitive theories 70–72, 122
intuitive (Type 1) reasoning 21, 30–34,
  58–59, 123, 135
invisible hand (hidden hand) 7, *8*, 12, 13,
  94, 123, 136
"isolation effect" 28, 39n1
Israel 6, 7, 106, 116, 118, 119, 131, 133
Italy 47, 116–118

Jost, J.T., Gaucher, D. and Stern, C. 79

Kahneman, D. 10; *Thinking, Fast and
  Slow* 30
Kaiser, T. and Menkhoff, L. 113
Kallaugher, K. 14
Katona, G. 47, 51
Keil, F.C. 3, 10
Keynes, J. M. 10
Keynesianism 34
Klein, N. 83; *This Changes Everything:
  Capitalism vs. the Climate* 78
knowledge retrieval 15, 27, 28, 31, 49
Krugman, P. 60

Labour supporters, on unemployment 43,
  44, *45*, 48
Laibson, D. 107
Landale, J. 62
Landau, M.J. et al. (2014) 66
Lapuz, J. and Griffiths, M.D. 105
"law" of supply and demand 11–12, 73
Law of Unintended Consequences (Cobra
  effect) 24, *25*
Lawson, T. 102
Lazear, E.P. 18
Lea, S.E.G. 106
Lea, S.E.G. and Webley, P. 102
Leiser, D. 28
Leiser, D. and Aroch, R. 55
Leiser, D. and Benita, R. 125–126
Leiser, D. and Drori, S. 47, 48, 118
Leiser, D. and Izak, G. 106
Leiser, D., Benita, R. and
  Bourgeois-Gironde, S. 31
Leiser, D., Bourgeois-Gironde, S. and
  Benita, R. 31, 74
Leiser, D., Duani, N. and Wagner-Egger, P.
  6–7, 107
lemming suicide myth 17

Lemon, A. 106
Levitt, S.D. and Dubner, S.J. 16
liberals 87–88, 90, 91, 92, 95, 126, 136
liquidity 69, 99, 100, 105, 107
LOC (locus of control) 90–92, 115,
  124, 125
Lotke–Volterra predator–prey model 16
Lotz, S. and Fix, A.R. 21
LTM (long-term memory) 26, 27–28, 30
Lunt, P. 43

McCaffery, E.J. and Baron, J. 28, 39n1
McLeay, M., Radia, A. and Thomas, R. 99
Macron, E. 122
Maduro, N. 102
"mailbox effect" 107
"make work" policies 14–15
Mankiw, N.G. 40, 50; Ten Principles of
  Economics 38
marginal costs 18
marginal returns 18
May, T. 62, 86
media and economics 4, 67–70, 78
"mental accounting" 107
Mercantilism 99
meritocracy 86, 87–88, 89, 92, *93*, 94
Merrill Lynch 56
metaphorical language 9, 60–75; economy
  as machine 68–69; economy as organism
  68; household 124; intuitive theories
  70–74; mechanical/animate 66–67; in
  media 67–70; in problem solving and
  decision making 65–67; source and target
  63; state budget as like household budget
  61–62, 124; stock market forecasting
  66–67; as structure mapping 63–65;
  targets 65
microeconomics 12–13
Miller, M., Reichelstein, J., Salas, C. and
  Zia, B. 113
minimum wages 32, 38
"misery index" 56
Mitchell, G. and Tetlock, P.E. 87
monetary value 29
money: emotional value of 102–104;
  fungibility 104–108
money illusion 50, 106
money supply (money stock) 98–101
MONIAC Hydraulic Computer (Phillips
  machine) 18–20, 69
Montaigne, M. de 96, 97
Monti, M. 116
Moore, J. and Newell, A. 27
Moore, M. 84; *Capitalism: A Love Story*
  (film) 78

164 Index

moral hazard 118
morality 11, 20–22; and capitalism 78, 83–94; and environmental policy 135; financial crisis 2008 31, 74; and price 124
Morris, M.W., Sheldon, O.J., Ames, D.R. and Young, M.J. 66–67
Morse, Sir A. 62
Mullainathan, S. and Shafir, E. 39n1
Murray, M. and Millar, R. 46

naïve thinking 11, 29, 38, 49, 50, 99, 118
narrow scoping 27–29, 31, 39n1, 49, 53, 122–123
national currency, emotions and 104
negative interest rates 34, 42
New York Times, The 69
Nigeria 127–128
non-market solutions 123
non-standard preferences 131, 135
numeracy 114, 115

Obama, B. 62
Occupy movement 77
OECD study of financial literacy 110–112
OECD Toolkit questionnaires 111
Okun, A. 56
O'Mara-Shimek, M., Guillén-Parra, M. and Ortega-Larrea, A. 69
opportunity cost neglect 33–34
Orange County News 4–5
organ donation 21–22
Orland, A. 52
outside goods 33

Pang, M.-F. and Marton, F. 12
"paradox of thrift" 34
partial equilibrium 24
"payment transparency" 105
Pennycook, G., Ross, R.M., Koehler, D.J. and Fugelsang, J.A. 32
pension systems 6, 111, 117, 118–119
Perry, R., Sibley, C.G. and Duckitt, J. 85
personal finances 131–134
personality, effect of 8, 90–92, *93*, 94, 114, 125–126
personalization 31
Pew Research Center 33
Phillips curve 52, 53, 57
Phillips machine *see MONIAC Hydraulic Computer*
Phillips, W. 18, 19
Pinker, S. 3, 71–72
Polanyi, M. 30
Potlatch 103
Pratto, F. et al. (1994) 85

predator–prey model 16
Prelec, D. and Simester, D. 104
present-time preference 115
price controls 123
prices 11–13; and currency 106; demand and supply 29; and inflation 41, 47–51, 53; inherence bias 124; intentionality bias 73; intrinsic 124; money supply 98–101; morality of 20–21, 24
procrastination 115
profit margins 21
profit-motive 83–86, 93
proportionality 50, 82, 87
psychology and economics 2–3, 20
public housing 32
public policy: financial literacy and 109, 115–119, 122–136; opportunity cost neglect 33–34
public policy analysis 37
public protests 116, 123
publication bias 113

Question Time (TV program) 6

Raghubir, P. and Srivastava, J. 105
Rasinski, K.A. 88
rational choice theory 109, 126
regulation of economy 24, 82, 85, 92, 129, 132, 133
Remmele, B. 133
Rentoul, J. 123, 124
Republican campaign 2012 62
retirement: age of 134–135; pension reform 117; planning for 6, 111, 113, 115, 116, 118–119, 132, 133–134
"retrospective" voting 40, 128
return expectations 36
risk perception 36–37, 125
risk reduction 111
Rodrik, D., *The Globalization Paradox* 38
Romney, M. 62
Roth, A. 21–22
Rotter, J.B. 91
Rubin, D. 54

salaries 49, 89
Salter, W.J. 29
Sanders, B. 77, 86–87
Savadori, L., Nicotra, E., Rumiati, R. and Tamborini, R. 47
Schneider, S.M. and Castillo, J.C. 88
Schumpeter, J. 102
Schwartz's Value Inventory 92
Scrooge McDuck 102, 103
SDO (Social Dominance Orientation) 85

Sgambati, S. 99
Shefrin, H.M. 36
Shefrin, H.M. and Statman, M. 107
Shiller, R.J. 40, 46, 51, 127
Shtulman, A. 14, 122
Silaški, N. and Ðurović, T. 68
Sloman, S. and Fernbach, P. 9, 124; *The Knowledge Illusion: Why We Never Think Alone* 92
Smith, A. 13
snow storms 24
SDO *see* Social Dominance Orientation
socialism 78, *80*, *81*
societal factors and unemployment 43
Soman, D. 104
Spain 58
speculative short-selling 21
Srnicek, N. and Williams, A. 123
Starmans, C., Sheskin, M. and Bloom, P. 88
Stigler, G. 2
stocks: dividends 106–108; folk beliefs 5, 7, 119; metaphorical language 63, 66–67, 69; MONIAC *18*; risk 111; tradeoffs 36–37
supply and demand 11–12, 13, 73, 96–98
supply-siders 29
system justification 79

Takahashi, H. 69
Tallon-Baudry, C., Meyniel, F. and Bourgeois-Gironde, S. 106
taxation: avoidance of 22; carbon tax 135; evasion of 101; folk theory 28–29, 33, 49; metaphorical language and 61, 127; political explanation of 4; and public policy 129; of wealthy 90
Taylor rule 57–58
Thaler, R. 1, 3, 104
Thorndike, E.L. 35–36
tool theory 102
tradeoffs 36, 37–39, 52–53, 88, 133, 134
treasury bonds 36
trilemmas 38–39
"the Trump trilemma" 38
"truthiness" 8
tsunami as metaphor 63–64
"tunneling" 39n1
Turkey 128

Uber 20
uncritical solutions 31
unemployment 40–48; causal links 43–44; causes and political affiliation 43–44, *45*; good-begets-good heuristic 54–59, 127; prevalent views 124; systemic and individual approaches 11; tradeoffs 38, 52–53
unforeseen effects 24
uni-dimensionality 35–37
United Kingdom: Brexit 32, 62, 79; MPs on economy 99–100; political affiliation and views on unemployment 43, 44, *45*, 48; survey 43–44, *45*
University of Michigan 47, 53, 57
US: background of voting members 127; Balanced Budget Amendment 136; inequality 79; presidential elections 62, 77, 79, 86–87; "the Trump trilemma" 38

van Bavel, R. and Gaskell, G. 46
Van Raaij, W.F. 114
Varoufákis, Y. 6
Venezuela 101, 102
Virgil 102
VOC (*Vereenigde Oost-Indische Compagnie*) 97
Vohs, K.D., Mead, N.L. and Goode, M.R. 103–104

Wall Street Journal, The 69
Wallon, H. 58
Washington Post, The 69
Wellman, H.M. and Gelman, S.A. 71
White Wilderness (film) 17
willful agent account 13
Williams, A.E. 66
Williamson, M.R. and Wearing, A.J. 22, 48, 53
Willis, L. 132
Winnie-the-Pooh 26
Winter, H. 37
WM (working memory) 26–27, 30, 123
World Economic Forum, Global Risks Report 2017 79

Ziv, I. and Leiser, D. 30
Zucker, G.S. and Weiner, B. 89

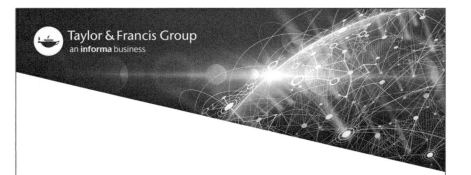